D1019989

Praise for *Personality at Work*

Personality at Work by Ron Warren provides a thoughtful framework to analyze one's own personality and strengths, but succeeds on the basis of its storytelling alone. I enjoyed having a seat at the table in the executive meetings of a number of the world's iconic companies. Mix in some science and the data that rolls out from it, informed by Ronald Warren's perceptive analyses and you have a thoughtful contribution to the leadership literature.

> —**Whitney Johnson**, Thinkers50, World's Most Influential Management Thinkers, author of critically acclaimed *Disrupt Yourself: Putting the Power of Disruptive Innovation to Work*

Ronald Warren does an excellent job of showing the importance of personality and behavioral skills at work in *Personality at Work*. With rich examples and relevant research he strongly makes the case that these are factors we can measure and change. These changes can lead directly to increased productivity and success. There's a lot to learn here for leaders and organizations everywhere.

> —**Steven Stein, PhD**, co-author of *The EQ Edge: Emotional Intelligence and Your Success*, CEO of MHS

I was impressed with Ron's work when I was CEO at my first company, Kenexa. However, he's even better in *Personality at Work*. A great combination of rigorous, empirical rationality and emotional connectivity using storytelling. Creating models for leadership or simply leading a great life is exceedingly difficult. Ron, as always, does it with humor, style, and grace. Enjoy the read and make your children read it as well.

> —**Rudy Karsan,** co-founder, Kenexa; founder, Karlani Capital

Personality matters. Personality is the polymer bonding knowledge and wisdom in teams to build resilience. In *Personality at Work*, Ronald Warren explains the elements of personality, that in turn explain how to perceive, think, act and communicate to build and lead effective teams and survive.

> —**Richard Champion de Crespigny**, Pilot in Command, Qantas Flight QF32

Want the truth on how to lead? Read this highly intelligent book. It draws on original research and high-drama real-world business cases aptly and deftly. Ron Warren has mastered leadership.

—**Robert Kaplan, PhD**, co-founder, Kaplan Devries; author of *Fear Your Strengths, The Versatile Leader,* and *Beyond Ambition*

Personality at Work is an essential read for those of us who develop leaders using evidence-based principles and techniques. *Personality at Work* represents a shift in the quality and sophistication of using personality in the development of leaders. I wish I had this book in the early stages of my work in leader development, but I also treasure it now—the relevance of *Personality at Work* can't be overstated.

As leaders are developed, the significance of personality can't be overlooked, and Ron Warren's *Personality at Work* is best-in-genre, it is entirely readable and pricelessly pragmatic. Warren's work helps any leader craft a data driven, tailored strategy for self-understanding and better leadership. I respect and admire Ron Warren's energy and intellect, and both shine through the pages of *Personality at Work*. Tap into the incredible potential between the pages of *Personality at Work*—I learned so much about myself reading it and I'm a better leader developer because of it!

—**Tom Kolditz, PhD, Brigadier General**, U.S. Army (ret); Professor Emeritus, U.S. Military Academy, West Point; Founding Director, West Point Leadership Center; Founding Director, Ann and John Doerr Institute for New Leaders

Want to know how personality plays into success? Look no further than Dr. Warren's terrific book. His decades of research into employee assessment provide practical insights for leaders at all levels.

—**Marshall Goldsmith**, executive coach, business educator, and *New York Times*-bestselling author, ranked the number one leadership thinker in the world by Thinkers50

Using compelling stories and data to back them up, Warren brings to life the critical importance of personality to effectiveness as a leader. That, combined with his unparalleled skill in translating the academic world of personality theory into something practical make this a must read for anyone looking to drive real organizational change. The LMAP has been one of the cornerstones of our Ignite! leadership development program, which has fundamentally changed the way we work at Clayton

Homes. Thank you for a powerful tool based on rigorous science and presented in a way that everyone can identify with.
—**Kevin Clayton**, president and CEO, Clayton Homes, Inc.

Having coached well over 350 leaders during the last 20 years, I found Ron Warren's *Personality at Work* filled with brilliant and actionable insights into the qualities that most frequently drive or block leadership effectiveness or success. In these times of immense uncertainty, volatility, and complexity, *Personality at Work* provides leaders with a well-guided vision and sound, scientific principles for what exceptional leadership looks like and what leaders can do to build it. Every committed and conscientious leader should have the close by for continued inspiration and guidance.
—**Greg Hiebert**, managing partner, Leadership Coach and Educator, leadershipForward

It's all about leadership. Leadership determines the success or failure of an organization. And leadership is driven by personality. Ronald bundles hard facts based on extensive research with practical stories. The book is a must read for those seeking insights into leadership principles and the importance of personality. It clearly helped to remind me about the importance of personality day in and day out.
—**Peter Mockler**, managing partner BearingPoint

This book peels away much of the mystery about how personality factors can determine success—or failure—for leaders. In clear and entertaining style, psychologist Dr. Ron Warren provides data- based strategies and tips for building a balanced personality profile, one that will help you succeed as a leader while avoiding common pitfalls and derailers. Essential reading for aspiring leaders in any discipline.
—**Paul T. Bartone, PhD**, Colonel (ret), U.S. Army; Professor and Senior Research Fellow, Center for Technology and National Security Policy National Defense University

Though I should be used to it by now, I am constantly astonished by Ron Warren's breadth of perspective, depth of insight, and ability to blend scholarly wisdom with practical application. I just cannot believe how Ron has combined such classic knowledge with cutting-edged research to draw such immediately applicable recommendations in *Personality at Work*. Without dumbing down a single element or overstating the implications of various studies, Ron accurately captures the subtle nuances of various schools of thought, in refreshingly plain English without all the academic jargon. Since I know personally many of the leaders cited in the book (Alan Mulally, Mark Fields, Doug Conant, etc.), I think Ron Warren has masterfully captured key truths in their sagas. *Personality at Work* is very useful throughout and thoroughly fun to read.

> —**Jeffrey A. Sonnenfeld**, Senior Associate Dean for Leadership Studies, Lester Crown Professor of Leadership, Yale School of Management

I cannot over-emphasise how valuable the LMAP and MMAP assessments are in stimulating self-reflection in managers and leaders. This includes the several hundred students who have used them in the MGSM MBA program. Ron Warren's book helps take the reflections deeper and further.

> —**Professor Richard J Badham BA**, Dip. Soc, PhD (Warwick), Macquarie Graduate School of Management, Macquarie University North Ryde Sydney

Ronald Warren's book offers leaders a great path to improve their leadership effectiveness. It is based on years of experience and understanding of how people work and behave in organizations. It is also a great reminder that the most important thing about any company is the people within. To presume this book does not apply to you would be missing a great opportunity.

> —**Philippe Bourguignon**, vice chairman, Revolution Places

In my 25-plus years of coaching and developing leaders, I have seen and used my fair share of assessment instruments. The LMAP 360 is, quite simply, the best I have seen. Using poignant real-life examples and a solid foundation of research, *Personality at Work* paints a compelling picture of why understanding and developing key aspects of personality should be at the core of executive development initiatives today. Striking the perfect balance of hard data and razor-sharp insights, the LMAP has been an ideal tool to help us truly awaken people and organizations to new possibilities and transform human potential into peak performance.

> —**Vergil Metts, PhD**, president and CEO Impact Associates, Inc.

I've worked with Ron and know how committed he is to using the best tools possible. I'm excited he's distilled what he's learned from his years of experience with thousands of clients.

> —**Cade Massey**, Practice Professor, The Wharton School

Warren proposes that an individual's personality is critical to success in the work situation, and in fact personality makes or breaks leadership. I have been using Warren's LMAP for more than five years in my executive coaching work in Asia, and can testify to the validity of these insights provided by this 360 assessment instrument. In *Personality at Work*, Warren argues his thesis based on research evidence. It provides insights into high-performance practices that leaders at all levels and stages in their career would do well to take on.

—**John Chan**, managing partner, Corporate Coaching Partners

This book identifies a combination of key traits that are correlated with successful leadership. A terrific guide for assessing the right stuff.

—**Samuel Barondes**, Robertson Professor, University of California, San Francisco; author, *Making Sense of People: The Science of Personality Differences*

Ron Warren has done it again—after bringing his insightful leadership process to numerous companies over the years, he now brings his knowledge and insight to all of us. *Personality at Work* provides fresh insights for leaders in ways that not only are provocative, but that have been proven to move the needle on a company's bottom line. This is a must read for anyone in a leadership role of any kind in business.

—**Dr. William Putsis**, Professor of Marketing, Economics and Business Strategy, Kenan-Flagler Business School, University of North Carolina at Chapel Hill; CEO, Chestnut Hill Associates

I met Ronald Warren the first time at the Yale School of Management in 2013 in his role as my coach with the LMAP 360. The differentiated content of personal attributes and at the same time the clear und understandable structure of the LMAP was and is the most valuable approach for reflecting myself. This happened at an important moment of my work life and helped me to work on myself in different personal topics. I honestly can say, Ron's coaching expertise and passion during the common work on the LMAP strongly impressed me over the years up to now. This book is a wonderful way through the LMAP method, not in a theoretical way. In truth, this book is *Ron* with all his extensive experiences and his deep passion.

—**Frank Henrich**, partner at BearingPoint, Berlin, Germany

Ron Warren captures the essence of how personality impacts effective leadership through compelling factual events that are backed up by scientific research.

—**Bill Sex**, president, New England Coaching

Ron Warren's book, *Personality at Work*, is compelling, impetuous and more gratifying than the familiar concepts of self-awareness and conscious choice. It is a must read for any leader desiring transformative behaviors in oneself, a team or an organization!"

—**Stephanie Duatschek**, Appointed Faculty, Georgetown University; used LMAP in former role of Vice President, Commercial Operations at MedImmune, an AstraZeneca Co.

Ronald Warren hits the nail on the head when he shows that personality IS behavior. I see this every day in my work in the C-suite, where the greatest influences on team effectiveness and performance are individual personalities and the team interactions that result. In today's landscape almost everyone is smart, competent, and putting in long hours, but too few leaders recognize that their personality is their key differentiator. This book clearly lays out how personality drives behavior and what leaders can do to bring their best self each day, all based on rigorous research and experience.

—**Gavin Fenn-Smith**, partner, The River Group

For years I longed for a 360 feedback tools that would be personality based; we focused too much on measuring competencies but paid inadequate attention to one of the critical leadership differentials. Dr. Ron Warren's LMAP tool was a precious discovery. I met Ron back in 2008 when I attended the Yale CEO College and he was my coach. I introduced Ron to Asia and brought him and the LMAP tool to Singapore. Since then, many have benefited from this leadership development tool and Asia has gotten onto LMAP's worldwide database. I have since used LMAP repeatedly to assist in executive coaching, and I am delighted that this book has finally come to fruition. It is an easy read, the explanation is clear and precise, but I find the descriptions on derailment factors and the appropriate remedial measures particularly useful.

—**Willie Chan**, retired CEO of Temasek Management Services, Singapore

After completing my LMAP 360 at Yale School of Management, I was a fan. This book is a must-read for Sales Managers, Results-oriented professionals, Coaches, and Parents like me, whose goal is to foster others' Best Self by advancing ours first. I specially recommend the Behavior action plan of the last appendix.

> —**Rogelio Medina**, sales manager, European team, Fortune 500
> Software Company

Many leaders think they know themselves well . . . Chances are you don't! In *Personality at Work* Ron has taken the hard data from his years of work with leaders and their teams on LMAP and articulates very simply how your personality— how you behave— matters. If you *listen*, your team will tell you; it's not about being everyone's friend, but the old maxim of "you reap what you sow" has never been clearer.

> —**Tim Dugan**, former CEO Chris O'Brien Lifehouse,
> Sydney Cancer Centre

Personality at Work propels readers to understand how personality affects behaviors at work and to reflect on how their own personality helps and hinders their success. Across these pages, Warren is an innately curious and an altruistically-motivated coach who masterfully balances fascinating case studies, evidence-based best practices, and personal anecdotes to help leaders relate to and motivate their employees. For many years, I have watched Ron Warren build 360-degree personality assessment to its largest scale in the history of organizational personality assessment. I'm glad that this book now offers a broader audience the benefits of his unique expertise that spans personality science, clinical psychology, and leadership coaching.

> —**Brian S. Connelly**, Associate Professor and Canada Research Chair
> in Integrative Perspectives on Personality, University of Toronto
> Scarborough

I experienced firsthand the LMAP360 instrument with Ron at Yale's CEO College. Ron has succinctly identified and clarified the intricate and complex linkages between personality and leadership, offering a holistic lens into the art and craft of leadership. Ron's real-world vignettes enable the reader to gain significant insights into how personality impacts the practice of leadership, provide lively descriptions of multiple personality styles in action, and create a paradigm for strategic, effective leadership. I highly recommend his unique and meaningful work.

> —**Sharafat (Shaz) Khan, PhD**, partner, Deloitte Consulting LLP

Most business books by psychologists focus rather absurdly on one or another small dimension of the person—from "sticking" to habits to body language—and while they make fun reads and are ego-gratifying for academics who get to show off their clever experiments, they do little to help a person who wants to develop. Ron has invested thirty years in integrating the best findings of his profession, pulling them together in a comprehensive assessment and coaching system, and developed the rare ability to help people make change, relatively quickly and enduringly.

Ron chose to build a book like one might design an executive program at a leading business school. He provides rich, compelling, almost novelistic stories of leaders in action, failing as well as succeeding, struggling with their personality traits and those of others, and seeking to develop the grit to carry on and the emotional intelligence to lead.

Ron's book is informed by his experience, and he seeks to communicate as much as he can in book form. Over several decades Ron led a living lab by collaborating with major organizations and their leaders, and in programs at HBS and Yale SOM. As such, he is in the position to offer a tour de force and delivers.

—**James Frederick Moore, PhD**, founder and CEO of GeoPartners
Research; author of *The Death of Competition* and McKinsey
Award-winning article "Predators and Prey"

Personality at Work

The **Drivers** and **Derailers** of Leadership

Ron Warren, PhD

New York   Chicago   San Francisco
Athens   London   Madrid   Mexico City
Milan   New Delhi   Singapore   Sydney   Toronto

1 2 3 4 5 6 7 8 9   LCR   22 21 20 19 18 17

ISBN   978-1-259-86035-5
MHID   1-259-86035-3

e-ISBN   978-1-259-86036-2
e-MHID   1-259-86036-1

McGraw-Hill Education books are available at special quantity discounts to use as premiums and sales promotions or for use in corporate training programs. To contact a representative, please visit the Contact Us pages at www.mhprofessional.com.

Contents

PART I
Personality in Action/Personality Measures

PART II
Deference: Derailers and Development

Acknowledgments

Ornaith Keane, co-founder of LMAP, gave cogent feedback on *Personality at Work* draft after draft after draft—while delighting clients. I am indeed fortunate.

Richard Carter wrote a chapter intended for *Personality at Work* before I did. Our writing styles were too different to marry, but Richard's finishing "Leadership in Healthcare" ignited my no-excuses, take-no-consulting gigs, sit and write and revise every day for two years. Richard's fingerprints are everywhere in *Personality at Work*.

Greg Hiebert, of leadershipForward, was our first LMAP 360 customer and believed in my work and me. These orders fed my family early on, and our collaboration at clients (with Paul Litten) made a lasting impression on my thinking.

Ilona Jerabek, CEO of PsychTests, has been a great partner for over a decade. Ilona is a part of the secret in the secret sauce (assessment logics) of LMAP 360. Ilona thinks out smart solutions, makes it fun, and then makes it so.

Tow Heng Tan has been a good friend and important supporter of my work ever since we met in Singapore in 2008. Tow: thank you.

Jeff Sonnenfeld (Yale School of Management) has been like a guardian angel in my career, introducing me to amazing people and opportunities. Yale SOM's integration of LMAP 360 into programs was a game changer. Programs at Yale gave me an arena to work with leaders and develop the language and material in *Personality at Work*.

Co-facilitators at Yale SOM programs: Roger Lipson, Vergil Metts, and Erica Dawson are exceptional thinkers and coaches, honest and fun. Roger and Vergil continue to deliver coaching at Yale SOM, and Erica now is Director of Leadership Programs, Engineering at Cornell University.

Richard de Crespigny, pilot in command of Qantas QF32 featured in Chapter 15, graciously read and edited my drafts. A year later—and though flying internationally, giving speeches for his best-selling QF32 book, and now writing a second book—he edited the production copy. Grit. Grit. Grit.

Allan Goldstein, training Captain, 747 fleet at UPS Air provided essential feedback on the aviation chapters. Bill Putsis (University of North Carolina at Chapel Hill) was so enthusiastic in his feedback early in my work on the book, which was contagious and helped me immensely. Thanks to William (Bill) Crocker, who has played a key supportive role in my career; you are a dear friend.

Kelli Christiansen, my literary agent, immediately understood *Personality at Work*, and weeks later *Personality at Work* found a home with editor Cheryl Ringer at McGraw-Hill Education. Patricia Wallenburg and Judy Duguid edited and produced masterfully.

My children, Kelly Kate and Will, heard me drone on about studies and stories of effectiveness and derailment as I worked these ideas out for many years. Angela Day, my best friend and lovely presence in my life, read, asked tough questions, and communicated *what worked* and *what did not* for endless drafts to help me find my writer's voice and always gave me space to write *Personality at Work*.

Carlton L. Ferrono. There'd likely be no *Personality at Work* without Carlton's contributions. Carl spent a year editing my drafts and bringing his magic to my mundane. We met eight times for a week in Chicago or San Francisco—his place or mine—to think, write, and edit. We consulted daily and he helped steer, augment, and polish my thinking and writing. Just one example: I spent a month researching the Fukushima Daiichi nuclear disaster. Carl would observe: human error yes, and ask, "Ron, exactly where are the personality links?" Without more explicit links, Fukushima didn't make the book, as he thought through and nudged me so that only the very best of our best would be included in the book.

Carl—dramaturg for Red Orchid Theatre in Chicago—then had the good timing and production sense to step back once McGraw-Hill contracted for *Personality at Work*, and empowered me to finish the book. This acknowledgement cannot do justice to the immense contributions of Carlton Ferrono to *Personality at Work*.

Introduction: Personality Matters

- ▶ A board-certified surgeon operates on the wrong knee of a patient. Afterward several members of the operating room staff acknowledge that they *thought it might be* the wrong knee but didn't speak up. The surgeon's reputation for being bad tempered is well known, and they feared "the Wrath of God."

- ▶ The captain of a commercial airliner repeatedly dismisses the concerns of his first officer. On approach for landing, the first officer comments five times about deviations in speed, altitude, and glide slope. Each time the captain ignores, dismisses, or vaguely responds. And then it's too late. The plane overshoots the runway and crashes into a ravine.

- ▶ A brilliant CEO runs executive meetings through fear and intimidation. He sees himself as the smartest person in the room, and objections or concerns around his decisions are met with razor-sharp criticism. Team members learn to keep their heads down. Open, honest communication fades away. Strategic and tactical blunders follow. The company, once looking at a bright future, falters.

The actions and interactions between individuals have a huge impact on outcomes in the workplace, as in life. This impact is played out every day, in every profession, at times with extraordinary results, at times with disastrous results. And although each of us has good days and bad days, something more is in play here, something that in common language, as in the social sciences, we call *personality*.

• • • • • • •

The impact of personality on work has been my professional focus for 30 years. *Personality at Work* lays out, in plain English with stories and hard data, the key personality traits that drive effectiveness and high performance and the common traits that derail and degrade effectiveness. And I am not just making this stuff up!

OUR DATA RUNS DEEP

Personality at Work builds on a decade of research using the LMAP 360 assessment. If you have never heard of LMAP 360, few have—100 percent of our sales are by referral. Our clients include Harvard Business School's Advanced Management Program, Yale School of Management's CEO College and Global Leader Programs, Temasek Holdings Global Leader Program in Singapore, Exelis Leaders at the Wharton School, Teach for America, Underwriter Laboratories, Clayton Homes, and over 30 hospital systems in the United States. Chapters 3, 5, and 7 explain the assessment, samples, and more.

The LMAP 360 measures a set of personality traits related to Task Mastery and Teamwork traits that drive high performance *and* common personality traits related to Dominance and Deference that derail effectiveness. Moreover, as I'll cite throughout the book, the LMAP findings fit well with contemporary personality and organizational psychology research.

A MATTER OF METHOD

But there are a few key differences in the LMAP 360 that informs *Personality at Work*. First, most of the prior research on the personality drivers and derailers has been based on *self-assessment* data. Self assessments have unique biases and questionable validity, but are logistically simple and quick to administer (see Chapter 7).

In contrast, the LMAP 360 research uses *360 feedback ratings* collected from 15 coworkers, colleagues of the leader. These tens of thousands of feedback ratings, not self-ratings, have high reliability and validity and are the basis of the findings in *Personality at Work*. As we shall see, while some leaders do indeed have insight into how their behavior is perceived by others, many do not.

GRIT, EQ, DERAILMENT—SHARED LANGUAGE

One of my goals with *Personality at Work* is to write for everyday professionals, making complex research in social psychology understandable and actionable for readers. So I explicitly use language and terms that professionals know. I refer to the Task Mastery Traits (Conscientousness, Achievement Drive, and Innovation) as *Grit*—even though the meaning in *Personality at Work* contrasts with Angela Duckworth's now popular research on Grit that is much more focused on the Conscientiousness facet and uses self-assessment.

Task Mastery Traits is an inelegant mouthful and the word *Grit* captures the essence of Conscientiousness, Achievement Drive, and Innovation as measured in LMAP. Historically, Grit has been used by psychologists to describe intrinsic drive, achievement need, competence motivation, conscientiousness, passion and inquisitiveness, and heartiness—and it is in this sense that I use the word *Grit*.

Similarly, I also use the well-known terms *Social Intelligence* and *Emotional Intelligence* (*EQ*) to describe the Teamwork Traits (Openness to Feedback, Helpfulness, and Sociability)—even though there are subtle differences debated in the literature. Yet, when leaders get high scores on the Teamwork Traits they are often described as having prominent EQ—reflecting that Teamwork Traits and EQ share *far* more commonalities than differences.

Personality at Work will cross-tab, cross-fertilize, and connect models and language that describe the multifaceted phenomenon of personality. I link to other personality and team leadership research and language: *personality traits* (Murray, Cattell, Hogan, Costa and McCrae), *Achievement Drive* and *Grit* (McClelland, R. White, Wm. Howell), *multiple intelligences* (Gardner, Goleman, Sternberg), *circumplex profiles* (Leary, Plutchik and Conte), *derailment* (Benz, McCall and Lombardo, Dotlich and Cairo, Goldsmith), *engagement* (Gallup, Kenexa), *positive psychology* and *flow* (Seligman, Csíkszentmihályi) and others.

It has become fashionable in the HR analytics community to be "content agnostic"—to offer clients just-in-time survey capabilities and number-dump formats. LMAP is anything but. The data that underlie LMAP are based on long-term observations of how leaders behave and how those behaviors facilitate or derail performance. The idea is to be *content-rich*—based on carefully collected and analyzed data over the last 15 years and interpreted in the context of other evidence-based work.

PERSONALITY IN THE TWENTY-FIRST CENTURY

At the turn of the century, it was the era of emotional intelligence. Studies convincingly showed that social and emotional intelligence were critical for effectiveness in leadership, teamwork, and communications. Some studies touted that EQ was more important to success than IQ or achievement drive. EQ was *the* new thing in schools and parenting and leadership.

For a few years building up to Duckworth's 2016 publication of *Grit—the Power of Passion and Perseverance,* much attention had been given to research touting how determination, persistence, and unwavering results orientation—Grit—was the key driver of success and "made high achievers special." Grit became *the* new, new thing in schools and parenting and leadership.

NOT GRIT OR EQ, GRIT + EQ

Duckworth makes an incisive observation: "As a psychologist, I can confirm that grit is far from the only—or even the most important aspect—of a person's character. . . . There are many other things a person needs to grow and flourish. Character is plural."[1] Plural is the LMAP 360 integrating Grit *and* Emotional Intelligence *and* Dominance *and* Deference into a personality profile. *Personality at Work* explains why it is the *combination* of personality traits—a personality profile—that either drives or derails performance.

Three key findings emerge from the LMAP 360 studies:

1. Elite leaders, the top 20 percent, have prominent Grit *and* EQ—and do not have prominent Dominance or Deference traits that degrade performance.

2. The remaining 80 percent—who vary from pretty effective to ineffective—have prominent Dominance traits (Rigidity, Hostility, Controlling, Hyper-competitiveness) and/ or Deference traits (Approval Seeking, Dependence)— sometimes with high Tension for spice . . . aka, normal professionals and leaders who populate the workforce.

3. The most effective of this 80 percent *also* have either prominent Grit *or* EQ.

Understanding the impact of the traits that drive high performance and those that derail it—and learning how to raise one's own effectiveness and satisfaction at work—is what *Personality at Work* is about.

PERSONALITY AT WORK IS ORGANIZED INTO FOUR PARTS

Part I, "Personality in Action/Personality Measures," consists of eight chapters. Chapter 1, "The Two Steves," tells the story of how Steve Jobs and Steve Wozniak built a relationship and Apple Computer around their shared Grit. And yet, despite their shared Grit, the personalities of Jobs and Woz could not be more different. The next six chapters alternate between real-life case studies of personality in action and a study of personality and how it is assessed. Chapter 8 deviates from that design appropriately so, as it focuses on deviance.

Part II, "Deference: Derailers and Development," has two chapters, both of which explore how deference behaviors interfere with decision making, risk taking, and assertiveness. In addition, Chapter 10 discusses accountability, risk taking, and confidence and offers seven methods for deferent personalities to develop higher-performance behaviors.

Part III, "Dominance: Derailers and Development," includes four chapters because there are so many dominant leaders. It opens with "The Dominant Personality of Our Time" for a further look at Steve Jobs's personality and leadership. The following chapter examines the damage that hostile leaders do to morale, team process, and productivity. Thankfully, most domineering leaders are *not* hostile, but they are negative, rigid, controlling, and competitive—common derailers that kill morale and degrade performance. The *sweet 16*, inspired by Robert Sutton's *dirty dozen*, closes Part III with 16 verbal and nonverbal, attitude and behavior adjustments and questions to ponder to gain perspective.

Part IV, "Leadership Drivers and Development," with four chapters, begins with the incredible story of Qantas Flight 32: An Airbus 380, the world's largest superjumbo jet with 469 onboard, had an uncontained explosion in Engine 2 that caused catastrophic damages. The hours-long, tenuous situation demanded flying skills, sustained leadership, teamwork, and communications if one of the worst aviation disasters in history was to be averted. Chapter 16, "Your Best Self—the LMAP Method," looks at how LMAP 360 is used by leaders and organizations, including best practices developed at Clayton Homes. Chapter 17, "Red Teams and WRAP," shows how to apply judgment and decision-making methods that can trump personality biases using collective intelligence. The WRAP model is adapted from Chip Heath and Dan Heath's model presented in their book, *Decisive*. Finally, the last chapter in the book, Chapter 18, "Insight in Action," wraps it all up.

Enjoy the read!

Personality in Action/Personality Measures

The Two Steves

It was 1968, the early days of Silicon Valley. Tidy bungalows sat among the orange groves, burgeoning electronics firms, and defense contractors. Twenty-year-old Steve Wozniak, who lived with his parents in San Jose, rode his bike over to his buddy Bill Fernandez's house to work together in the Fernandez garage where they'd been building electronic gadgets together for years. Fernandez, a senior from Homestead High School, invited a sophomore schoolmate, Steve Jobs, who lived nearby in Los Altos. Bill was excited to introduce them because he knew that both were *really* into electronics. Despite their five-year age difference, they hit it off immediately. Woz remembers himself and Steve Jobs— "skinny and wiry and full of energy"—sitting on the sidewalk, telling stories about shared interests in pranks and electronics, a germinating friendship. Then,

> Steve came into the garage and saw the computer (this was before it blew up) and listened to our description of it. I could tell he was impressed. I mean, we'd actually built a computer from scratch and proved that it was possible . . . for people to have computers in a really small space. . . . Steve and I got close right away.[1]

Within a few years, they cofounded Apple Computer, a collaboration that would make them wealthy, iconic figures. Known personalities. In the early years, the differences in Woz's and Jobs's personalities helped to fuel the partnership: Woz, by nature shy and eager to please, focused on the back room: designing and building the electronics; Jobs, the never-satisfied go-getter and visionary thinker, drove Woz and the business that would become Apple.

Yet their personality differences ultimately undermined their partnership, as their attitudes—toward status, collaboration, treatment of fellow employees, and the type of organization they would build—led to their split by late 1981.

WOZ

Steve Jobs said that when he met Steve Wozniak, he was the first person who knew more about electronics than he did. Little wonder that the 15-year-old Steve Jobs was impressed with Woz. Few could match Woz's sheer intellectual firepower: in sixth grade his IQ was measured at 200. Their friendship blossomed fast, and they began working on pranks and projects together.

The young Woz was fortunate to grow up in an enriched environment bent on nurturing his intellect, particularly in math and the sciences.

Born to a white-collar family, he lived in one of the upper-middle-class suburban neighborhoods and attended schools in the emerging Silicon Valley. His father, Jerry Wozniak, had been a football star at California Institute of Technology (Caltech), was trained as an engineer, and was a rocket scientist at Lockheed Missiles & Space. His mother, Margaret, was also a strong presence: college educated and an activist for education, equal rights, and the community. Woz recalled that in third grade he practiced multiplication flash cards with his mom until he was proficient.[2]

His father was teacher, mentor, and role model and provided Woz with rigorous training in electronics that allowed him to learn and understand sophisticated engineering concepts in the fourth grade that "usually . . . come . . . much later for people."[3]

Jerry Wozniak believed that people's highest achievements were expressed in engineering, which could take society to a new level. He looked down on sales, marketing, and business leaders who ran corporations, teaching Woz to always be in the middle and not in a leadership position. Woz accommodated and, like his father, became an engineer, saying, "That's what I wanted to be" and that he was too shy to be a "business leader like Steve."[4]

If his parents and schooling provided him a strong foundation for his childhood identity, the interpersonal world of adolescence would be much more challenging. Woz was shy and introverted.[5] Though not uncommon in adolescents, these traits became more prominent over time and manifested as low confidence, tension, fearfulness, and low assertiveness. Woz had been a good athlete and popular prior to middle school, but this changed into a series of "terrible years" where Woz felt socially isolated and saw himself as unpopular.[6] Woz was insecure and afraid to speak for fear of saying the wrong thing.

He took refuge in his electronics and found comfort working alone, focusing intensively, solving complex problems. It was one area where Woz felt he could stand out and build his confidence. Never a show-off, Woz found approval, recognition, and a sense of belonging in science. Here, Woz was at the top, not the bottom, of the social hierarchy.

In eighth grade, Woz won a U.S. Air Force contest, competing against students entering university. Woz designed and built a sophisticated calculator with 100 transistors, 200 diodes, and 200 resistors on 10 circuit boards. On the college boards, Woz had perfect 800 scores in science and math, but not in chemistry, where he scored "only" 770.[7]

Woz's brilliance, however, did not find an academic focus as a freshman at the University of Colorado. He felt bored and constrained by courses and spent most of his time playing bridge with guys in the dorm and doing pranks. While introverted and shy, one-on-one or in small groups with the guys, Woz was very funny, affable, and well liked. He was smart but unassuming, easygoing and generous with others. More down-to-earth and community-minded than personally ambitious, he enjoyed intellectual challenges but was not interpersonally competitive. Challenged by a project, Woz had unmatched perseverance, self-direction, and critical thinking skills, but he had no desire to rigidly follow university curriculum rules and regulations.

In a computer class, Woz programmed the university mainframe to print reams of paper saying "Fuck Nixon." He followed up by programming it to calculate Fibonacci numbers infinitely. The Fibonacci prank cost five times more than the budget for the entire class; the university put Woz on probation for "computer abuse"[8] and threatened to bill him thousands of dollars to reimburse costs. Woz agreed to continue his education elsewhere. (He got an A+ in the class.)

He returned home to live with his parents, take courses at De Anza College, and work part-time as a programmer at Sylvania. Each night he'd think through how to improve on Sylvania's computers, upgrading chips and using fewer parts to reduce costs while maintaining performance.

Woz's prodigious intellect and innovative efforts were not limited to Sylvania. He was building computers *in his head*, always using fewer chips while improving performance.[9]

Despite Woz's hippy appearance and antiwar politics, he did not drink alcohol, use drugs, or enjoy much Bay Area free love. He felt like an outsider, and was treated as one. As noted earlier, his mother, Margaret, was a social activist, and Woz was also left of center, but his efforts to join a hippie cohort were unsuccessful. He says that the hippies he tried to hang with did not trust him "because I wouldn't do drugs" and describes this as "a hard time for me."[10]

STEVE JOBS

[Steve Jobs] showed me how brave he was by scoring free chips just by calling the sales reps. I could never do that. What one of us found difficult, the other often accomplished pretty handily. Examples of that teamwork are all over this story.

—Steve Wozniak[11]

Except for both men having Silicon Valley roots, their family backgrounds, ages, appearances, and temperaments were very different: Woz at 20 was an arrested adolescent, whereas Steve Jobs was a precocious, intense, willful young teenager. He was lean and angular in body and had a sharp, inquisitive mind. Jobs comfortably inhabited the hippy counterculture look, and he was already experimenting with sex and drugs at age 14.

Like Woz, Jobs was intellectually gifted. His fourth grade standardized test scores led the school to recommend skipping fifth and sixth grades; Jobs's parents approved skipping just fifth grade. But even that decision proved very challenging, as Jobs began sixth grade in a new school and was bullied by the older boys. He was miserable, hated the school and classmates, and began cutting classes.

Jobs responded to this adversity with a proactive position: he relentlessly lobbied his working-class parents, who could scarcely afford it, to move to a better school district in Los Altos. As Jobs later recalled, "I insisted they put me in a different school," and they eventually conceded. Even as a schoolboy—literally a *preteen*—Jobs exerted tremendous will and took control.

This may have been a fateful event in Jobs's life—as if Jobs decided that he would never again be bullied and that, if he used his wits and will to bend others, he could get his way. But Jobs's tough exterior was also brittle. A few years later, Jerry Wozniak aggressively questioned Jobs's justification for a 50-50 partnership split in Apple, given that Woz had created the intellectual property. Jobs was quickly reduced to tears (Woz insisted that it was a fair split).[12]

Ever confident, assertive, and willing to take risks, at 12 years old, Jobs looked up the phone number for Bill Hewlett (the H of HP: Hewlett and Packard) and asked for spare parts he needed to build a frequency counter for a school project. Hewlett, one of the nice guys of Silicon Valley, not only gave Jobs the parts; he offered him a summer job. Jobs recalls that HP had "a remarkable influence on me . . . formed my view of what a company was and how well they treated their employees (coffee, donuts, breaktimes) . . . it was clear that company recognized its true value was its employees."[13] This was a lesson that Jobs espoused throughout his life, though he did not walk this talk as a leader.[14]

Unlike Woz, Jobs never just wanted to "fit in" and belong, but to dominate and control his environment and others. As he accumulated power throughout his life, Jobs's unwavering belief in himself and his ideas, his need to govern every aspect of his environment, and his perseverance became legend.

Jobs and Woz's complementary talents, interests, and personalities found focus in their first project together—the blue box. The illegal venture was part antiauthoritarian prank, part moneymaking opportunity, and a harbinger of things to come.

THE BLUE BOX—1971

. . . it gave us a taste of what we could do with my engineering skills and his vision.

—Steve Wozniak[15]

If it hadn't been for the Blue Boxes, there wouldn't have been an Apple. I'm 100% sure of that. Woz and I learned how to work together, and we gained the confidence that we could solve technical problems and actually put something into production.

— Steve Jobs[16]

Woz, now a junior in college at Berkeley, read in *Esquire* magazine how hackers built a "blue box" to replicate the AT&T phone sound tones to make free long-distance calls. Woz told Jobs—still in high school— about it, and they excitedly gathered information, and Woz built a digital blue box to use in pranks. Woz claims it was honest fun. In his book, he refers to himself as the "ethical phone phreak." He writes that despite having his own blue box—built to place free calls anywhere in the world—because of his ethics, he paid huge phone bills![17]

Steve Jobs, rebellious and always on the lookout for a business opportunity, suggested they sell the blue boxes to students at Berkeley. The young entrepreneurs and their customers felt justified ripping off the AT&T monopoly during the Vietnam War, which generated strong antiestablishment sentiments on campuses.

If, for Woz, the ethical phone phreak, this was just another prank, for Jobs the experience was transformational. Jobs said that what he learned from this first venture was that he and Woz, two guys in a garage, could build a product and "control billions of dollars of infrastructure in the world . . . us two could control a giant thing."[18] For Jobs, this kind of leverage was intoxicating and fed his deep need for self-efficacy, impact, and power. Jobs also wielded power interpersonally: with the blue box, Jobs had convinced Woz to cross his previously defined ethical barrier, to see and do things *his* way. Jobs was already *the* leader.

They built the blue boxes for $40 each and sold about 100 of them for $150 each. Then they were robbed at gunpoint; and because of this and the fact that Jobs was soon leaving for college, they ended the venture.

REED COLLEGE

Jobs's need to do things his way—as well as his sense of entitlement to do so—played out with his selection of Reed College. Jobs's parents wanted Steve to attend college within the California university system, which had top-rated programs that were affordable. But Jobs insisted that if he were to attend *any* college, it had to be Reed College, a costly private college in Oregon. Because his parents, who had adopted Steve, had committed to his birth mother that Steve would attend college, they made the major sacrifices required to accommodate Steve.

As a freshman, Jobs had no interest in sticking to the conventional curriculum prescribed by the school authorities. Instead, Jobs dropped out—bypassing tuition, grades, and educational credits—but continued to audit classes that interested him. Jobs may have been academically unfocused, but he continued searching for knowledge and direction. He joined a commune, regularly dropped acid, and bounced back and forth between Oregon and the Bay Area. He took off to India with his close friend Daniel Kottke, looking for deeper meaning and purpose. Jobs returned to the Bay Area and began partnering with Woz on new ventures. After traveling the world, it was back at home where Jobs would find the meaning and purpose he'd sought abroad.

ATARI—1974

Jobs saw an ad for work at Atari, an early video-game maker, and showed up unannounced and unkempt, insisting he would not leave until the company gave him a job. The personnel director almost called the police, but instead called Al Alcorn, the chief engineer at Atari, who met with Jobs. Alcorn recalls that Jobs was intelligent and very passionate about tech: "I saw something in him," and Jobs was hired.

Coworkers at Atari soon began to complain that Jobs was "impossible to deal with," was callous and condescending, and had repellent body odor. But Jobs was good at debugging games, so Alcorn and Atari CEO Nolan Bushnell assigned him to a night shift. Bushnell didn't find Jobs's smell, odd behavior, or "prickliness" as a big issue; "I kind of liked him," he said, and to put him on the night shift (when no one else worked) was "a way to save him."[19]

Even after being assigned to the night shift, the 19-year-old Jobs maintained his superior attitude and continued to feel entitled to do or say whatever he wanted including, when he ran into other Atari employees, "informing them they were 'dumb shits.'"[20]

The Atari Project

Throughout this time Woz and Jobs remained close: Jobs would stop by Woz's apartment for dinner, talk shop, and play Atari's hit game Pong for hours on end. Nolan Bushnell contracted with Jobs to help Atari build the successor to Pong, Breakout. Bushnell knew Jobs would work with Woz, who knew how to reduce chip count and increase performance.

The contract was for $700 with delivery due in four days. Woz worked nonstop nights and delivered a low chip count. Jobs did not tell Woz that he and Bushnell had negotiated a large bonus for a low chip count and only paid Woz $350. Woz discovered that Jobs was paid several thousand dollars more than he'd told Woz, who said, "He wasn't honest with me, and I was hurt. But I didn't make a big deal about it or anything."[21]

This incident highlights a few things: First, it reflects Woz's conflict-avoidant personality and his rationalizing inappropriate treatment to maintain the relationship. Woz minimizes the difference between what Jobs was paid and what was shared with him as "a bit more" (when he tells the story in interviews and in his book)—though several thousand dollars is a hell of a lot more $350. Second, it reflects Jobs's self-centeredness and his callous disregard for a friend's loyalty, contributions, and feelings, as well as his sense of entitlement to operate outside the rules of ethical conduct. Later in life, Jobs denied, then rationalized, then avoided discussing this breach. Woz, Alcorn, and Bushnell confirm the story recorded in the official Apple Museum timeline as "Jobs cheats Woz out of $5,000."[22]

THE HP AND HOMEBREW YEARS

Woz, through an introduction by friend Allen Baum, got a job in the calculator division at HP. For Woz, who pined for a full-time, stable job at a respected technology giant, this was a personal and professional dream come true. Like his father, Woz was now an engineer in an engineering firm in the Silicon Valley. Woz had arrived; he said he'd planned on working at HP for life.[23]

Woz was proud to be working at HP, but his genius went unrecognized, and he was not challenged by the work. It looked fortuitous when HP began recruiting talent from the calculator team to build a desktop computer. Woz told the project manager that he wanted to be assigned to the project and was willing to do *any* kind of work to contribute and just be part of the project—"even be a measly printer interface engineer. Something tiny."[24] HP did not select Woz for the project even though Woz was well known to be highly skilled in the work.

While HP did not provide the opportunity for Woz's imagination to soar, the Homebrew Computer Club did. The club drew engineers and their children, a generation raised with electronics and prepared to take technology to the next level. Allen Baum invited Woz to accompany him to the club's first meeting in 1975; there, along with 30 others, they saw the then state-of-the-art Altair computer and its microprocessor specs. Woz knew he could improve on the specs and went to work to build a better, faster, cheaper computer: the prototype of the Apple I.

Woz built the computer from scrounged, low-cost spare parts, and a few months later he had a working model to show to Jobs. Jobs— of course—asked for new features: networking, memory storage, and disk drives, and he got to work finding better-quality components. Woz was impressed with Jobs's ability to acquire upgraded components from Intel. Unlike Woz, Steve Jobs was neither too shy nor too insecure to take risks, to be bold, to ask for things from others.[25]

Jobs was trying to sell Woz on going into business together, but there were several obstacles: Woz's loyalty to the hacker creed and to HP, his employer. The hacker ethos promoted at the Homebrew Club was to openly learn from and share work for the benefit of the entire community—not for personal profit. Woz later said that he had no plans to sell his work and that he'd have preferred to have the technology available for free for everyone.[26]

Woz was also a loyal and honest employee and wanted to bring his PC work to HP—he felt it was the right and ethical thing to do as HP's employee. But for reasons we will never understand, HP had no interest in the work of its brilliant, intensely loyal, hardworking employee. Woz later said, "I don't know what they were thinking."[27]

After his 12-hour workdays at HP, Woz continued laboring intensively into the nights on the Apple I. On June 29, 1975, Woz finished the prototype, a fully operational machine that ran BASIC, cost under a thousand dollars, and was about the size of an electric typewriter.

It took almost a year for Jobs to convince Woz to start a business together, and on April 1, 1976, Jobs, now 20, Wozniak, 25, and Ron Wayne[28] cofounded Apple Computer.

THE APPLE I

In May 1976, Jobs, Woz, and Wayne had a "product launch" at the Homebrew Computer Club and showed an assembled kit attached to a keyboard and TV monitor. The Apple I was a hobbyist, specialty product—like a Heathkit—a set of component parts and directions on how to assemble a circuit board. Built for people like members of the Homebrew Club, this was in no way anything like a personal computer for the mass consumer market.

Paul Terrell, who ran the Byte Shop in Palo Alto, was impressed with the unmatched performance of the Apple I and placed an order for 50 units to Jobs. But Terrell did not order 50 "kits" requiring assembly; instead he ordered 50 *assembled* units—for $500 each. Terrell's stroke-of-genius customer requirement transformed into a visionary idea for the integrated personal computer that Jobs took personal credit for in the years that followed.

On June 30, 1976, Jobs excitedly called Woz with news: a $25,000 order! To buy the parts to build the units, Allen Baum and his father, Elmer, loaned Jobs and Woz $5,000.

But the difficult, precise, and time-consuming nature of the assembly work showed that this was not a viable business in the long term. After the first 50 computers, Wayne quit. The two remaining partners needed assembled circuit boards, so Jobs sold his VW van, Woz sold his calculator, and they hired a friend to design a circuit board that could be mass-produced.

Woz was already working on the Apple II that would be a true personal computer. Where the Apple I was envisioned and engineered to be a hobbyist's machine and *only as an afterthought* was sold as a personal computer, Woz had built the Apple II from the ground up as a personal computer with color, higher-resolution graphics, sound, slots to attach external game paddles, etc.—a true plug-in and play design.[29]

To scale up from a garage to a manufacturing operation would require capital, and Jobs asked Bushnell for advice and introductions to investors. Don Valentine, a pioneer of venture capital, visited the Jobs garage but was not favorably impressed by the business or the partners. Valentine thought Apple needed a stronger marketing and distribution strategy and a business plan. Additionally, he thought Jobs argumentative and was turned off by Jobs's lousy hygiene and his Ho Chi Minh beard. But Jobs pressed Valentine for next steps and was referred to Mike Markkula, a former Intel executive.

Markkula Buys In

Markkula, who'd retired a multimillionaire at 30, knew both technology and—having himself been mentored by the Silicon Valley's premiere company leaders—the start-up business.[30] He visited the garage, was amazed by the Apple II prototype, *got it*, and was *in*. He recognized the genius of both Woz's and Jobs's work and the opportunity. Where most in the Silicon Valley saw personal computers as limited to the hobbyist market, Markkula saw the future and told the Steves that Apple Computer would be in the Fortune 500 in two years and launch an industry.[31]

Jobs and Woz were both wowed by Markkula. Woz said, "He was the nicest person ever" and was particularly impressed with Markkula's big house overlooking the Silicon Valley, his beautiful wife, "the whole package."[32] Jobs and Woz were impressed with Markkula's early success and riches; but more importantly, his vision for Apple as a revolutionary and disruptive industry impressed Jobs deeply. Markkula became a father figure, mentor, and role model for Jobs to rely on, learn from, and emulate.

Markkula joined the Apple team, bringing the critical strategic marketing, distribution, business planning, and adult supervision that Apple needed to succeed. He would also provide an immediate $92,000 installment of a $250,000 investment.

But now the plan hit a bump in the road: Markkula would only invest and join the Apple team with Woz as a full-time employee. Woz did not want to leave his engineer's job at HP, which he saw as his job for life. Furthermore, he was uncomfortable with the idea of being in a start-up venture where he believed, as a founder, he'd be required to "push people around and control what they did . . . become someone authoritative."[33]

Jobs went into overdrive to work every angle to convince Woz to join. He called on Woz's family and friends to encourage him to leave HP and join the venture, emphasizing how much fun it would be. Even Woz's mother, Margaret, who did not like or trust "Steve Job-less," supported the plan. Still Woz did not waver.

It was Allen Baum who ultimately understood Woz's passions, fears, and values and deftly reframed Apple as an engineering opportunity. Markkula, Jobs, and others would fill management and leadership roles while Woz would remain an engineer. "I needed to hear one person saying that I could stay at the bottom of the organizational chart, as an engineer, and not have to be a manager. He told me I could do it and never get into management. I called Steve Jobs right away."[34] Woz was in.

APPLE COMPUTER TAKES OFF

In January 1977, Apple Computer incorporated and would introduce the affordable Apple II ($1,295) at the West Coast Computer Faire in April. Markkula took leadership and outlined Apple's three core principles moving forward:

▶ Have *empathy* for the customers' experience and understand their needs better than any other company.

▶ *Focus* exclusively on critical business activities; eliminate all non-mission-critical activities that dilute focus.

▶ *Impute* quality into every level of the customer relationship by using quality technology, design, and marketing.

These principles helped form the foundations of Jobs's developing business mindset. Years later he paid homage to Markkula: "When you open the box of an iPhone or iPad, we want that tactile experience to set the tone for how you perceive the product . . . Mike taught me that."[35]

ONE LAST STAND FOR THE ENGINEER

Woz, who by nature was accommodating and nonconfrontational, already anticipated difficulties working with the willful and controlling Jobs. But in a conflict around the design of the Apple II, Woz the engineer took a stand.

Jobs wanted to control the user's experience and wanted only two slots, for a printer and modem. Woz knew that tech-savvy users would want to add circuit boards and peripherals and insisted on eight slots. "This time I told him, 'If that's what you want, go get yourself another computer.' . . . I was in a position to do that then. I wouldn't always be."[36]

Woz, the engineering workhorse, used his trump card and prevailed. In the future he had little leverage, as he'd opted out of formal leadership.

APPLE II

Prior to the Faire, Markkula coached his young, unpolished partners to impute professionalism around everything associated with the Apple brand. Markkula instructed them how to dress, talk, act and interact, and demonstrate the product.

Jobs followed Markkula's lead; gone was the dirty, smelly, barefoot hippie; he cleaned up well. Woz wasn't interested in playing professional. The arrested adolescent Woz (and buddies) distributed 8,000 leaflets for a nonexistent Zaltair Computer. Woz knew that Markkula would not approve of a prank at such a high-profile event and that it would "give the wrong image to the company." That's what any professional type would've said. But hey, they were dealing with Steve Wozniak."[37]

Jobs's recollection was that "we stole the show." Apple II became a huge success, and Apple Computer was on its way.

THE APPLE YEARS

Business cycled up fast. Woz was status averse, disliked all the attention, and found that it distracted from his work. The brash Jobs grabbed the mantle of leadership firmly with both hands. Though they did not discuss it at the time and may not have even been consciously aware of it, the two Steves had very different visions of the kind of organization and culture in which they wanted to work and could flourish.

Woz wanted to perfect the Apple II, while Jobs moved onto the new Lisa and Mac technology. Woz wanted a family atmosphere, flat with minimal hierarchy, where all were treated with respect and consideration. Jobs liked being the face of Apple, enjoyed being recognized as the genius authority of the computer revolution, and began accumulating the accoutrements of wealth, status, and power.

By age 23 Jobs was worth $100 million (1983 dollars) and enjoyed the newfound money, beauty, power, and control. He consistently said that the money was unimportant to him and that the really important things to him were *the company* and *the people*.[38] Those who worked with Jobs would absolutely agree to the central importance of the company, but Jobs's relationships with people rarely conveyed that he believed they were important to him.

The success of Apple reinforced Jobs's sense of self-importance, and in his arrogance he ran roughshod over others. Woz claimed Jobs "never treated me rudely," but Woz—like others who observe hostile, bullying behavior even when not directed at them personally—*was* affected. Jobs mercilessly belittled two programmers Woz had hired, one of whom was Randy Wigginton, then 18 years old, who said Jobs would glance at his work and tell him "it was shit without having any idea what it was or why I had done it."[39] Wigginton, who went on to program MacWrite and other key Apple IPs, proved to not be a total shit.

THE NEXT BIG THING

As Jobs became the public face of the personal computer revolution, his leadership within Apple grew increasingly disruptive. Apple had many projects under way. Apple employee #31 was Jef Raskin, who had written his PhD on graphical user interfaces (GUIs). Raskin urged Jobs to visit Xerox PARC, where Raskin knew engineers there doing groundbreaking work. In late 1979, Jobs visited and had a transformative experience with the GUI and mouse to navigate. Years later, when Jobs recalled the GUI—*the* foundation for Apple design—he neglected to mention Raskin and diminished the Xerox PARC GUI work itself, saying, "[I] remember it was very flawed, was incomplete, they'd done a bunch of things wrong . . . but still the germ of the idea was there."[40]

In 1979, Apple announced the Lisa Computer for release in 1981 for less than $2,000. Lisa would be the first PC applying Xerox PARC technology with mouse/GUI navigation. Jobs had also negotiated a $100 million investment in Apple from Xerox in 1980. Ken Rothmuller was the Lisa project leader until 1980, when Jobs insisted on adding new features that Rothmuller saw would make it impossible to meet two sacrosanct goals: deliver on time and at a reasonable price. Rothmuller could not get on board and was fired. In 1981, with Lisa now two years behind schedule, Jobs recruited 15 key Xerox employees to work on it. Lisa was released in 1983 for $9,998—a price with no market.

Safe in isolation, Woz refined and upgraded his beloved Apple II, which was released on time for $1,395, won the 1984 Industrial Design Excellence Award, and anchored the most successful Apple products for the next decade.

Despite the fact that the Apple II provided the bulk of revenue[41] and was loved by the public and Apple staff, Jobs took every opportunity to publically disrespect and belittle the Apple II as old, past technology and *not* Apple's future. This was a serious morale killer that promoted ill-informed and ugly divisiveness at Apple.

In addition to the Lisa mess, Jobs also foisted himself onto the Macintosh team, where he quickly fostered dissent at project leader Jef Raskin. Within a year, Jobs forced Raskin out (who then resigned). Woz said, "Some of my very best friends in Apple, the most creative people in Apple who worked on the Macintosh, almost all of them said they would never, ever work for Steve Jobs again. . . . It was that bad."[42]

1980—THE BIGGEST IPO SINCE FORD

In late 1980, Apple went public, valued at $1.79 billion. Jobs made $217 million in the IPO, but his reputation as mean-spirited and with-holding was further cemented when early employees were not included in the stock option plan.[43] Incredibly, this included Daniel Kottke, Jobs's soul mate from Reed and travels to India. Kottke, Apple employee #12, who had started work in the Jobs garage and remained a full-time employee, had assumed he had earned founders' stock. "I totally trusted Steve," he said, "and I assumed he would take care of me like I'd taken care of him, so I didn't push." But Jobs avoided Kottke: "He just would not talk to me. He kept me waiting outside his office for hours, on multiple occasions . . . he would just be on the phone endlessly until I went away, because he didn't want to talk to me."[44]

Ron Holt, an Apple manager aware of the situation with Kottke, offered to match whatever number of stock options Jobs would give to Daniel. Jobs infamously replied, "OK. I will give him zero."[45] Jef Raskin also got no stock.

By contrast, generous Woz had created "The Woz' Plan," where engineers and marketing staff could buy 2,000 shares at a low option price. Those who participated were able to buy a house and have some security in their life. Woz also gave stock to 40 employees left out of the IPO—Randy Wigginton, Daniel Kottke, Bill Fernandez, and others. He recalled, "I gave each of them stock worth about a million dollars."[46] With his stock proceeds, Woz bought a dream home for himself and his new wife, Alice. They soon divorced, and she kept the house.[47]

PARTNERS NO MORE

Within a year of the IPO, the short collaboration between Woz and Jobs was over. Jobs's profile rose as Apple's undisputed leader and driving force, while Woz grew disengaged.

With proceeds from the IPO, Woz bought a Beechcraft airplane. In 1980, he'd gotten his private pilot's license, and he and his girlfriend, Candi, took trips around California. On February 7, 1981, Woz, along with Candi and two others, crashed on takeoff from Scotts Valley. The NTSB investigation said the plane stalled while climbing on takeoff, bounced down the runway through two fences, and came to rest on an embankment. Pilot inexperience and premature liftoff were the probable causes of the crash.

All four onboard were hurt, but Woz was the worst injured, with head injuries and anterograde amnesia for five weeks. This traumatic experience led to him make two decisions. First, he married Candi in June, and they moved into a spectacular house on the summit of the

Santa Cruz Mountains. Second, Woz decided to leave Apple to return to UC Berkeley and finish college, enrolling as Rocky Raccoon Clark. While he would return to Apple after Berkeley, his position would never be more than as a figurehead founder.

CHAPTER 2

Silicon Valley Grit

Steve Wozniak and Steve Jobs spent almost 10 years in garages working together and tinkering with and mastering electronics projects. What drove them was their shared *Grit*—a blend of Conscientiousness, Achievement Drive, and Innovation—the behavioral drivers that focused their IQ and intellectual curiosity and was the common denominator on which *their relationship* and *Apple Computer* were built.

Except for Grit, Woz and Jobs differed in almost every other aspect of personality, which made their *overall personalities* strikingly different:

▶ **Jobs wanted to be in control, in the lead.** Beside his formidable Grit, Jobs was extremely *domineering*—intensely inflexible, aggressive, controlling, and competitive. These personality traits, not his Grit, were why Jobs saw a binary world. Jobs was so self-centered and self-absorbed that he was less capable and less willing to collaborate with others. Empathy is rare enough in dominating personalities, but Jobs was also hostile—mean, nasty, and ungracious with others—the exact opposite of behaviors that constitute key aspects of social and emotional intelligence.

▶ **Woz aspired to be a great engineer, *not* a great leader.** Woz channeled 100 percent of his Grit into the engineering;

he wanted to be on a team, not lead a team. Woz's ambitions were all about building technology, not building power or authority or status as a company leader. He earnestly believed that formal authority clashed with his introverted, easygoing, generous, and accommodating nature. Woz was raised to be suspicious of the company man and to understand how power corrupts.

Woz recognized Jobs's talent for promoting, networking, marketing, and funding—the exact roles and situations where Woz was most uncomfortable and that he wanted to avoid. Precisely because Woz was accommodating and just wanted to do great work, he was a perfect complement to the stubborn visionary, the controlling and competitive natural showman, Steve Jobs. Woz's deferential personality, shyness, and introversion all led him to *consciously opt out of leadership* at Apple where Steve Jobs was *all in*.

EQ AND SOCIAL INTELLIGENCE

Aside from the traits of Grit, Dominance, and Deference, there is one other important behavioral dimension and leadership asset in which neither Woz nor Jobs excelled: *EQ and social intelligence.* Neither had the social and emotional intelligence needed to effectively manage himself and interpersonal relationships or to attain high-performance leadership—though for dramatically different reasons.

Jobs was too dominating and Woz too deferring. Jobs's bossy, authoritarian style suffocated teamwork and communications and eroded morale. Woz's shy, unassertive, conflict-avoidant personality impaired his ability to speak up, address conflict constructively, and fill a team leadership–versus–follower role. When Jobs mistreated others, Woz might feel awful about it, but he would not intervene, behave like a leader, and stop it. Though Jobs's behavior conflicted with Woz's personal values (and for that he felt bad), Woz did not act on his values to help shape and define the culture.

Jobs seized the lead, Woz colluded-by-accommodation, and the behavioral fabric of an Apple culture was woven: in the behaviors demonstrated and tolerated by leadership. Woz left Apple with a reputation as being well liked, and in fact revered, and as being respectful and considerate of others. While Woz never aspired to lead, he might have developed stronger team leadership skills had he not become wealthy and free to do what he wanted. He moved on to his other passion projects and away from the unhappy corporate culture at Apple. Unlike most professionals, Woz could afford the luxury of choices that many professionals do not have if their career choices include management or leadership roles.

LEADING TALENTED PROFESSIONALS

Steve Jobs not only aspired to be a great leader; he became one, albeit with shortcomings. The early Apple story speaks to grit, dominance, and deference, but not much about EQ and social intelligence as key team leadership behaviors. Only after being forced out of Apple did Jobs finally learn about effective team leadership behaviors from John Lasseter and Ed Catmull at Pixar—a topic discussed in Chapter 11, "The Dominant Personality of Our Time." We will explore how Jobs matured and grew and how he didn't.

Professionals with a gritty and domineering style sometimes point to Steve Jobs as evidence and validation that domineering behaviors can be a foundation for great leadership . . . *If it worked for Steve Jobs, why won't it work for me?* In short, if, like Steve Jobs, you have a gritty, hostile, domineering style *and* $100 million at age 23, then expressing hostile, domineering behaviors might be a risk you can afford to take. But do not overlook the fact that it was Jobs's hostile, domineering behavior at Apple that derailed him out of a job. He self-funded his next decade of work—which is not something most professionals can do.

• • • • • • • •

A key reason for writing this book is that the most successful leaders have Grit and EQ, but far more leaders and aspiring leaders have prominent deference or domineering behaviors.[1] Just like Woz and Jobs (and the author), 75 percent of professionals have prominent Dominance or Deference traits that negatively impact performance.

A growing body of research identifies that behaviors associated with Grit and EQ operate as "high-value skills" (in the words of *Fortune Magazine* editor Geoff Colvin) *that facilitate and drive leadership*, teamwork, and communications.[2] Yet far more commonly we see professionals who struggle in their careers because they do not effectively manage prominent Dominance or Deference traits that *interfere with and derail leadership*, teamwork, and communications.

STONE AGE MAN IN THE INFORMATION AGE

Why are counterproductive dominance and deference behaviors so common? These behaviors are seen throughout the animal kingdom. These behaviors in our ape relatives often look and feel so familiar, so like those of humans. Dominance and deference behaviors are deeply rooted in our evolutionary programming—essentially stone age behaviors. These behaviors developed to keep order in the primitive environments in which we evolved over millions of years (see Figure 2.1), and now, in modern complex workplaces, these behaviors can be counterproductive.

Watch video interviews of Jobs and Woz, and you will see how both were driven to build technology that would serve as new, meaningful tools for humankind—to make a difference. They have passion and persistence, competence and ambition, focus and engagement, *Grit*. Throughout their careers, in the face of obstacles, difficulties, and derailments, they persevered to start again . . . to express their passion and drive for innovation and results.

Video will also reveal Jobs's aggressive, dominating nature and Woz's more cooperative, nonthreatening style. You can almost see predator

FIGURE 2.1 | HUMAN EVOLUTION

Stone Age Man in the Information Age

Stone Age	2.5 million to 10,000 years ago
Agrarian Age	8,000 BC to 1900
Industrial Age	1900 to 1995
Information Age	1995 to 2015
Information/Consumer Age	2015 to

Stone Age = 99.9% of Human Evolution

and prey—the deeply rooted dominance and deference behaviors in the two Steves.

PHYLOGENY AND ONTOGENY

Grit and EQ are behaviors that appeared later in human evolution (species phylogeny) and in individual development (personal ontogeny), and in many people, these behaviors only emerge well into adulthood—if ever. Yet we see basic dominance and deference behaviors emerge in toddlers. For some, the more highly evolved behaviors of Grit and EQ require the full maturation of the frontal cortex—in the mid-twenties. This is a critical pivot point for those of us who need to think before we act in order to exercise our Grit or EQ. Grit often requires careful planning and thinking about projects and work; EQ/Social Intelligence often requires careful thinking about people and relationships. Many of us, much of the time, do *not* think before we act.

PERSONALITY TRAITS AND PROFILES

To understand the impact of personality on work, we must define our terms, and then it helps to visually represent the personality traits and how they interact—to construct a Personality Profile.

Personality traits are the building blocks of personality, and each specific trait represents habitual patterns of thoughts, feelings, motivations, and behaviors. It is the sum of the personality traits and their interaction that forms an individual's personality. These are the topics we explore in the next chapter, "Personality Traits and Profiles."

CHAPTER 3

Personality Traits and Profiles

HOW MANY PERSONALITY TRAITS EXIST?

The MIT personality traits web page lists 638 "traits." This long list includes synonyms that describe the same traits. For example, *Hostility* is closely related to the meaning of traits such as *Angry, Cantankerous, Argumentative, Abrasive, Vindictive, Hateful, Unctuous, Treacherous, Sadistic, Reactive, Predatory*, and the list goes on and on—with another 30 words! So as you can see, there are not 638 meaningfully different personality traits.

By the 1950s, psychologists had identified and classified the personality traits we measure today. Although we use a range of labels for the key traits, psychologists agree that between 10 and 15 traits reflect the important individual differences associated with effectiveness at work. Moreover, there is high agreement on which personality traits facilitate and drive individual and team performance and which impair and derail it.

TRAITS INTERACTING

The *gestalt*, where the whole is greater than the sum of its parts, is a central concept in personality theory. So whether you measure 5 or 10 traits, the fact remains that individual personality traits do not operate

The Big Five Personality Model

Factor analytic studies have identified a set of five broad personality traits or dimensions that occur universally across cultures, genders, and generations. Psychologists call it the five-factor model (FFM), or the Big Five.[1] The Big Five dimensions (also referred to by the acronym OCEAN) are like the least common denominators of personality, with each dimension anchored by opposite behaviors:

Dimension		Opposite Behavior
Openness to Experience	⟷	Cautious/Pragmatic
Conscientiousness	⟷	Careless/Disorganized
Extraversion	⟷	Introversion/Reserved
Agreeableness	⟷	Argumentative/Detached
Neuroticism	⟷	Confident/Secure

in a vacuum, independent from one another; rather, they dynamically interact with one another. Compare two sociable individuals who nonetheless behave differently because one is confident and the other insecure. Their shared sociability will be expressed uniquely through a range of verbal and nonverbal behaviors. But because of their dissimilar traits of confidence and insecurity, their behavior will differ. Now consider the impact of combining not 2 traits, but 13 (as in the LMAP 360 described later in the chapter), and you can see that there is a lot of variability in the behavior of people.

TIMOTHY LEARY AND THE INTERPERSONAL CIRCUMPLEX

How can this dynamic whole of personality traits be represented? This is the question that Timothy Leary addressed in his doctoral dissertation at Berkeley and refined in his groundbreaking 1957 book, *The*

Interpersonal Diagnosis of Personality. Leary set out a complex, integrated model of human personality that described how personality is organized and how traits interact conceptually and statistically, and he represented his model in a simple graphic. He called it the *Interpersonal Circumplex* (see Figure 3.1).

Tim Leary was an amazing, charismatic, and sometimes very difficult character. Recruited to Harvard University by David McClelland in 1957, he was fired for scandals at the Harvard Psilocybin Project in 1963. President Nixon called him "the most dangerous man in America." But generation-leading intellectuals and artists including Huston Smith, Aldous Huxley, Marshall McLuhan, John Lennon,

FIGURE 3.1 | THE INTERPERSONAL CIRCUMPLEX (LEARY, 1955)

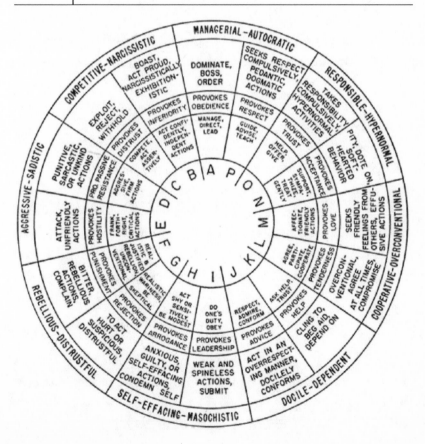

Allen Ginsberg, Jack Kerouac, and Ken Kesey saw Leary's genius, and he became a leader of the countercultural movement. (See Appendix A for more on Leary.)

Fast-forward a half century: Leary, a leader of the anti-establishment movement of the 1960s and beyond, today would see many derivatives of his Interpersonal Circumplex in *establishment* training programs across the world. Just a very few of the Circumplex-based personality assessments are shown in Table 3.1.

While businesses and the world at large have transformed into a 24/7, globally interconnected world, one thing that has not changed much is people. The same traits and behaviors that operated as assets and liabilities in the industrial age function similarly in the information age. The world around us evolves at an unprecedented faster rate all the time, as technology pushes beyond Moore's law of 18-month cycles to the next generation. But humans don't evolve according to Moore's law, and we remain essentially *stone age* humans in the *information age*.

LMAP 360

The LMAP 360 is a multirater assessment—meaning it has self-ratings *and* collects ratings from multiple feedback raters who know the leader well. All raters respond to 135 assessment items (e.g., "friendly," "brags about winning," "self-confident") using a 5-point rating scale to rate how much a behavior describes the leader—from "Not at all" to "A great extent." Feedback raters also rate the leader's effectiveness in five performance areas and provide comments (this is described in greater detail in Chapter 5).

Figure 3.2 shows an example of an LMAP 360 Profile, which displays the results as a circular graph with the center point as zero and four concentric circles marking the 25, 50, 75, and 100 percent quartiles. The ratings are converted to percentiles by comparing a leader's scores with those of a representative sample.[2] Traits with higher scores have

TABLE 3.1 | THE LEARY LEGACY—CIRCUMPLEX PERSONALITY ASSESSMENTS

Leary (1957)	Schaefer (1959, 1961, 1964)	Lafferty (1971)	Wiggins (1995)	Kaplan & Kaiser (2006)	LMAP 360, Warren (2002, 2006, 2016)
Helpful	Democratic	Humanistic	Helpful	Supports	1. Helpfulness
Affiliation	Cooperative	Affiliative	Sociable	Listens	2. Sociability
Self-Effacing	Accepting	Approval	Absolving	—	3. Approval Seeking
Dependent	Protective	Dependence	Dependent	Empowers—Excessive	4. Dependence
Fearful	—	Avoidant	Abasive	—	5. Tension
Distrustful	Possessive	Oppositional	Rigid	Versatility—Low	6. Rigidity
Hostile	Authoritarian	Power	Dictatorial	Forceful—Excessive	7. Hostility
Aggressive	Authoritarian	Power	Controlling	Takes Charge	8. Need to Control
Competitive	—	Competitive	Competitive	—	9. Competitiveness
Ordering	Persistence	Perfectionism	—	Order	10. Conscientiousness
Responsible	—	Achievement	Ambitious	Executes	11. Achievement Drive
Independent	Imagination	Self-Actualization	Confident	Innovation	12. Innovation
—	—	—	—	—	13. Open to Feedback

Key: — not specifically measured

FIGURE 3.2 | THE LMAP 360 PROFILE

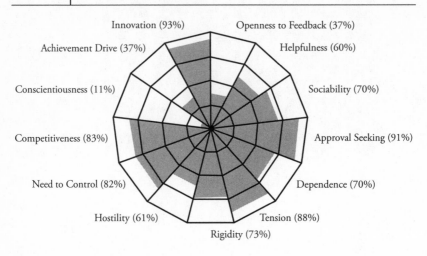

the greatest impact on a person's behavior and appear as the longest and largest-shaded areas. Traits with the lower scores have the least influence on a person's behavior and appear as smaller shaded areas.

Who Is in the Representative Sample?

The LMAP sample is composed of already successful professionals. Most are college educated, have 10+ years of experience in a management or matrix management role, and have professional expertise in engineering, finance, medicine, law, accounting, IT, etc. All work in reputable firms and organizations. Most are rated as being in the top 25 percent compared with others.[3] The LMAP 360 ratings do not measure a leader's intelligence or job-specific technical knowledge or skills, but rather the behaviors needed to work with and through others and to produce quality results.

Who Is the Rater?

When we refer to relationships between a leader's personality and performance, we refer to the person's personality expressed in behavior based on coworker feedback ratings, not self-ratings. The differences between self- and feedback ratings are addressed in Chapter 7, but keep in mind that feedback ratings reflect how observers see a leader behaving, and these ratings are strongly related to leadership effectiveness. Self-ratings reflect how a leader thinks he or she behaves, and such ratings are weakly linked to effectiveness.

THE LMAP 360: FOUR KEY DIMENSIONS

The LMAP clusters closely related traits into four dimensions of behavior (see Figure 3.3):

1. Social Intelligence and Teamwork

2. Deference

3. Dominance/Domineering

4. Grit and Task Mastery

Let's take a deeper look at each one.

FIGURE 3.3 | FOUR KEY DIMENSIONS

1. Social Intelligence and Teamwork Traits

These traits are strongly positively associated with interpersonal skill and leadership effectiveness (see Figure 3.4). In combination, they reflect the kinds of attitudes and behaviors associated with emotional and social intelligence and a positive, optimistic presence. Cooperation, collaboration, trust, and an ability to enjoy time spent with others are hallmarks. The Teamwork sector is made up of three traits:

▶ Openness to Feedback

▶ Helpfulness

▶ Sociability

OPENNESS TO FEEDBACK

Openness to Feedback indicates a leader's interest in and efforts to seek out and use feedback from others. A high score points to open-mindedness, intellectual curiosity, flexibility, and a demonstrated interest in others' views. These are key aspects of Carol Dweck's *growth mindset*.[4] A low score suggests a narrow-minded, inflexible approach and disinterest in others' points of view.

FIGURE 3.4 | TEAMWORK TRAITS—SOCIAL AND EMOTIONAL INTELLIGENCE

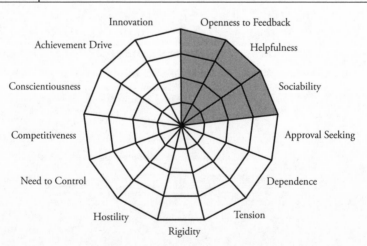

HELPFULNESS

Helpfulness measures qualities associated with emotional intelligence: interpersonal sensitivity, consensus building, and interest in working with others. Individuals with high scores are patient listeners, are optimistic, and use encouragement to motivate performance. Helpfulness is not a measure of friendliness or extraversion: introverts, ambiverts,[5] and extraverts can all equally score high (or low) on this trait.

SOCIABILITY

Sociability measures an interest in and ability to maintain warm interpersonal relationships. A person with a high score on Sociability loves to interact with others and is a friendly and socially skilled "people person." Because the Sociability scale does not assess stimulus-seeking behavior, it's not a pure measure of extraversion, although it is correlated with it.

> Introverts can have strong teamwork skills with high scores on Openness to Feedback and Helpfulness. Extraversion is seen in the combination of Sociability and Approval Seeking.

2. DEFERENCE TRAITS

Deference is negatively correlated to leadership effectiveness (see Figure 3.5). The inhibition and lack of assertiveness impairs teamwork and communications, as we examine throughout the book. Professionals high in Deference avoid confrontation and prefer others take the lead, but they also show humility and loyalty as behavioral assets. These traits are the core of the Deference sector and are associated with unassertive, passive behavior:

- ▶ Approval Seeking
- ▶ Dependence
- ▶ Tension

FIGURE 3.5 | DEFERENCE TRAITS

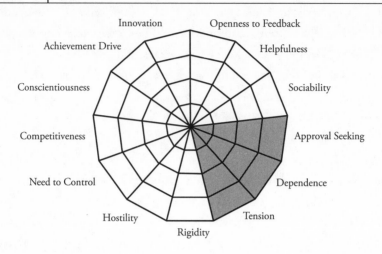

APPROVAL SEEKING

Approval Seeking measures the need to seek out and gain the support and acknowledgment of others. People with a high need for approval place a priority on fitting in and "going along to get along." They compromise to avoid the discomfort of confrontation even when confrontation is appropriate. They can be reticent to a fault to take the lead, and they can be overly optimistic. Rebels do not typically score high on this scale.

DEPENDENCE

Dependence measures the need to seek direction and guidance from others. High scores reflect a preference to be in the role of follower, to maintain the status quo, to play it safe, and to limit risks. Dependent people feel at the mercy of events and believe events happen to them, which is referred to as "external locus of control." They react to events rather than initiating them. In addition, they are easily intimidated and are uncomfortable with conflict or change.

TENSION

Tension reflects the tendency to worry and feel anxious. A certain level of anxiety functions to keep us alert, but very tense people see problems everywhere, reducing their capacity to learn and experience joy, creativity, and confidence. Tension is contagious and creates discomfort and doubt in others. Anxiety and tension further inhibit the reserved person, causing the person to remain stuck in ready, aim, aim, aim, aim . . . unwilling to fire.

Tension co-occurs with deference and dominance. Tension can further amp up type A, dominating personalities, with their heightened sense of urgency. Their impatience can trigger ready, fire behaviors— without the careful aim and thinking through of details or consequences—examined in Chapter 4, "Team Process and Personality," and in Chapter 6, "Flying Lessons."

We readily see Tension in Jobs and Woz, who had very different ways of expressing their anxieties and worries: Jobs projected it outward through perfectionism and hostility, while Woz internalized his anxieties, which further fed his insecurities.

3. Dominance/Domineering Traits

The traits associated with Dominance focus on getting and maintaining control (see Figure 3.6). Drive, decisiveness, and passion are assets. But

FIGURE 3.6 | DOMINANCE/DOMINEERING TRAITS

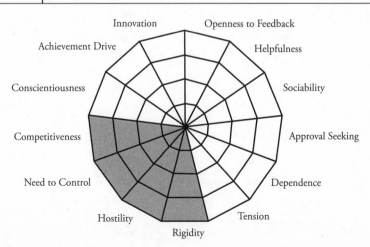

self-centeredness and inflexibility are liabilities that decrease teamwork and leadership effectiveness.

There are four traits at the core of Dominance/Domineering:

▶ Rigidity

▶ Hostility

▶ Need to Control

▶ Competitiveness

RIGIDITY

Rigidity measures the tendency to be stubborn and resistant to alternative points of view. In Carol Dweck's model these are people with a *fixed mindset*. Rigid thinkers enjoy arguments and debates and raise a lot of issues, not with the intent to find common ground but in order to find fault and be "right." They like being a devil's advocate, and they tend to focus on finding problems rather than solutions.

HOSTILITY

Hostility is the tendency to become irritable and angry in response to everyday frustrations and challenges. Hostile leaders are intolerant of people, situations, or work that does not match what they want and expect. They are easily offended and antagonized and feel justified reacting to what they perceive as provocations with heated arguments. Rather than finding ways to reduce conflict, they escalate and go on the offensive.

NEED TO CONTROL

Need to Control measures the tendency to be authoritarian, adversarial, and pushy. Controlling people feel a need to dominate situations and exercise or flex their power and influence. They are opinionated, see things as black and white (i.e., there's my way or the wrong way), and state their opinions directly. They tend to take things personally and make things personal, which is not an asset for teamwork.

COMPETITIVENESS

Competitiveness measures the need to compete with and outdo other people. While many forms of competition are appropriate and healthy, high scores on this scale indicate a tendency to set up win-lose situations rather than win-win scenarios. Most businesses operate as teams and need team members to collaborate rather than compete with each other, so the ability to create win-win scenarios is essential.

Steve Jobs likely would have very high scores on all these traits. Indeed, in many ways, he is the archetypal hostile, domineering leader, as described in Chapter 11, "The Dominant Personality of Our Time." In contrast, Woz would likely have scored very low on these traits.

4. Task Mastery Traits—Grit

Average or higher Grit and Task Mastery traits (see Figure 3.7) are common among leaders who routinely must plan and execute against high standards. Even leaders with just one elevated aspect of Grit—a CPA with high Conscientiousness and low Innovation, for example—can be very effective, especially when complemented by Teamwork traits. Grit

FIGURE 3.7 | TASK MASTERY TRAITS—GRIT

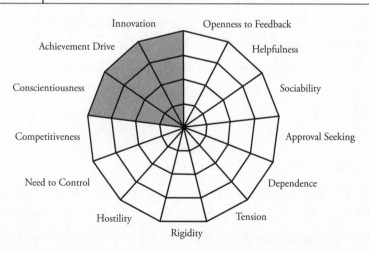

is a word long used by psychologists to describe achievement and competence drives, intrinsic motivation, passion, and inquisitiveness and this is it's meaning in *Personality at Work*. The three traits that form this powerful, high-performance combination are:

▶ Conscientiousness

▶ Achievement Drive

▶ Innovation

CONSCIENTIOUSNESS

Conscientiousness[6] measures the need to produce high-quality results through self-discipline, persistence, and attention to detail. Conscientious people focus on their work and put forth strong efforts to attain results. Professionals who are conscientious tend to be more effective on the job. But carried to the extreme, conscientiousness can lead to perfectionism and a sense that good enough never is. In contrast, too little conscientiousness suggests a lack of attention to detail and disorganization.

ACHIEVEMENT DRIVE

Achievement Drive measures a leader's ambition, initiative, confidence, and passion for work. High achievers enjoy solving intellectually challenging problems and like work that tests and stretches their abilities. They are pragmatic, set aggressive goals, and have strong internal standards of excellence. High achievers seek and need stimulation and do best when given opportunities to exercise their judgment, skills, and abilities. Achievement Drive is highly correlated to personal work productivity and leadership.

INNOVATION

Innovation measures an individual's inquisitiveness, curiosity, and confidence to try new things. Innovative people are independent-minded, have a strong sense of commitment to learning, and are not stuck in following convention or thinking within the box. They are creative idea generators who enthusiastically seek opportunities to turn possibilities into realities.

Steve Jobs would score very high on Conscientiousness, Achievement Drive, and Innovation: he was hardworking and detail-oriented, set high-quality standards, was innovative, and was very ambitious to be a successful capitalist business leader. Woz, like Jobs, was hardworking and detail-oriented, set high-quality standards, and was innovative. But he was less traditionally ambitious—Woz left Apple to become a public school teacher, and he aspired to be an engineer and a hacker and to contribute to the collective community rather than achieve personal profits or big-business aspirations.

• • • • • • •

What is most relevant and important for leadership effectiveness is not to focus on any one individual trait, but instead to understand how the 13 traits interact and form an overall Personality Profile—and how these "gestalt" profiles are related to leadership effectiveness and organizational outcomes.

That is the focus in the next chapter, which shifts the level of analysis away from LMAP Profiles and on to compelling, real-world case studies of *personality in action* that illuminate just how team process and outcomes are shaped by a leader's personality.

CHAPTER 4

Team Process and Personality

The people process is more important than either the strategy or operations processes. After all, it's the people of an organization who make judgments about how markets are changing, create strategies based on those judgments, and translate the strategies into operational realities. To put it simply and starkly: If you don't get the people process right, you will never fulfill the potential of your business.

— Larry Bossidy and Ram Charan, *Execution*[1]

Team process is what keeps organizations operating at every level and phase of every business. This is true in the execution of all work, whether it be in the executive suite, the cockpit, the operating room, or the shop floor.

Consider AIG's central role in the global financial meltdown of 2008.[2] The losses at AIG were so large that the U.S. government had to step in to avoid the risk of even greater damage to the world financial system. It provided $182 billion in emergency funds to AIG and installed new management.[3] The damage and ineptitude at AIG was so great that it prompted Iowa Senator Charles Grassley to suggest that the leadership at AIG should follow the Japanese example and "resign or go commit suicide."

Remarkably, the catastrophic losses at AIG were not the result of a broad, general slowdown; rather, they were directly related to one division: the Financial Products (FP) unit. The FP unit was led by Joe Cassano, a fiercely independent, arrogant manager with an explosive temper and near-delusional belief in his own assessment of the market.

Until 2001, AIG's FP division was led by Tom Savage, "a trained mathematician who understood the models used by AIG traders to price the risk they were running—and thus ensure that they were fairly paid for it. He enjoyed debates about both the models and the merits of AIG Financial Products' various trades. Cassano knew a lot less math and had much less interest in debate."[4] For years, Cassano reported to Savage, who kept him in check. Across AIG FP the view of the boss was remarkably consistent: Cassano was "a guy with a crude feel for financial risk but a real talent for bullying people who doubted him."[5]

When Tom Savage retired, Cassano became the CEO of FP. After the fall of AIG, colleagues interviewed by Michael Lewis detailed what this meant for the organization. In his aptly titled article, "The Man Who Crashed the World,"[6] Lewis detailed how Cassano's personality was at the core of the AIG meltdown:

> The culture changed. . . . The fear level was so high that when we had morning meetings, you presented what you did [with the intention to] not upset him. And if you were critical of the organization, all hell would break loose. . . . Under Joe the debate and discussion that was common under Tom [Savage] ceased. . . . The way you dealt with Joe was to start everything by saying, "You're right, Joe."[7]

"A.I.G. FP became a dictatorship," said one London trader. "Joe would bully people around. He'd humiliate them and then try to make it up to them by giving them huge amounts of money."[8]

By 2005, just four years into Cassano's tenure at the helm of FP, there were signs that the U.S. housing bubble would burst. Major business publications ran cover stories about how intertwined the mortgage and financial markets had become, and economists were worried. So were members of the FP team. One courageous member raised this issue: "If U.S. homeowners began to default in sharply greater numbers, AIG didn't have anywhere near the capital required to cover the losses. When he brought this up at a meeting, his reward was to be hauled into a separate room by Joe Cassano, who screamed at him that he didn't know what he was talking about." Cassano dismissed the multiple warnings and cautions, like this one, that FP team members tried to provide him.[9]

Unfortunately, we all know the consequences of Joe Cassano's failure to listen to members of his own team. Cassano wasn't a thief—more than 95 percent of his own money was tied up in AIG. He wasn't a status seeker or social climber, either: "He wore crappy clothes, drove a crappy car, and spent all of his time at the office," wrote Lewis. Nor was he a spendthrift or personal risk taker: Any money that wasn't invested in AIG Cassano invested in Treasury bonds.

So what drove Joe Cassano?

Those who know him best say it is Cassano's dominating personality. A toxic mix of inflexibility, competitiveness, the need to control, and hostility led to Cassano's arrogant disregard and contemptuous dismissal of input from others. As Lewis wrote:

> Traders left behind, much as they despise him personally, refuse to believe Cassano was engaged in any kind of fraud. The problem is that they knew him. And they believe that his crime was not mere legal fraudulence but the deeper kind: a need for subservience in others and an unwillingness to acknowledge his own weaknesses. "When he said that he could not envision losses, that we wouldn't lose a dime, I am positive that he believed that," says one of the traders. The problem with Joe Cassano wasn't that he knew he was wrong. It was that it was too important to him that he be right.[10]

• • • • • • •

The personality traits of a leader create the conditions that allow for open discussion of different perspectives that leverage team intelligence or, as the Cassano example vividly demonstrates, make it difficult if not impossible for team members to contribute input, observations, and differing perspectives. Such leaders can turn team members who work under them, no matter their gender, into "yes men."

Cassano created a toxic environment that subordinated the team's collective intelligence to what Joe himself thought. Fortunately, however, leaders can also make their team better. Witness what took place at Campbell's Soup when Doug Conant took over in 2001.

When Conant was named president and CEO of Campbell's Soup Company, the company was in free fall. One of the world's most iconic brands "was trailing the S&P 500 and falling precipitously, the core businesses were in disrepair, the organization was in shambles, and Campbell was the poorest performer of all the major food companies in the world."[11] It was a dispirited and dispiriting place to work. Its managers were stressed and burned out from successive cost-cutting and other drive-down-the-costs measures and from the drive-up-the-numbers management philosophies that immediately preceded Conant.

Moreover, all employees, from senior management to the production line, were unhappy, unmotivated, and disengaged.

Engagement, a Gallup metric[12] widely used to survey the cultural health and landscape of an organization, was at historic lows at Campbell's. Under the new leadership of Conant, however, employee engagement doubled in two years, from less than 2 to 1 at his arrival in 2001 to 4 to 1 in 2003. Doubling the employee engagement ratio over two years may seem like solid progress, except for the fact that Gallup's gold standard for employee engagement is 12 to 1. The 4-to-1 result was not good enough for Conant. His goal was to exceed Gallup's gold standard. For good reason: To Conant, "improving that ratio is not about becoming nicer; it is about becoming more effective. It is about engaging people and moving forward faster, instead of tripping up and slowing down. It is about gaining commitment instead of settling for compliance."[13]

Conant applied a leadership model he'd honed in turning Nabisco Food Company from a laggard to an industry leader. In that assignment, he developed a leadership approach, called TouchPoints, which he describes as being "tough-minded on the issue and tenderhearted with people." Conant has described this as:

> being present in the moment and feeling confident you can deal with whatever happens in a way that is helpful to others—and by extension, to yourself and your organization. TouchPoints do not replace the leadership models that work for you. Instead they infuse them with energy. They offer a way of working that is ideally suited to the vagaries and demands of today's organizations.[14]

This model became the foundation and fulcrum point of what Conant saw as his and Campbell's mission: "to lead in a way that's going to build the world's most extraordinary food company."[15] A turnaround approach built around being tenderhearted with people using interpersonal interactions may sound "too soft" to be successful in a hard business with low margins like food manufacturing. But Conant's tenderhearted approach was integrated with a tough-minded philosophy. It was not a matter of *either-or*; it was *both-and*: tough-minded on issues and results *and* tenderhearted and empathetic with people.[16]

Conant's commitment to cultural turnaround was unwavering. To him, engagement was the issue, and his own team needed to either get with the program or move on. For many, Conant's approach proved too tough; by 2003, 300 out of 350 Campbell global executives had retired, resigned, or been terminated.[17]

In 2006, Conant's tough-tender culture had taken hold and cascaded through the organization. In successive years, employee engagement grew dramatically: first 6 to 1; then 9 to 1, 12 to 1, and finally, in

2010, 17 to 1. At the same time, Campbell's Soup Company also began to flourish in the marketplace and beyond. Conant demonstrated obvious pride and satisfaction in describing the extraordinary accomplishments of the Campbell team under his leadership.

By 2009, the company was outperforming both the S&P Food Group and the S&P 500. Sales and earnings were growing, the core businesses were thriving, the employees were highly engaged in their work, the company was increasingly being recognized for its progress with workforce diversity and inclusion, and Campbell was ranked as one of the ten most socially responsible U.S. companies.[18]

Cassano and Conant demonstrated wildly different leadership styles, both of which were driven by distinct personalities. But are their stories merely anecdotal outliers? Is there any empirical evidence that personality drives team process and affects hard business outcomes?

TEAMWORK, DECISION MAKING, AND BUSINESS RESULTS

> *George W. Bush has famously described his leadership role as being "the decider." But deciding how and when to decide is as important as making the final decision . . . without contextual intelligence, being a "decider" is not enough.*
>
> —Joseph Nye, *The Powers to Lead*[19]

A growing body of research demonstrates that leaders set the tone and serve as role models for how leadership, teamwork, and communications are—and should be—conducted in organizations. Information age studies[20] have found that team process defined by the quantity, quality, and logistics of interpersonal dynamics on a team dramatically impacts engagement, team creativity, customer satisfaction, and financial performance. Based on studies across many types of organizations, it appears that not only does process matter; in many cases it trumps other important factors.

In 2010, Dan Lovallo and Olivier Sibony[21] published a longitudinal study of the impact of team process on business decisions and results. Over the course of the five-year study, they looked at 1,048 business decisions. They analyzed how decisions were made and the impact of those decisions in terms of revenue, profits, and market share. These were not small decisions (the color of the furniture in the boardroom), but major decisions around product releases, changes in organizational structure, and mergers and acquisitions. Given the importance of these decisions, teams in the study had rigorously collected and analyzed key metrics, financial models, and marketplace analytics.

Lovallo and Sibony were interested in exploring several questions about the process by which leadership teams make decisions, including:

▶ What kinds of processes do teams use to help expose and illuminate faulty logic or assumptions that underlie the financial analyses?

▶ What kinds of discussions do teams have about possible black swan events?

▶ How do teams explicitly seek and explore contrary opinions so as not to be blindsided by the "facts" and assumptions that underlie decisions?

In this vein, Lovallo and Sibony interviewed the teams to understand the kinds of team processes that they employed to help them reach a decision, asking (as summarized by Chip and Dan Heath), "Had the team explicitly discussed what was still uncertain about the decision? Did they include perspectives that contradicted the senior executive's point of view? Did they elicit participation from a range of people who had different views on the decision?"[22]

What Lovallo and Sibony found was that *the processes that the teams used in making decisions were six times more important than the analysis of financial and marketplace variables.* They concluded that "superb analysis is useless unless the decision process gives it a fair hearing."[23]

As we shall see, getting a fair hearing can be far more difficult than it sounds.

MIND GAMES

How is it possible that an organization's culture and teamwork processes can trump other important factors such as strategy, analysis, and operational processes? Perhaps this is the thrust of the business truism—often attributed to Peter Drucker—"culture eats strategy for breakfast." The Lovallo-Sibony findings suggest that, just as flight crews use checklists and cross-checks to minimize crew errors during critical phases of flight, smart organizations use team process as a cross-check in making critical decisions. The authors write:

> It does not mean that analysis is unimportant, as a closer look at the data reveals: almost no decisions in our sample made through a very strong process were backed by very poor analysis. Why? Because one of the things an unbiased decision-making process will do is ferret out poor analysis. The reverse is not true; superb analysis is useless unless the decision process gives it a fair hearing.[24]

What are the characteristics of a strong, unbiased decision-making process? Lovallo and Sibony suggest that it is by fully leveraging the team's collective intelligence that biases and assumptions are surfaced, examined, and overcome. We know a leader's personality can either reinforce the utilization of team intelligence or undermine it. Recall Joe Cassano, who despite the serious doubts and concerns that team members raised, was absolutely certain of his perspective: he was *strong but wrong*.[25] Moreover, Joe Cassano is no outlier: Lovallo's and Sibony's interviews with executives showed that significant decision-making problems are actually quite routine:

Candid conversations with senior executives behind closed doors reveal a similar unease with the quality of decision making and confirm the significant body of research indicating that cognitive biases affect the most important strategic decisions made by the smartest managers in the best companies. Mergers routinely fail to deliver the expected synergies. Strategic plans often ignore competitive responses. And large investment projects are over budget and over time—over and over again. . . . only 28 percent thought the quality of strategic decisions in their companies was generally good, 60 percent thought that bad decisions were about as frequent as good ones, and the remaining 12 percent thought good decisions were altogether infrequent.[26]

BIASES, BELIEFS, AND COGNITIVE ERRORS

Findings from the emerging field of behavioral economics indicate that a wide array of common biases, beliefs, and cognitive errors routinely interfere with problem solving and sound decision making. Lovallo and Sibony discuss five types of biases and methods to keep them in check:

▶ Counter pattern-recognition biases *by* changing the perspective

▶ Counter action-oriented biases *by* recognizing uncertainty

▶ Counter stability biases *by* shaking things up

▶ Counter interest biases *by* making them explicit

▶ Counter social biases *by* depersonalizing debate[27]

Daniel Kahneman, the Nobel laureate, psychologist, and leading behavioral economist, says that the odds of defeating biases in a group setting increase when discussion of them is widespread.[28] In our work, we have observed that a leader's personality either creates the conditions for robust team discussion to confront these biases or does not.

Good Process Is Good Business

Chip Heath and Dan Heath, in reviewing Lovallo and Sibony's and other studies, say *good process is good business*. If this is true, then what are the components of good process? What are the interpersonal processes and communication building blocks that make good team process? Are there relevant research studies—particularly of communications in business settings—that provide a starting point and pathway to understanding?

To answer some of those questions, let's turn to research conducted by Alex Pentland and colleagues at MIT's Human Dynamics Laboratory. This research illustrates which team processes are associated with performance. Pentland sampled teams across industries and work settings, from teams in call centers to customer-facing teams in banks and from innovation teams in high-technology firms to staff in postoperative wards in hospitals. Over seven years, about 2,500 people in 21 organizations were studied for many weeks.

The study used electronic badges that unobtrusively captured a hundred data points a minute to measure individual and interpersonal behaviors between team members, tracking who interacted with whom, for how long, and their tone of voice and body language. Studies took place over a period of several months to establish patterns. Pentland explained that the research focus was to identify the variables that make teams "click." He observed that even when the research team members did not understand the issues and content of the work of the teams they studied, they "could sense a buzz in a team" that signified the click factor. The MIT studies concluded that "the key to high performance lay not in the content of a team's discussions but in the manner in which it was communicated."

Pentland was seeking what he describes as the "it factor" of high-performing teams. He noted that, "with remarkable consistency, the data confirmed that communication indeed plays a critical role in building successful teams. In fact, we've found patterns of communication to be the most important predictor of a team's success."[29] The researchers found this result held across teams, functional expertise, and industries. In addition, high-performing teams shared five characteristics:

1. Everyone on the team talks and listens in roughly equal measure.

2. Members face one another, and their conversations and gestures are energetic.

3. Members connect directly with one another—not just with the team leader.

4. Members carry on back-channel or side conversations within the team.

5. Members periodically break, go exploring outside the team, and bring information back.[30]

Consistent with the notion that personality style often has a greater influence on managerial and leadership effectiveness than IQ or educational achievement, Pentland found similar parallels with regards to team effectiveness. Like emotional intelligence researchers, Pentland's team found that:

Individual reasoning and talent contribute far less to team success than one might expect. The best way to build a great team is not to select individuals for their smarts or accomplishments but to learn how they communicate and to shape and guide the team so that it follows successful communication patterns.[31]

Pentland's research identified three components of communication associated with higher team performance: energy, engagement, and exploration.

▶ *Energy* represents the number and nature of the interactions between team members. Face-to-face is the most valuable form of communication, then phone and videoconference, with e-mail and texting the least valuable.

▶ *Engagement* represents the distribution of attention and interactions between team members. "If all members of a team have relatively equal and reasonably high energy with all other members, engagement is extremely strong. Teams that have clusters of members who engage in high-energy communication while other members do not participate don't perform as well."[32] This is particularly challenging for decentralized teams who operate by phone.

▶ *Exploration* represents the extent of communications that team members have with people outside their team. "Successful teams, especially successful creative teams, oscillate between exploration for discovery and engagement for integration of the ideas gathered from outside sources."[33]

Teamwork Maps

Pentland's work was designed to study how teams operate, but just as importantly, it was designed to help participating teams identify and improve their performance. The study produced *teamwork maps* that allowed team members to see interaction patterns and the impact of their behaviors on team process. When individuals made adjustments in their behavior, team effectiveness increased, and this was particularly important when energy or engagement was low. Teamwork maps acted as a catalyst for team members to inquire into their own behavior patterns:

Are they trying to contribute and being ignored or cut off? Do they cut others off and not listen, thereby discouraging colleagues from seeking their opinions? Do they communicate only with one other team member? Do they face other people in meetings or tend to hide from the group physically? Do they speak loudly enough? Perhaps the leader of a team is too dominant; it may be that she is doing most of the talking at meetings and needs to work on encouraging others to participate. Energy and engagement maps will make such problems clear. And once we know what they are, we can begin to fix them.[34]

While the methodology, approach, and unit of analysis of the MIT research differ from the Lovallo and Sibony studies, both show the often-unappreciated significance of team process and interactions to hard outcomes. Similarly the MIT research is different from the Losada studies presented next. But the key findings are strikingly similar: the nature of communications within teams has a significant impact on team productivity and bottom-line financial results.

THE LOSADA LINE

In 1999, organizational psychologist Marcial Losada published "The Complex Dynamics of High Performance Teams."[35] The study showed that leaders not only need to have a balance of positive and negative communications with other team members but also need to provide it in the right amounts.[36] This has become known as the Losada line: a line that marks a tipping point at which the ratio of positive to negative feedback triggers higher performance on a team.[37]

In Losada's study, 60 strategic-business-unit leadership teams at a large information processing firm conducted meetings in a boardroom that Losada had set up. The business teams conducted their meetings just as they would back at the office. Behind one-way mirrors, Losada and his research associates used video cameras to record every comment made by every individual during the hour-long meetings. The video was then meticulously coded for communications between team members, along three lines of study:

▶ *Positive* or *negative* comments:

- Positive comments include "That's a great idea," "I agree with that," etc.

- Negative comments include "We shouldn't consider doing that," "I disagree with you," etc.

▶ *Self-focused* or *other-focused* remarks:

- Self-focused refers to anyone internal to the company.

- Other-focused is anyone external to the company.

▶ *Inquiry* or *advocacy* verbalizations:

- Inquiry is asking questions to explore an idea.

- Advocacy is promoting the speaker's position.

The researchers then drew from independent performance measures of profitability, customer satisfaction ratings, and evaluations from superiors, peers, and subordinates to categorize teams into three performance levels: high, mixed, and low performers:

▶ High-performing teams were "by all accounts, teams doing amazingly well—they were flourishing. They earned profits and were well-regarded by all with whom they did business."[38] These teams constituted 25 percent of the sample.

▶ Mixed-performing teams had both high and low scores on performance measures. They were the largest group at 45 percent of the sample.

▶ Low-performing teams were unprofitable and had poor customer satisfaction ratings and subpar 360 evaluations. They composed 30 percent of the sample.

Losada's key finding was that high-performing teams had a dramatically higher ratio of positive to negative comments than mixed- or low-performing teams:

▶ High-performance teams: a 5.6-to-1 ratio of positive to negative comments

▶ Mixed-performance teams: a 1.9-to-1 ratio of positive to negative comments

▶ Low-performance teams: a 0.36-to-1 ratio of negative to positive comments—nearly three negative for each positive comment

Losada and other researchers have concluded that team success is partly a function of the ratio of positive comments to negative comments. A team process that accentuates positives and minimizes negatives helps to create an environment where team members feel secure and motivated to better understand, explore, and discuss concerns, alternative perspectives, and options, leading to sound decision making. Team members who feel secure and motivated are more energized and engaged than those in an environment where inputs are criticized and discounted. Negativity is exhausting and de-motivating.

While speaking up may come naturally to team members of higher rank or those who are confident and assertive, a positive process serves as a catalyst to encourage greater participation from those who are more introverted, shy, or insecure, as well as those in less senior positions. Creating a positive team process in which team members do not fear being "wrong," because ideas are "more grist for the mill" and built upon, reinforces cognitive diversity. This positive process allows for an evolution of ideas based on the team's collective intelligence, rather than on just those of more senior or dominating team members.

Losada also found two other important communication patterns. First, high-performing teams showed a balance of inquiry and advocacy—like *engagement* in the MIT research. Team members spent as much time asking questions in order to better understand others' points of view as they did in promoting their own ideas. Team members on the lowest-performing teams asked few questions and spent most time advocating their own ideas and solutions. Like Joe Cassano at AIG, in low-performing teams, it's not uncommon for a few dominant voices, in a self-promoting competition for air time, to crowd out others. Dominant team members need to actively solicit input and inquiry from the quieter, more deferential team members and to do so in a positive tone. Dominating leaders also are more effective when they reach out and encourage participation from all team members, drawing out and drawing upon their ideas and perspectives.

Second, the highest-performing teams demonstrated a balance of self-focus and focus on others, while the lowest-performing teams focused almost exclusively internally on ideas within the company—like *exploration* in the MIT research.

Consistent with the MIT research, internal focus drives the "not invented here" syndrome, in which organizations resist knowledge and approaches from outside their organization (or even a different division or silo within the same company). Outward focus is exemplified by benchmarking, in which organizations specifically seek out best practices both in their particular industry and beyond. This is known as "proudly found elsewhere."[39] This approach is featured in design thinking and collective innovation that actively seek to take advantage of the best ideas that come from outside a company.[40]

Losada's research identified three communication processes that together create an environment for greater employee engagement and better business outcomes: positivity, the generous use of inquiry, and outward focus. Let's see how these communication processes played out in transforming Ford Motor Company—but before we do, it is important to clarify what positivity does *not mean*.

What Positivity Is Not

I want to be clear on a few aspects of positivity and its role in leadership that sometimes are confused or misunderstood:

▶ A positive leadership orientation does not mean avoiding constructive criticism or confrontation. Instead it supports a constructive confrontation model in which issues are depersonalized, addressed objectively, and oriented toward finding solutions. In contrast, a leader with a personality that focuses on negatives, places blame, and personalizes issues risks alienating the many team members who do not respond well to negativity.

▶ A positive leadership orientation does not mean being Pollyannaish and putting a positive spin on everything. It means looking at even difficult situations with forthrightness and candor with the intent to remediate the situation.

▶ Finally, a positive leadership style does not mean that positivity is the only behavioral trait important for leadership.[41] Positivity, empathy, integrity, social skills, trustworthiness, achievement drive and grit, conscientiousness, innovation and creativity, and flexibility all interact and contribute to the personality and character of a leader. Personality traits shape leadership style and significantly influence how leaders execute their roles and responsibilities.

TRANSFORMING FORD

Ford Motor Company was a mess by the early 2000s, after a decade of inferior engineering, declining market share, and plunging stock prices. Nothing less than a total transformation of the company was required at Ford for that iconic carmaker to survive. The transformation of Ford began when Alan Mulally joined in 2006. He had been aggressively recruited by Boeing in 1969 and joined right out of college as an engineer. He rose rapidly into program management positions and led the flight deck design team for Boeing's revolutionary 757 and 767 platforms, which had:

▶ The first all-digital flight deck in a commercial craft, surpassing even Airbus designs at the time

▶ The same flight deck in both the 757 and 767, allowing for a single commercial pilot rating to fly two different airplanes[42]

▶ The first two-person flight crew and two-jet-engine airplane approved for long-distance, transoceanic flight

The transformations continued as Mulally rose to become vice president and general manager of the Boeing 777 project. In 1997, he was named senior vice president of Boeing Commercial Airplanes and the president of the Information, Space, and Defense Systems. In 1998 and 2001, respectively, he became president of Boeing Commercial Airplanes and CEO of the division. Given the formidable competition from Europe's Airbus Industries, many considered Mulally's stewardship of Boeing's engineering and business process transformation as a vital reason Boeing remained an industry leader.

When Mulally joined Ford in 2006, he held a news conference, and one of the questions posed to him was whether he was considering any acquisitions or mergers. He answered, "Yeah. We're going to merge with ourselves."[43]

The problems on Ford's executive management team were rife, and decades-long dysfunctional patterns were well entrenched in the culture. Executive meetings were known for sarcasm, jokes at the expense of others, and a notable absence of cooperation, encouragement, or support. "There was often nastier cutthroat competition inside Ford than against the other car companies that Ford was supposed to be besting in the marketplace—especially between different Ford brands and regions."[44] Being evasive, shifting blame, keeping multiple sets of books, and failing to take responsibility or acknowledge problems were all hallmarks of the culture. There was no "One Ford."

Mulally had to begin transforming the culture from the top down by reconstructing and reframing the executive team meetings that began on September 28, 2006:

Key to Mulally's reform was his judgment that Ford lacked a unified global strategy and that executives, in order to evade criticism or blame, refused to share critical information about troubled operations with one another. So Mulally introduced mandatory weekly meetings of senior leaders at which each was required to report on progress (or lack of it) using green, yellow or red signals. He heaped praise on executives willing to disclose difficulties.[45]

Initially Mulally met resistance to the rules—attendance at all meetings was mandatory, no phones allowed, no side-conversations, no jokes at the expense of other team members—and to the process. He responded to resistance with "Trust the process"[46] and offered encouragement with "The neatest thing about this process is that we're going to get back together next week. I just want to know that you know what's happening, because I'm going to see you again next week—and I *know* you're going to make progress by then."[47]

From the Boardroom to the Employee Cafeteria to the Sales Floor

Mulally was a role model for transformative behaviors not only in executive meetings, but throughout the company, shunning the executive lunchroom and status to eat in the employee cafeteria. He stood in line with his tray, introduced himself to whoever was in line next to him, and reached out to all employees, asking for suggestions and ideas to help turn the firm around. He authentically solicited and valued input from all levels of the organization.

In March 2007, Mulally spent four hours on the showroom floor at Village Ford outside Dearborn, Michigan. He introduced himself to customers, saying, "Hi, I'm Alan. I'm from Ford. I'm just helping out here today," and sold several cars. Mulally then took Village Ford dealer Jim Seavitt to lunch at a local burger joint. Seavitt said, "He really engages people. I can tell you, he's not your father's CEO."[48]

It was during these mandatory weekly meetings that Mulally set Ford's new tone, insisting on transparency and open, honest, and direct communications. Executives were no longer allowed to have their direct reports present for them in meetings; instead, executives had to be accountable and informed "on business realities, not politics or personality. That was the old Ford. . . . The new Ford was all about the numbers . . . 'the data sets you free.'"[49]

Finally, as November approached, Mulally had outlined the process that the team would follow, and reports began. During the first reporting meeting, not one executive reported any problems on his or her watch. Mulally stopped the meeting and said, "We're going to lose billions of dollars this year. Is there anything that's not going well here?"[50] During the second meeting, one senior leader, Mark Fields, came in with a report that showed a red signal, and Mulally applauded.

Members of the executive team were surprised that Fields was in attendance the next week. They figured he'd be fired for disclosing a problem, but he was there, with even more red and yellow signals on his report. Another executive offered ideas for solving the problem.

The following week, each member of the executive team had red and yellow signals on their reports. The transformation was beginning.

Mulally intuitively understood what the MIT and Losada studies revealed about teamwork and communications. He insisted on mandatory attendance in each of these meetings (can't attend, don't be on the executive committee), absolute focused attention in the meeting (no phones or computers for other work), and accentuation of positives even when it meant acknowledging problems. These were drastic departures from the old Ford culture.

Refusing Bailout Funds as a Communication

Shortly after Mulally joined Ford, the federal bailout program following the global financial meltdown became available. GM took in $50 billon, Chrysler $11 billion. Many were shocked that Mulally did not add easily available billions for some extra running room. Mulally asked Congress to support funding for GM and Chrysler, important competitors for a robust U.S. automobile industry, saying how jobs were at risk not only at the other manufacturers but for their suppliers as well. Of the Big Three car companies, Ford was the only one that did not declare bankruptcy. Instead, Mulally got to work on the real problems at Ford: the Ford culture.

In not taking funding, Mulally clearly communicated his core and consistent message: we will succeed on our hard work and smart use of Ford's internal resources.

Mulally's leadership helped break down the silos within Ford, using its natural competitiveness and the combined intelligence of the Ford managers and employees to resolve the quality issues that had plagued the firm for years. His leadership style was to facilitate and encourage open, honest, and direct communications to confront and resolve problems that previously had been taboo. Eventually, a new, more open, transparent environment emerged where teamwork and peer problem-solving skills became the norm. If, for example, someone reported he or she was having problems of a particular kind, another team member would say, "Hey, we had a problem like that a few years ago and found this to be helpful." Over time, the team did in fact "merge with itself," and a stronger "One Ford" evolved within years. Ford since has performed admirably in a highly competitive, quickly transforming automobile market.[51]

When team members respect each other and see each other as additional resources—rather than internal competitors—the team can collaborate and focus on "getting it right" rather than "being right." In this type of environment, people feel more valued, included, and purposeful, and they have greater access to information and resources from other teams. In high-level interdepartmental executive meetings, team members are more willing to share what they know and to learn from each other (blind men touching different parts of the elephant) when the focus is on shared problems to be solved rather than an internal competition to be won.

When Mulally retired from Ford Motor Company on July 1, 2014, he passed the reins to Mark Fields, who had been the first executive to openly discuss his problems with other members of the executive team. In April 2016, when this chapter was completed, Ford Motor Company reported its largest profit for any quarter in its long history.

CHAPTER 5

Personality Profiles and Effectiveness

We have seen how personality traits are the building blocks of personality and recognize that there are distinct Personality Profiles that reflect the prominence and interactions of the personality traits. We've seen research on team effectiveness in organizations and can identify links between behaviors and outcomes—both positive and negative.

In this chapter we will look at the clear and specific relationships between LMAP 360 Personality Profiles and effectiveness: effectiveness in output of productivity and results, in teamwork, and in overall leadership. We start with a description of a central measure of effectiveness, the LMAP Effectiveness Ratings, and then look at LMAP 360 Profiles associated with high, mixed, and low effectiveness.

LMAP EFFECTIVENESS RATINGS

In addition to collecting responses to 135 behavioral assessment items and comments from coworkers, we also collected ratings of the leader's effectiveness using a 7-point scale ranging from the bottom 2 percent (1) to the top 2 percent (7) (see Exhibit 5.1).[1] Below are the five areas of effectiveness with the average score in parentheses:

▶ Performance compared with that of others in a similar position (5.68)

▶ Ability to get along with others (5.81)

▶ Ability to produce results (5.81)

▶ Leadership ability (5.59)

▶ Overall effectiveness in his or her job (5.75)

Exhibits 5.1 and 5.2 illustrate how effectiveness ratings are reported (and Appendix B shows a complete set of effectiveness ratings).

You may be surprised to see that scores that range from 5.59 to 5.81—the top 15 to 20 percent on the rating scale—translate to "average."[2] It can be very sobering for a leader to receive effectiveness ratings that are "about average."

Some leaders initially misinterpret their raw scores of 4s or 5s on the 7-point rating scales as indicating they are doing really well. They don't realize that compared with a very talented workforce—with sample averages of 5.81 on "Ability to get along with others" and "Ability to produce results"—a score of 3, 4, or 5 is well below average.

EXHIBIT 5.1 | EFFECTIVENESS RATINGS: "ABILITY TO PRODUCE RESULTS"

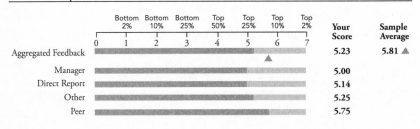

	Bottom 2%	Bottom 10%	Bottom 25%	Top 50%	Top 25%	Top 10%	Top 2%	Your Score	Sample Average
	0	1	2	3	4	5	6	7		
Aggregated Feedback									5.23	5.81 ▲
Manager									5.00	
Direct Report									5.14	
Other									5.25	
Peer									5.75	

EXHIBIT 5.2 | EFFECTIVENESS RATINGS: "ABILITY TO GET ALONG WITH OTHERS"

	Bottom 2%	Bottom 10%	Bottom 25%	Top 50%	Top 25%	Top 10%	Top 2%	Your Score	Sample Average
	0	1	2	3	4	5	6	7		
Aggregated Feedback									3.94	5.81 ▲
Manager									4.00	
Direct Report									3.14	
Other									5.60	
Peer									3.25	

Personality Profiles and Effectiveness

The organizational psychology research shows systematic, statistically significant, meaningful relationships between 360 personality measures, effectiveness ratings, and the rater comments.[3] Sometimes the contents of the 360 feedback is common knowledge to all but that leader, whose self-image and self-concept include being a highly effective leader.

This begets the question: If "everyone knows" that a professional in a leadership role is average or mediocre or worse in that position, how do these leaders keep their jobs?

The fact is, high standards have been set: *employers, customers, vendors, and team members want and expect far better than average.* We know many professionals are promoted by organizations into leadership roles because they were great at something else. Some are brilliant or misplaced individual contributors; others have skills or certifications required to operate the business. Some have formal or informal tenure or are there as a result of nepotism, and others may be suboptimal due to many common economic, social, psychological, and health challenges in life. This is how it works in many organizations and for many leaders. 360 feedback helps a leader develop the self-awareness and sometimes the humility to raise his or her game to become a better leader.

HIGH-PERFORMANCE PROFILES = GRIT + TEAMWORK

Profiles in which the most prominent traits are in Grit /Task Mastery and Teamwork/Social Intelligence are what we call Top-Heavy Profiles. Leaders with Top-Heavy Profiles are rated in the top 10 percent of leadership due to exceptional abilities to drive projects and results and work well with people. Their feedback raters write comments like these: "The best boss I've had in my career. A real role model." "A star. I've not seen a challenge he can't handle." And "Yes, she really is that good and handles it all with seeming ease and grace."

As you'll see, there is considerable variability in Top-Heavy Profiles that express a leader's individuality and uniqueness. Some profiles have high scores on all the high-performance traits; others have high scores on a few. Correspondingly, there is wide variation in the counterproductive derailer traits. What these profiles share is the *predominance of the six Grit and Social Intelligence traits on the top of the profile with the relative lesser prevalence of the seven derailment traits.* See Figure 5.1.

FIGURE 5.1 | HIGH-PERFORMANCE BIG-PICTURE AND DETAIL-ORIENTED PROFILES

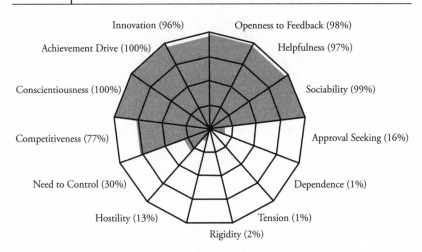

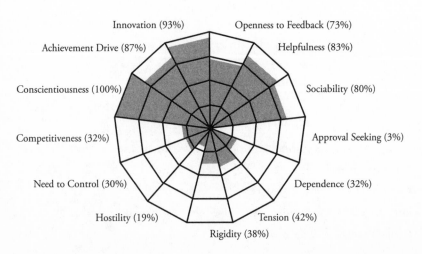

Unlike the profiles in Figure 5.1 that have both high Conscientiousness *and* high Innovation, some high-performance leaders have high Conscientiousness *or* high Innovation. The former are more detail-oriented (see Figure 5.2); the latter are big-picture-oriented (see Figure 5.3).

FIGURE 5.2 | HIGH-DETAIL–AVERAGE-INNOVATION PROFILE

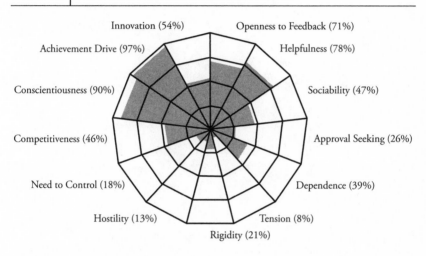

FIGURE 5.3 | HIGH-INNOVATION–LOW-DETAIL PROFILE

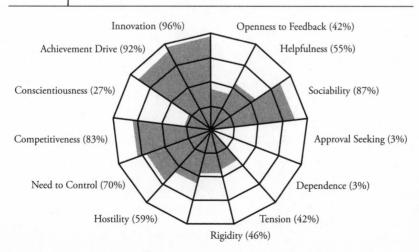

A third of the most effective leaders have high scores *only* in Grit and Social Intelligence with below average (less than 50 percent) on derailment traits. But *more often than not*, leaders with prominent Grit and Social Intelligence also have prominent derailers—like the profiles shown in Figures 5.4 and 5.5.

FIGURE 5.4 | TOP-HEAVY ACCOMMODATING PROFILE

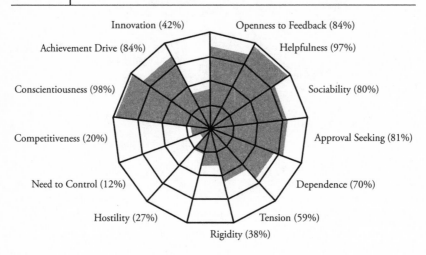

FIGURE 5.5 | TOP-HEAVY HIGH-CONTROL PROFILE

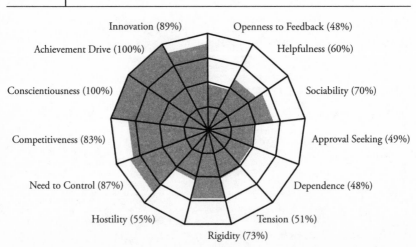

FIGURE 5.6 | TOP-HEAVY PROFILE WITH MIXED FEATURES

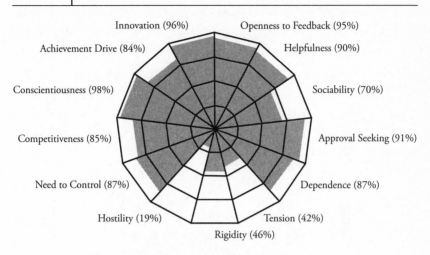

Finally, some high-performing leaders have prominent Grit and Social Intelligence and also a wide distribution of prominent derailers—like the profile in Figure 5.6.

MIXED-EFFECTIVENESS PROFILES

These profiles have prominent Grit *or* Social Intelligence *and* prominent Deference *and/or* Dominance. In terms of leadership effectiveness, leaders with this Personality Profile could be described as one-dimensional—they excel with people *or* projects, but not both.

MIXED-EFFECTIVENESS PROFILES:
SOCIAL INTELLIGENCE + DEFERENCE = RIGHT-SIDERS

Profiles with prominent Social Intelligence *and* Deference are referred to as *Right-Siders.* Right-Siders have a personality well suited for effective teamwork but are not effective when leadership requires being assertive, being decisive, and holding others accountable to deliver results. There is considerable variation within Right-Siders. Figure 5.7, for example, offers a profile of a Right-Sider who is extraverted, and Figure 5.8 shows a profile of an introverted Right-Sider.

Right-Side Profiles that have at least one *average or higher* Grit trait—like those shown in Figure 5.9—are far more effective. With the addition of a strong results orientation and initiative, leaders with these types of profiles demonstrate dramatically increased effectiveness compared with other socially skilled, deferent leaders.

FIGURE 5.7 | SOCIABLE (AND EXTRAVERTED) RIGHT-SIDER

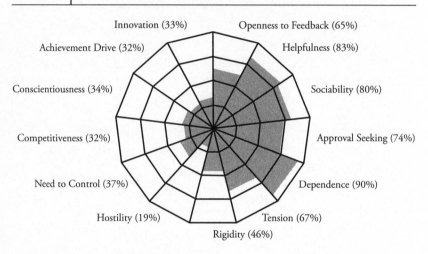

FIGURE 5.8 | INTROVERTED RIGHT-SIDER

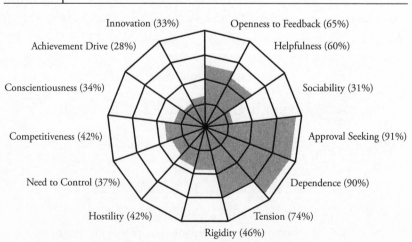

FIGURE 5.9 | RIGHT-SIDE PROFILES WITH ONE AVERAGE OR HIGHER GRIT TRAIT

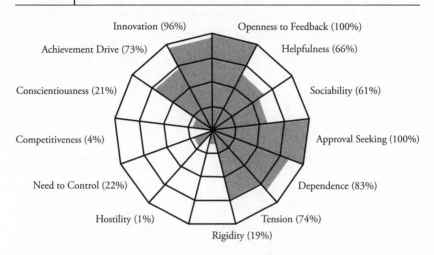

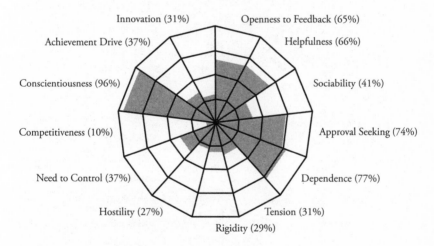

MIXED-EFFECTIVENESS PROFILES:
GRIT + DOMINANCE = LEFT-SIDERS

Profiles with prominent Grit *and* Dominance are referred to as *Left-Siders*. These leaders are effective in delivering project results but lack interpersonal and teamwork skills. There are more Left-Siders in leadership roles than any other profile type. In fact, there are so many that there are sections of bookstores dedicated to Authoritarian, Aggressive,

Angry, Abusive, Aggravating, type A leaders. Very frequent though not very popular, there are many variations of Left-Siders.

The two profiles shown in Figures 5.10 and 5.11 are similar—but also show some significant differences. Notice in Figure 5.10 the

FIGURE 5.10 | HIGH SCORES ON ALL TASK MASTERY AND DOMINEERING TRAITS

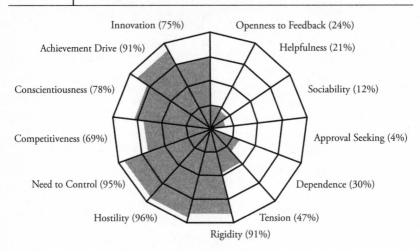

FIGURE 5.11 | HIGH SCORES ON SOME TASK MASTERY AND DOMINEERING TRAITS

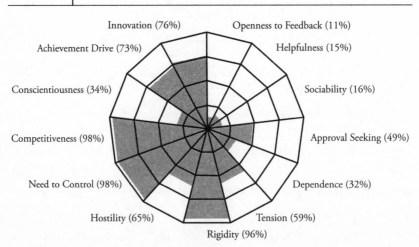

high scores on *all* the Task Mastery and Domineering traits, similar to what I'd expect for Steve Jobs. The prominent Conscientiousness and Hostility traits amplify the challenges for this leader to control the tendency to micromanage others, to be civil, and to work collaboratively on a team. In contrast, the leader with a profile similar to the one in Figure 5.11 will be similarly driven and intense, but much less organized and detail-oriented and not overtly angry and irritable.

Leaders with Left-Side Profiles with at least one *average* or higher Teamwork trait, like the profile in Figure 5.12, have dramatically increased effectiveness compared with high-Grit/high-Dominance leaders without social skills.

A Left-Sider with *average* Social Intelligence, like the profile shown in Figure 5.12, has enhanced abilities to listen, collaborate, and take advantage of the team's collective intelligence—which leads to superior outcomes in project results and in employee engagement.

FIGURE 5.12 | GRIT/TASK MASTERY AND DOMINEERING PROFILE WITH AVERAGE EQ/SOCIAL INTELLIGENCE

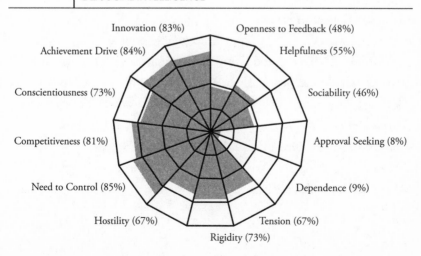

Advocates of strengths-based training discount the value of improving a behavioral weakness. They argue that, at best, improvement in an area that is not already a strength will lead to average but not outstanding performance in that particular behavior. But behaviors interact, and replacing deficits with even average behavioral skills provides tremendous synergistic upsides. Spend an hour around a high-Grit–high-Dominance leader who demonstrates virtually no encouragement, helpfulness, and interpersonal engagement and compare that with an hour spent with a high-Grit–high-Dominance leader *who also has about-average* listening and interpersonal skills; the experiences will be quite different.

There are significant advantages for professionals to develop *average behavioral skills to replace deficiencies*—but it is essential for leaders whose roles demand behavioral competence in areas that do not come to them naturally.

LOW-EFFECTIVENESS PROFILES = DEFERENCE OR DOMINEERING OR DEFERENCE + DOMINEERING

About 20 percent of leaders who complete an LMAP 360 are perceived by their coworkers as having prominent Deference or Domineering traits or both Deference and Domineering traits, *and below-average Grit and EQ/Social Intelligence*. These are leaders who are rated as the least effective, and because of the shape of the profiles, we refer to them as Bottom-Heavy Profiles. These leaders lack the work ethic, ambition, and innovation skills driven by Task Mastery traits as well as being short on the team leadership skills needed for high performance. Figures 5.13, 5.14, and 5.15 illustrate some of the variety seen in Bottom-Heavy Profiles.

FIGURE 5.13 | DEFERENTIAL – CAUTIOUS PROFILE

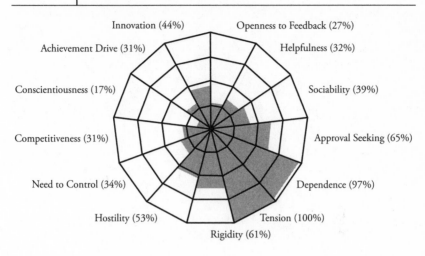

FIGURE 5.14 | DEFERENTIAL + DOMINATING PROFILE

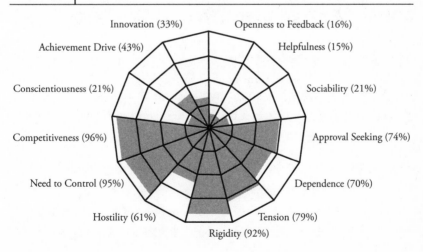

FIGURE 5.15 | DOMINEERING-TENSE PROFILE

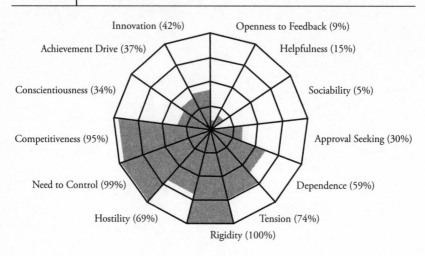

THE NORMAL 80 PERCENT

Because only about 20 percent of professionals have a Top-Heavy Profile, all of us 80 percenters who have some prominent derailers are by definition *normal.* We are not the outliers!

In this vein, the intent of the LMAP 360 assessment is not to find fault or weakness, nor is it to "clone" leaders and to transform all of us into Top-Heavy Profiles. More modestly, the goals are to raise our self-awareness of:

▶ Which behaviors are effective and which are ineffective—based on research, not hearsay or an anecdote or a marketing rap.

▶ Differences between how we think we behave (self-ratings) and how others perceive us behaving (feedback ratings). For leaders especially, it is critical to understand and appreciate that *team members* interact with a leader based on their *perceptions of the leader's behavior*—not the leader's intentions or self-concept, or not uncommonly, an idealized self-image.

▶ Our ability to make conscious choices in our behavior and to modify and mitigate counterproductive behaviors in order to more effectively fulfill our work roles and responsibilities . . . and to have a more satisfying, positive work experience.

With the LMAP 360 process, most leaders are able to quickly identify one behavior to start, stop, or improve. Selecting *only one* behavior to change seems limiting; yet simply stopping one behavior—like interrupting—can be transformative for a leader, a team, or a critical situation.[4]

Finally and importantly, the results of the LMAP 360 act as a catalyst to take the time to consider: *Is the character you are, the character you want to be?*

CHAPTER 6

Flying Lessons—Crew Leadership, Teamwork, and Communications

Every second, somewhere around the world, a plane takes off and another lands. Every second.

At any given moment, 700,000 people occupy the sky, their lives in the hands of a flight crew composed of a captain and one or two flight officers, working with air traffic control. In commercial aircraft, the captain is the undisputed leader of the flight crew. As in other work settings, his or her personality sets the tone, crew dynamics, and efficacy in the flight deck. Unlike most settings, however, in the highly compressed time and space constraints of commercial flight, the split-second decisions, actions, and interactions of this team can make the difference between life and death for all aboard. In few other settings are the stakes higher or the relationships between personality and leadership more dramatically played out than in the flight deck of a commercial jet.

Crew error consistently ranks as the leading contributing cause of commercial airline accidents. National Transportation Safety Board (NTSB) investigations have found that three out of four planes would not have crashed had the crew utilized effective leadership, teamwork, and communications. Often, it is the interaction of dominant and deferential crew members' personalities that leads to crew breakdowns. Since 1981, the Federal Aviation Administration (FAA) has required that every 18 months every commercial pilot complete crew resource management (CRM) training that focuses on enhancing and practicing leadership, teamwork, and communications skills in order to maintain situational awareness and assure a safe flight.

This chapter and Chapter 15, "Leadership in Action—Qantas Flight 32," both look at the relationship of personality to team dynamics and flight safety at the extremes. At one extreme, we observe the behaviors and interactions of flight crews who, *as a result of their dysfunctional, ineffective behaviors and interactions, crash fully functioning, perfectly operable aircraft.* In Chapter 15, we examine the other extreme: *where only the effective behaviors and interactions of the flight crew allow them to successfully fly and land a catastrophically damaged aircraft*—a plane that, *had it crashed,* would have crashed due to massive equipment failure.

While the aviation examples are extreme and extraordinary, the behaviors demonstrated are anything but. The examples contrast common, ordinary behaviors and interactions on the flight deck that create highly divergent and extraordinary outcomes. Leaders can learn key lessons from the behaviors demonstrated on the flight deck because they are mirrored by how people act and interact every day in the workplace.

WHAT'S THE DIFFERENCE BETWEEN A DUCK AND A COPILOT?

It is April 5, 1976. An Alaska Airlines Boeing 727 is beginning its approach into Ketchikan. The Ketchikan flight service center reported a cloud ceiling of 800 feet, 2 miles of visibility, light snow, fog, and 5-knot winds. Officially the weather was "inclement" but nothing that would shake the ready confidence of Captain Richard Burke, who had landed at Ketchikan more than 50 times previously, at times in far worse weather. The flight service center advised the crew that braking conditions on the runway were "poor." The captain later testified that he didn't hear the braking warning, but another crew member testified that he *had* heard and noted the warning. As the following black box transcript indicates, this was not the only example of listening problems that overconfident Captain Burke had on this day (we will return to the italic text).

First officer (FO): *Below the glide slope there, Rich?*

Captain: *Yeah, well, we know where we are out here . . . we're alright.*

Flight engineer (FE): *Don't you worry; the fox is going to have it wired.*

FO: *I hope so.*

FE: *Oh yeah.*

Captain: *No problem.*

FO: *This a little faster than you normally fly this, Rich.*

Captain: *Oh yeah, but it's nice and smooth. We're going to get in right on time, maybe a little bit ahead of time. We got it made.*

FO: *I sure hope so.*

FE: You know, Rich, you know the difference between a duck and a copilot?

Captain: What's the difference?

FE: Well, a duck can fly.

Captain: Well said.

FO: *Seems like there's a bit of tail wind up here, Rich.*

Captain: *Yeah, we're saving gas . . . help us get in a couple of minutes early too.*

(Note: The airplane is now flying 40 knots too fast and 200 feet too low.)

FO: *Rich, you're just a little below the MDA here* (minimum descent altitude).

Captain: *Yeah, we'll take care of it here.*

FO: *You're going just a little bit high.*

Captain: *Well, gear down.*

Captain: Final check [checklist].

(Flight engineer begins checklist.)

FE: No smoking signs?

FO: It's on.

FE: Flight and nav instruments?

FO: They're cross-checked.

FE: Landing gear?

FO: It's down.

FE: Speed brakes?

(Ignored.)

FO: *You really look awfully high, Rich.*

FE: Speed brakes?

(Ignored.)

Captain: 5 degrees.

FO: 5 degrees?

Captain: 15 degree flaps . . . 25 on the flaps.

FO: *Rich, you're really high . . . you're gonna need 40 [degree flaps] is what you need here, to ah to get this thing down. There are . . . uh there aren't . . .*

FE interrupts: You want the speed brakes on?

(Ignored.)

FO: I don't think you're gonna make it, Rich. If you don't get this sucker on the ground . . .

FE: Get it down, Rich.

FO (sounding frantic): I don't think you're gonna make it. I don't think you're gonna make it.

FO: You're not gonna make it.

(Plane over runway now.)

Captain: We're going around. Oh darn.

FO: 130, 140 knots.

FE: It isn't gonna stop, Rich.

FO: We're not gonna make it, Rich. Great job, Rich. I told you . . . Jeez . . .

(Sound of impact is heard on the cockpit voice recorder as the plane, with no mechanical problems, overshoots the runway.)[1]

In what should have been a routine flight and landing, one passenger died, and many were seriously injured during the accident you just read about.

Please take a few minutes to reread the *italicized sections* of the transcript and focus on those crew interactions.

What Went Wrong?

The NTSB investigation determined that the crash resulted from the captain's "faulty judgment in initiating a go-around after he was committed to a full-stop landing following an excessively long and fast touchdown from an unstabilized approach" and "pilot's unprofessional decision to abandon the precision approach."

The NTSB conclusions are right, *but* it is more complicated than that.

First, each crew member had opportunities to short-circuit the communications breakdown. Let's look at some specifics:

1. The captain could have listened to the FO and adjusted the approach.

2. The FO could have advocated more assertively to get the captain's attention.

3. The FE could have said, "Hey Rich, the FO has a point. We don't need to get in early. . . Let's do this by the book."

Second, the plane crashed because of the captain's unwillingness to use the monitoring feedback from the FO. Third, the captain abrogated his responsibility to manage and lead the crew as a functional, operational team.

Throughout the landing approach, the FO accurately monitors and advises the flying captain on deviations to the standard approach parameters four or more times (in italic text). However, each time he speaks up, he mitigates the communication by saying "a little" or "a bit." After the flight engineer tells an awful joke at the first officer's expense (difference between a duck and a copilot), the first officer communicates even more indirectly saying, **"Seems like there's a bit of tail wind up here, Rich,"** hinting that the plane is going too fast. These types of minimized communications have little impact on the self-reliant, noncooperative, passively hostile personality of the captain, who responds to the FO's mitigated communication about the plane's altitude ("You're going just a little bit high") *with an absolutely dismissive* "Well, gear down." These crew communications are like a road map for how *not to* collaborate.

Deconstructing Human Interactions in Aviation Accidents

LMAP presentations begin by showing a video reenactment of this Alaska Airlines accident (I encourage you to see this video for yourself.[2]) Participants are shocked by what they hear. Audiences initially focus on the *captain*—his poor leadership, lack of listening, and controlling, noncollaborative style. They use words like *arrogant, smug, stubborn,* and *dangerous* to describe him. Inevitably someone says, "Hey, what about that *first officer?* Why is he so tentative; hinting and suggesting things to the captain? If the landing does not work out right, he could die! If I were in that cockpit and it was my life on the line, I'd be a lot more assertive!" When this comment comes up, I ask, "So exactly what would *you* say to the captain? Imagine you are in that cockpit and *you've* now made four inquiries about flying too fast and too high. What exactly would *you* say?"

I've asked hundreds if not thousands of leaders the same question, and the response is always something general like, "Well I'd sure be more assertive than that" or "I'd say we have to go around once I thought

---

Think About It

Who among us has not been in the passenger seat of a car and the driver is going too fast. You might say something like, "Is this a little faster than you normally drive, Rich?" Rich, confident and unconcerned, says, "Oh yeah, but it's nice and smooth. We're going to get there right on time, maybe a little bit ahead of time. We got it made." You now face a challenge: do you escalate and say, "No really, Rich, I asked that you slow down," or do you let it pass because you'd already said something, Rich has dismissed your concern, and Rich is giving you a ride?

If you are a person who dislikes conflict and avoids confrontations, you are more likely to let it pass, which may or may not be fine in the car. But as a commercial airline pilot, you have the *professional obligation*—an ethical responsibility—to speak up to assure a safe flight.

Reciprocally, if you are a commercial pilot flying a plane and other crew members even just hint you are deviating from standards, you have the *professional obligation* to listen up and take very seriously their monitoring role in the flight. *You need to listen.*

things were off." This inability to have the right words at the right time without much time to think is the reason that pilots train how exactly to deal with situations like this. This training is especially important for deferring types who avoid confrontation and for confident, aggressive types who are lousy listeners. As noted earlier in the chapter, the training is called crew resource management.

CREW RESOURCE MANAGEMENT TRAINING

We can change switches and instruments, but not human nature. We're all just "normal" neurotics who must be taught to know and live with our problems and weaknesses.
—Former Deputy Head of Flight Safety, Swissair

In 1981, when United Airlines was the first airline to implement crew resource management, CRM was sarcastically called "Captain's Charm School." But with decades of accidents and CRM training, pilots now understand that leadership, management, and communications are mission-critical for safe, efficient flight. CRM focuses on problem solving and decision making, conflict management, stress management, circadian disruptions, human-machine interfaces and interactions, chain of events, and situational awareness.

CRM curricula emphasize the review of accident transcripts, analysis of investigation reports, and study of video re-creations of near misses and accidents to allow pilots to discuss and learn from what went wrong in accidents. While sometimes it can feel like Monday-morning quarterbacking, it is not rare to hear "but for the grace of God go I."

INQUIRY AND ADVOCACY—CORNERSTONES OF EFFECTIVE COMMUNICATION

Inquiry and advocacy are both forms of assertiveness taught in CRM training—and essential tools for all professionals (that we refer to throughout the book).

▶ *Inquiry* refers to proactively asking questions to get information from all the available resources in order to maintain high situational awareness.

▶ *Advocacy* refers to expressing your ideas, concerns, and perspectives to others in order to help others see a situation as you see it, and thus raise the group's situational awareness. CRM teaches pilots that it is a *professional obligation* of all crew members to inquire or advocate even in interpersonally uncomfortable or difficult situations.

COMMUNICATIONS RESEARCH

An NTSB study of accidents (1978–1990) involving crew error found that 75 percent of the crew errors related to "monitoring/challenging or assertiveness."[3] Clues to this are uncovered in studies by Ute Fischer and Judith Orasanu[4] on crew communications. The studies examined how commercial airline pilots call attention to problems and get action on them from other crew members who differed in rank.[5]

Fischer and Ute first set up the situation where over the course of the flight you (the monitoring pilot) have observed the flying pilot making "errors" and "oversights." In one scenario:

You notice on the weather radar an area of heavy precipitation 25 miles ahead. The flying pilot is maintaining his present course at Mach .73 (560 mph), even though embedded thunderstorms have been reported in your area and you encounter moderate turbulence. You want to ensure that your aircraft will not penetrate this area.

The studies found that when pilots were given a choice of communications on a list, the pilots identified the correct option, regardless of their rank. But when asked to "request action of another crew member," the pilots behaved according to rank—captains issued commands, and FOs used hints.

When captains are monitoring an FO flying the plane, they are direct and explicit in issuing commands to assure corrections are made. FOs monitoring a captain making errors will use indirect and mitigated communications to *influence* the captain to make corrections—they *hint*. We see this exact communications dynamic play out in the Alaska Airlines accident, and it helps explain the research that shows that most accidents, *by far*, happen when the flying pilot is the captain—which seems counterintuitive.[6]

This research points to the compelling need for training in inquiry and advocacy—particularly for first officers when monitoring the flying captain. *This is even more important when the FO's personality predisposes him or her to be reserved, nonassertive, or conflict avoidant.*

Reciprocally, this research also points to the need to train captains to be better listeners and for them to encourage other crew members to speak up regardless of rank. *This is even more important when the captain's personality is rigid, controlling, and independent-minded.*

Remember, in three out of four airline accidents, crew error is the leading contributing cause, and three out of four crew errors are communication breakdowns.

Practice—Rehearsing for Reality

Communications skills can be taught and improved with practice. Personality assessments help pilots identify the specific kinds of communications skills that are critical for them to develop. A method used in a CRM course I cofacilitated illustrates the challenges and opportunities of this work.

Some exercises are designed for dyads, so when there is an odd number, a facilitator pairs off with a participant-pilot. I was paired with an FO whom I knew from our work together on a pilot training committee. Edwin came across as a competent and responsible person and a very eager to please FO. A true southern boy who was "raised right," he was polite and very considerate. It sometimes felt that he was just too agreeable, careful to never offend anyone and skilled at avoiding conflict. This stood in contrast to my own direct, impatient, and Chicago-bred abrupt style.

Though professionally he was fast-tracked into emerging leadership roles, Edwin had a follower's mindset. On his 360 assessment, the written comments by crew members noted that he unfailingly deferred to authority and sometimes seemed so rule bound that he came across as inflexible. Comments suggested that he "drop the false humility and instead be confident and humble" and that he should "quit obediently following the rules and take more of a lead in creating the right rules." To develop, Edwin would need to leverage his competence, conscientiousness, and earnest commitment to safe operations by becoming more outspoken and by showing more initiative rather than looking to others for direction.

Edwin and I practiced inquiry and advocacy skills through role play. For Edwin, these were rehearsals for reality, practice to prepare for a future situation where greater assertiveness on his part was required to assure a safe flight. When confronted with a situation that required him to respond with behaviors that did not come naturally, he needed to practice exactly what to say and how to say it.

I played the role of a rigid, aggressive, overconfident captain (I was amazed how easily I was able to get into that role). When Edwin, playing the role of first officer, would hint or politely suggest an action, I'd blow him off.

I did this repeatedly, forcing Edwin to speak much more assertively without minimizing. I pushed him hard, and at one point Edwin got angry and began yelling at me, drawing looks by everyone in the room. This proved a breakthrough for Edwin, who had been taught to *keep a lid on it and never lose control.* We could then discuss how being direct in communications was not the same as losing control. Being assertive and direct facilitates necessary constructive confrontations—something

Edwin avoided. He came to see he could call upon several levels of assertiveness between being a pushover and blowing his top.

We practiced different words and alternative ways to inquire, to state a position without equivocation, to frame and reframe questions and statements. We practiced until Edwin found the language he was comfortable with and was prepared to use. Even if these behaviors never came naturally to Edwin, he now had a script, had practiced that script, and simply had to say it aloud one more time when needed for real.

Notice that this exercise is not designed to remake Edwin's personality, but to give him the tools to use when the situation required—tools that he was not naturally equipped to use without repeated practice.

Nor was this exercise designed to make Edwin an expert in assertiveness; rather it was to help Edwin develop communication skills that are "good enough." He needed to develop these skills to a level that they would no longer be problematic in his role as a commercial pilot. Edwin could see this exercise wasn't intended to correct his personal shortcomings, but to provide him with the communication tools he needed to fulfill his professional duties. Edwin realized that as he grew into leadership roles, his behavior would need to change.

Three years later I ran into Edwin at a flight-training seminar.[7] He pulled me aside and said, "I need to thank you for something." A situation had arisen where he had to put into practice the very skills we had rehearsed. "It was late at night. It had been a long flight in lousy weather. The flight deck was cold, everyone was tired and more than ready to land and call it a day. The captain was flying, and we were being bounced around. First we were too high, then a little low, and the approach was never quite stabilized. At first I thought, the odds are we'll be okay. But then I thought, nah, I've got to say something. So I told the captain, 'I think it would be a good idea to go around.' I was relieved and surprised when the captain said, 'Good idea. Man, I know we all just want to get in, but this approach feels off to me, too. Let's go around and we'll try again.'"

AVIATION SAFETY

Despite the extreme stories in this chapter, commercial flying is extraordinarily safe. For every major accident, there are literally millions of safe flights—9 million annually in the United States alone. There are hundreds of thousands of unremarkable flights, as well as untold instances of unsung leadership where flight crews have dealt with any number of equipment failures and potentially life-threatening situations without fanfare, simply in the line of duty. And there are those flights that are by any measure remarkable: flights where against all odds the flight crew is successful in bringing a catastrophically disabled plane safely home. These flights, and in particular their captains and their crews, deservedly so, become the stuff of legend. Chapter 15 tells the story of such a flight, *QF32*.

CHAPTER 7

Personality Is Behavior—Self-Ratings and 360 Feedback

Many people think of personality as a strictly internal experience and phenomenon, something that is in our minds as motivations, thoughts, and feelings. As if behavior—how you act and interact in the world—is distinct from personality.

Psychologists generally agree that behavior is a core aspect of personality, as reflected in these definitions of personality by three thought-leading psychologists:

▶ "The most outstanding and salient impressions a person creates on others"[1]

▶ "The pattern and regularity of behavior over time"[2]

▶ "A person's typical behavioral traits and characteristics"[3]

Historically, personality assessments have been based on self-ratings that reflect our internal or actor's perspective of personality—unquestionably an essential aspect of who we are and how we experience the world. But others interact with us based on their observations of our behavior, not our intentions or actor's perspective. In large part, this is why 360 feedback is now a best practice in leadership development programs. Nonetheless, self-assessments are widely used for employee selection and development, and despite being subject to a range of biases, they are inexpensive and easy to administer, and some are well researched. So let's first take a look at self-ratings and what they measure.

Robert Hogan[4] describes the internal experience as identity, or the "actor's view of personality . . . personality from the inside . . . the person you think you are; your hopes, dreams, aspirations, values, fears, and theories about how to get along, get ahead, and find meaning."[5] This internal actor's view of personality provides a powerful rationale and logic for self-assessments. Moreover, some aspects of personality are best understood from the inside-the-body experience. Consider introversion, where the need to have private time and to regulate exposure to stimulation is an internal phenomenon, *not* an externalized behavior that others reliably recognize. Observers sometimes misinterpret an introvert's reserve and reticence in social situations as being "uppity," "snobbish," or "superior." In fact, that introvert's internal state is the opposite of feeling superior; he or she feels out of place, uncomfortable, sometimes inadequate.

But unlike introversion (or anxiety and tension), even masterful self-assessment developers like Hogan say that "it is empirically well established that people's self-stories are only tangentially related to their past performances, and in many cases are radically discrepant with them . . . so subjective and even fanciful."[6]

Subjective? Fanciful? Is Hogan being hyperbolic? Nope; let's take a look at some examples.

HOW CAN EVERYONE BE ABOVE AVERAGE?

David Myers conducted a famous study in which professionals were asked to rate their own social and leadership skills.[7] One hundred percent of the respondents claimed that they were in the top half in social skills. One in four respondents placed himself or herself in the top 1 percent in social skills. Only 1 in 50 said he or she was in the bottom 25 percent in leadership capability. This kind of *self-enhancement* is what

Garrison Keillor refers to as the Lake Wobegon effect, "where all the men are strong, all the women are pretty, and all the children are above average." Self-ratings suffer from the *social desirability bias* and often reflect how people think they should be rather than how they actually are.

In a now classic set of experiments, Justin Kruger and David Dunning found that people who are not conscious of their deficits tend to grossly overestimate those skills.[8] Paradoxically, they are more confident of their capabilities than people who actually have the skill or capability. Dunning explains this gap as a "deficiency in self-monitoring." Self-monitoring seems (to me) akin to the "observing ego," or mindfulness, or self-awareness—and needed for insight.

Perhaps nothing makes this point more strongly or humorously than a study in the *British Journal of Social Psychology*.[9] A survey of 79 convicts in an English prison found that the convicts rated themselves *higher than average* on a range of positive attributes, including morality and kindness. The exception was law-abidingness in which they scored about average. Psychologist Constantine Sedikides (University of Southampton) says the results speak to how important it is to maintain a positive self-image and how inflated opinions of self-worth can be extraordinarily resistant to change—even with indisputable contrary evidence.

Brian Connelly, industrial psychologist and professor at the University of Toronto's Rotman Business School, applies sophisticated statistics to study *enhancement biases*. In a *Journal of Personality* article, Connelly describes how people who overestimate their agreeableness and conscientiousness (the traits most predictive for effectiveness on the Big Five) performed worse on the job than those who did not overestimate these traits.[10] Connelly describes this as the "Michael Scott" phenomenon.

Michael Scott is the out-of-touch office manager on the television comedy show *The Office*, who has so little insight into how others perceive his behaviors that it is painfully comical. Connelly says, "One possible thing would be for those applying for jobs to nominate someone else to rate their personality rather than doing it themselves, and then you might have a better workforce. . . . If we're basing all the responses on self-reports, which is the norm, rather than having somebody else giving them the feedback, then we may be handing people's biased perceptions right back to them."

LMAP 360 FEEDBACK RATINGS

If self-ratings reflect the *actor's view* of personality, *reputation* is what Hogan calls the *observer's view of personality*. Even a self-assessment guru like Hogan understands how critical *reputation* is:

> Affection and status are granted on the basis of reputation—people hire us, fire us, marry us, loan us money, and otherwise support us based on our reputations. Consequently, smart players will reverse the natural order of their thinking and pay close attention to how others perceive and evaluate them.[11]

Hogan could not be more right and reifies what many researchers have found: it is *feedback ratings, not self-ratings, that significantly correlate with job performance.* Let's look at feedback ratings to get a sense for how they uniquely contribute to a more complete picture of personality and how feedback can sometimes bring welcome news or more a more challenging reality check.

When we report the results of the 360, we show multiple profiles: the Self Profile and Aggregated Feedback Profile and also ratings split out by Peers, Direct Reports, Manager, etc.[12] in the LMAP Report—though we will only show Self and Aggregated Feedback in the examples that follow.

SELF-EFFACEMENT

As part of a leadership development program for a client, I was asked to debrief the LMAP 360 assessment results, by phone, with a professional named Miriam. Miriam provides a great example of a person who is very talented, self-effacing, humble, and perhaps too falsely modest as an emerging leader (see Figure 7.1). Miriam might restrain her own growth as a leader if not for the feedback from others, which helps in her maturation process besides bringing welcome news.

FIGURE 7.1 | MIRIAM'S LMAP 360 PROFILES

Self Profile

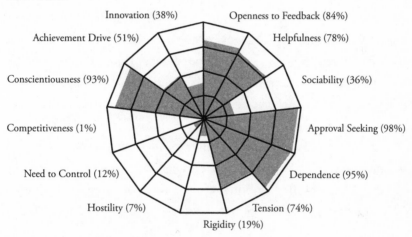

Aggregated Feedback Profile

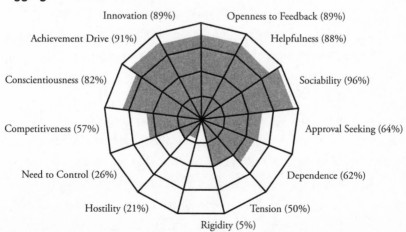

Miriam's Self Profile reflects that she sees herself as a very positive, patient, open-minded, and deferring person. She recognizes that she excels in helpfulness and is supportive of others despite her being slightly introverted. She sees herself as very conscientious but perceives herself as about average in Achievement Drive and low average in Innovation. Miriam's unassuming and modest self-ratings are consistent with her upbringing: "Don't go getting a big head . . . don't draw attention to yourself . . . in a room of leaders, don't presume to be in their league and assert your point of view."[13]

In contrast to her Self Profile, Miriam's aggregated feedback is nothing short of extraordinary. Uniformly—across Manager, Peer, and Direct Report ratings—others view her as a rising star with intellect, creativity, Grit, EQ, very strong interpersonal skills, and a genuinely humble nature. Others see in Miriam a professional who excels in Conscientiousness, Achievement Drive, and Innovation. They recognize her humility and generosity in giving credit to other team members. In written comments provided by teammates, they suggest she seek out the spotlight more to assure she gets the recognition she deserves. They do recognize Miriam's private, introverted manner but see her making the effort to exercise great interpersonal skills—something she does not give herself much credit for but does acknowledge as accurate.

Miriam was raised to never see oneself as "better than others or better than average" and to carefully and humbly wait for permission before stepping out into an assertive, leadership role—which would be *in bad taste to presume.* But her coworkers want her to be more assertive, to stop holding herself back, and to take the lead where she has the talent, support, and a following of coworkers.

The 360 feedback provides Miriam with a "reality check" and allows her to see that it is not presumptuous to take the lead when team members want that of her. She has their trust, and that can be used to help her build her confidence. These insights lay the foundation and direction for coaching Miriam to a higher level of contribution (and success) that she would not have pursued if she were limited to her self-perceptions.

SELF-ENHANCEMENT

Sometimes feedback reports bring less welcome and challenging news, especially for leaders who view their behavior through rose-colored lenses. Sometimes gaps emerge that force leaders to confront their identity—and consider *the character you thought you were, the character that others experience*, and *the character you want to be.* In this crazy, busy world, this is not a common line of thought and inquiry.

The leader who enhances self-ratings can be in for a shock when those ratings are compared with feedback ratings. One painfully common pattern is the leader who thinks of himself or herself as flexible, with an open mindset and welcoming of ideas from others. Others experience the opposite—a stubborn person who can outdebate others from intellect and rank and is inflexible with a closed mindset. Marcus was such a leader, and I'd been hired to deliver his feedback. Dr. M—as he was known in the facility—was an MD, healthcare CEO, and respected industry thought leader who consulted for the U.S. Congress on healthcare issues. Marcus exuded power, authority, self-confidence, and arrogance (see Figure 7.2).

Marcus rated himself as very high in Grit and about average in Social Intelligence and in Dominance, ratings that reflect his self-image of a brilliant, successful, open-minded, easygoing leader. He related to me that he has a very positive presence in the hospital and is friendly with everyone—he even knew the names of several janitors.

Aggregated feedback (and written comments) agreed with Marcus's view of his impressive Grit—he worked hard, was an innovator and visionary, and took on great challenges. But where Marcus self-rated Dominance behaviors (Rigidity, Hostility, Need to Control, Competitiveness) as low, his feedback raters gave very high scores on all the Dominance behaviors. They experienced Marcus as so rigid and controlling and harsh with others, that he undermined teamwork and communications and left a trail of hurt feelings and damaged relationships. The LMAP 360 feedback ratings were supported by written com-

FIGURE 7.2 | DR. M'S LMAP 360 PROFILES

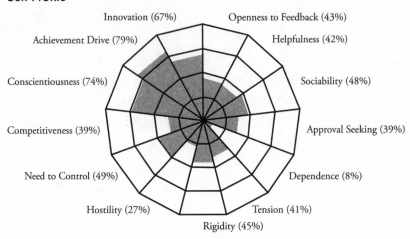

Self Profile

Innovation (67%)
Openness to Feedback (43%)
Achievement Drive (79%)
Helpfulness (42%)
Conscientiousness (74%)
Sociability (48%)
Competitiveness (39%)
Approval Seeking (39%)
Need to Control (49%)
Dependence (8%)
Hostility (27%)
Tension (41%)
Rigidity (45%)

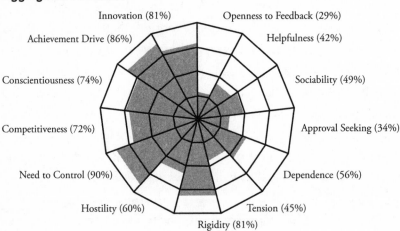

Aggregated Feedback

Innovation (81%)
Openness to Feedback (29%)
Achievement Drive (86%)
Helpfulness (42%)
Conscientiousness (74%)
Sociability (49%)
Competitiveness (72%)
Approval Seeking (34%)
Need to Control (90%)
Dependence (56%)
Hostility (60%)
Tension (45%)
Rigidity (81%)

ments: "Dr. Marcus needs to stop being so inflexible . . . nothing around here can happen without his approval—from low-level decisions to the most strategic. This is not sustainable and good people are leaving to go elsewhere" . . . "Dr. M rarely changes his mind on something and usually has made up his mind before a so-called discussion to 'reach a decision.' He is tremendously resistant to input, ideas, and opinions that differ from his own" . . . "No one wants to take him on in a debate that you can't win and won't have any influence on the outcome anyway. Dr. M calls all the shots."

Marcus dismissed the comments. He vigorously debated definitions of words like *rigid, open-minded, listening, micromanaging,* and *considerate.* He went into a long philosophical discourse on differences between perception and reality. He insisted that "others just don't understand me. I'm one of the most flexible, open-minded people you'll ever meet." I was getting exhausted from what felt like a wrestling match.

I finally said to Marcus, "Let's turn this around. Let me ask what would you say to a colleague—say a fellow physician—who received feedback from 18 work associates that they'd personally selected to give feedback and then your colleague insisted the feedback was absolutely wrong?" He threw up his hands, shrugged, and reluctantly acknowledged, "I guess I'd have to say, maybe you don't need a second opinion . . . there's something in this feedback you need to understand . . . even if you don't like it." It was at this point that we got down to work. In the months that followed, Dr. M implemented his Leadership Development Plan that stressed listening without interrupting others, being very open to input from team members, and taking time from his busy schedule to slow down and ask employees how they are doing and if they had suggestions for improving the quality of their work.

PERSONALITY: HARDWIRED OR SOFTWIRED?

> *Personality: The pattern of traits characterizing an individual person, trait here meaning any psychological characteristic of a person, including dispositions to perceive different situations similarly and to react consistently despite changing stimulus conditions, values, abilities, motives, defenses, and aspects of temperament, identity or personal style.*
>
> —Benjamin Wolman, *Dictionary of Behavioral Science*[14]

Dr. Wolman and many other twentieth-century psychologists believed that personality was "hardwired" and unchangeable. Laypeople who adopt this perspective do so to their detriment, as the belief provides a ready excuse for not managing one's externalized behavior. Understanding that *personality is behavior* allows for broader intervention and change strategies—even if you can't stop the urge to interrupt, stop the behavior—please. Thoughts, feelings, emotions, moods, and behavior are always in play—and interacting. But even if you never master the *urge* (impatience to interrupt), you can control the *behavior* of actually interrupting.

Recent studies in psychology and neuroscience have revised beliefs. We now believe personality is softwired rather than hardwired. It operates within a biologically set range and can flex within that range to adapt to internal and external factors. (In fact, the inability of individuals to adapt their actions and interactions to fit situations in their personal and work life is a key diagnostic sign of a *personality disorder*, seen in about 20 percent of the population.)[15]

Let's unpack this sentence: *Personality* (1) *is softwired rather than hardwired and operates within a biologically set range* and (2) *can flex within that range to adapt to internal and external factors.*

1. Personality . . . is softwired rather than hardwired and operates within a biologically set range. For instance, introverts are more private and reserved and less outspoken than extraverts. But within introverts as a group, and within each introverted individual, is a range. Some introverts have a very limited range and find interacting in groups very difficult. Some introverts have a wide range and have such outstanding social skills that even people they work closely with do not know they are introverts. I've spoken with hundreds of introverted leaders—whose jobs require good social skills—and they describe "putting on their social skills when they get dressed for work in the morning." At the end of the day, these introverts need their private time because they feel *exhausted* and *depleted* from a day of social stimuli and interpersonal demands. In contrast, at the end of the day, extraverts want to go out for

What's a Personality Disorder?

Everyone has personality traits, and many people have personality traits that interfere with their achieving success and satisfaction. Simply interfering with high performance and personal satisfaction does not equate to a personality disorder. A personality disorder is a chronic pattern of feelings and behaviors that significantly deviate from the cultural expectations, is resistant to change, and causes significant impairment. Estimates are that 20 percent of people have a personality disorder.[16]

What kinds of feelings and behaviors characterize a personality disorder? Here are a few examples of disorders: the *dependent personality* passively allows others to assume responsibility for major areas of life . . . subordinates own needs . . . lacks self-confidence. The *histrionic personality* shows an incessant drawing of attention to oneself . . . is perceived by others as shallow and lacking genuineness . . . vain and demanding. The *narcissistic personality* has a grandiose sense of self-importance . . . entitlement . . . interpersonal exploitativeness.

Once when I presented this list to a large audience, one of the people shouted out, "Hey! Wait a minute, that's my team!"

drinks, hang out and socialize with other people. Extraverts are *energized by* and *thrive on* social stimuli.

Consider the trait *Tension*, the tendency to feel anxious and worry. Imagine that the entire range for Tension goes from 1 to 10. Some people are very tense; their normal set range is from 7 to 10. Other people are naturally very calm, and their normal set range is 1 to 3. In a low-stress situation, the tense person might be in the low end of his or her range: 7. In a high-stress situation, the tense person goes to the high end of his or her range: 10. In contrast, a calm individual will normally operate in the 1-to-3 range. However, if you put a normally calm individual in a highly abnormal situation—in a war, for instance—that person may become far more anxious than his or her normal set range. In fact, some research suggests that PTSD in part resets the range for key behavioral characteristics.

2. Personality . . . can flex within that range to adapt to internal and external factors. People and behavior are complex, and the more sophisticated the person, often the more complex the behaviors. Roger Lipson, an executive coach, tells a story about a smart, honest, multi-talented CEO of a manufacturing firm in the Midwest. The CEO was direct and straight talking with everyone. He unfailingly showed great respect and consideration to the operations staff, even when disagreements or conflicts arose. Yet he was also known to be very aggressive and exhibit angry displeasure with the senior management team. Roger asked him how he could behave so differently to these two groups.

The CEO explained that his behaviors reflected not just his personality but also his values. Within his value system, "at $18.00 an hour, operations staff don't earn much and sure aren't paid enough to hear the CEO yell at them." On the other hand, he said, "I pay the management team pretty damn well . . . enough that, if I'm pissed off about something, I'm not going to watch what I say or how I say it." He also believed that his tough, unforgiving style with the management team was needed to "keep them on their feet." Roger asked, "Who keeps you on your feet? Who critiques your work?" The CEO said that because he had such high standards, he could critique his own work.

What is interesting is that the CEO managed his behavior to match his *value system*, which led him to be very specific in the kinds of behaviors he demonstrated to specific constituencies.[17]

CAN PERSONALITY CHANGE?

In our work with clients, we are clear that the goal of the assessment is *not to transform your personality, but to modify a specific behavior* to raise your effectiveness as a leader (pilot, team manager, etc.). Given the nature of our work, we are most focused on modifications to the *behavioral* side of personality: that which people demonstrate in their actions and interactions with others. An example makes this clearer: Anne is a brilliant, ambitious, but not very socially skilled engineer who feels an almost overwhelming sense of urgency to get things done as fast as possible. She is a very quick thinker and convinced that her mind works faster than most other people's. She has an internal personality makeup that drives her off-putting behavioral habit to interrupt others. Chances are, she will always feel a strong internal sense of urgency and the impulse to interrupt others.

But is Anne literally compelled to interrupt others? Or can she learn to control this interrupting behavior? Anne initially says, "I know it's not right to interrupt, but I just can't stop myself in the moment." Yet when asked if there are any situations when she is *not* likely to interrupt, Anne readily acknowledges that she does not interrupt the CEO where she works and recalls that in graduate school she did not interrupt her dissertation chair. Anne also said she controls herself and does not interrupt important customers, "even though I sometimes want to." Anne has an insight and laughs, "I guess I have more control over this than I thought." While Anne may not (yet) have control over the *internal sense of urgency* that drives her behavior of interrupting others, she realizes that she does have control over and flexibility around the *external behavior* of interrupting—it is just that she very selectively chooses to exercise control. Anne agrees to practice listening without interruption by exercising greater deliberate, conscious control over her counterproductive interrupting behavior.

Is it possible that Anne could also modify her internal urges? To change not just her external behavior of interrupting others but also her internal experience of urgency? The research suggests that this is indeed possible with great practice and discipline. But because this sense of urgency is part of Anne's personality DNA, she is far more likely to decrease rather than eliminate the sense of urgency altogether. Yet the importance of Anne's success in simply decreasing (versus eliminating) her sense of urgency should not be discounted. There are multiple positive outcomes:

▶ Because Anne is less distracted by the urge to interrupt, her *internal experience* in listening will be less stressful for her.

▶ In terms of her *external behavior*, she will be less likely to interrupt.

▶ Anne's *interpersonal interactions* improve because others will not respond to her interruptions with verbal or nonverbal (rolled eyes, grimace, sigh) feedback that they don't appreciate being interrupted.

▶ The flow of information, now unimpeded, makes for *more effective communication*.

We compare modifying externalized behaviors (versus internal experience) to picking low-hanging fruit: these behaviors are the most easily modified and controlled and often the most efficient way to assist professionals with changing counterproductive personality attributes. Even if Anne's internal experience of urgency does not change initially, through the practice of not interrupting others, she is able to build better listening skills into her behavioral repertoire, resulting in an increased sense of self-efficacy and positive feedback from others.

Top 10 Behaviors to Start, Stop, or Improve[18]

1. I will start to give people my undivided attention and not use my computer or smartphone when we are in a conversation.

2. I will start to ask the tough questions that I ordinarily feel uncomfortable asking because I want to be "nice" to everyone.

3. I will stop yelling at work—I will speak to others with respect and consideration.

4. I will stop overanalyzing things and start taking more calculated risks.

5. I will give more verbal recognition and reinforcement for good work done by others on the team rather than assume they know I've noticed.

6. I will improve my listening skills; I will listen patiently and ask follow-up questions.

7. To be more helpful to my direct reports, I will start to ask them weekly how projects are progressing and ask if they need my additional support.

8. I will be more tolerant and listen more to others and do this in a way that people feel valued versus diminished.

9. I will start to delegate more work to several of the talented individuals on the team who are ready to take on more and coach them to success.

10. I will start to be more assertive and say what I mean and mean what I say without sugarcoating my words.

INSIGHT IN ACTION

For most people, the gap between their habitual behaviors and their efforts to consciously and thoughtfully manage those behavior is *huge*, even when they know intellectually that those behaviors are dysfunctional or ineffective. Most personality patterns are unconscious, ingrained actions and reactions; more often than not in our everyday lives, we operate in "automatic" or "autopilot" mode.[19] We often rely on default behaviors and do not consciously think about, manage, or guide our thoughts, feelings, and behaviors. Moreover, it becomes a self-fulfilling prophecy to believe that one's personality traits are hardwired and unchangeable ("That's just the way I am") or to rationalize or justify our behavior ("If I'm not demanding or critical, people will slack off"). This allows us to avoid taking responsibility for our attitudes and behaviors, even when we know they are counterproductive and interfere with our personal and professional life. Anne's self-fulfilling prophecy was that she had no control over her annoying habit of interrupting others. Only when she thought through the exceptions (with the CEO, her dissertation chair, and important customers) was she able to see that, in fact, she could manage and change this behavior.

Just like Anne, we often don't realize that we can exercise tremendous choice in our behavior, because we so seldom take the time and effort to think it through. It is in the gap between unconscious habitual behaviors and conscious and thoughtful management of those behaviors that the opportunity for improving leadership, teamwork, and communications exists.

CHAPTER 8

Things Are Crazy at Work

This book focuses on the relationships between normal personality traits and work performance. The traits measured in the LMAP 360 are normal traits and behaviors—not abnormal or psychopathology. And yet . . .

PSYCHOPATHOLOGY AT WORK— AN ASIDE TO PERSONALITY?

Almost all of us have worked with a colleague with self-management or interpersonal issues that we suspect are related to psychiatric, substance, or personality problems (or have a family member or friend experiencing psychological problems). And we read about spectacular examples:

Germanwings copilot Andreas Lubitz, whose history suggests chronic depression with acute suicidal and psychotic features that led him to crash Flight 9525 (recall, nobody at the airline suspected Andreas Lubitz had psychiatric problems, but his doctors knew he should not fly). Lubitz is just one of *at least* eight pilot suicides-by-plane-crash from the period 2002–2013.[1] These are extremes outside the analysis of relationships between personality and flight crew performance. Yet, incidents like these raise intriguing questions we explore in this chapter beginning with some definitions and distinctions.

In the American Psychiatric Association's *Diagnostic and Statistical Manual of Mental Disorders* (DSM)—the bible of psychiatry—thought and behavior disorders are divided into two domains or axes:[2]

Axis 1. Clinical Psychiatric Disorders (e.g., major depression, anxiety disorders, bipolar disorder, schizophrenia, etc.)

Axis 2. Personality Disorders (e.g., borderline, narcissistic, dependent, etc.)

Now, consider the demographics for each axis:

▶ (Roughly) 20 percent have Axis 1 Clinical Psychiatric Disorders—these are episodic behaviors (a manic mood episode, episodes of hearing voices).

▶ (Roughly) 20 percent Substance Abuse and Dependence (also considered Axis 1)

▶ (Roughly) 20 percent have Axis 2 Personality Disorders— these are chronic behaviors.

That is a lot of people—though it absolutely does not mean 60 percent of people have a DSM disorder, because many are *dual-diagnosed* with (generally) a disorder on each axis (e.g., bipolar disorder + alcohol dependence + borderline personality disorder; anxiety disorder + dependent personality disorder; major depression + alcohol abuse; etc.).

Just consider one class of disorders, anxiety disorders, the most common. These Axis 1 disorders include panic disorder, generalized anxiety disorder, posttraumatic stress disorder, phobias, and separation anxiety disorder. With a 12-month prevalence of 10+ percent, this is obviously a population large enough to support television commercials for medications specifically for social phobia.

To be clear, anxiety disorders, major depression, bipolar disorders (and substance abuse) are Axis 1 disorders and are serious and well represented in the professional ranks. In part, newer medications for some

> ## The Hard Money Costs for a Few Clinical Disorders
>
> The estimated costs for the clinical disorders vary by the tens of billions; here are a few:
>
> ▶ Anxiety disorders: $40 billion in healthcare costs and lost productivity[3]
>
> ▶ Major depression: $44 billion
>
> ▶ Bipolar disorder: $45 billion
>
> The main costs for people suffering from major depression are from absenteeism, whereas those with anxiety disorders are less likely to miss work; thus they can generously share their worries and tensions with fellow workers.

disorders effectively inhibit future episodes and provide long-term stability. Professionals take psychiatric medication—just as asthmatics or diabetics take meds, and nobody at work knows.

However, the most severe Axis 1 clinical disorders—and especially the psychotic disorders and those of the severely mentally ill—are uncommon in professional ranks; but bipolar, depression, anxiety, and substance abuse disorders are absolutely well represented in the professional ranks.[4] Putting aside for this discussion the presence of Axis 1 disorders in the professional ranks, let's turn to Axis 2, Personality Disorders.

THIS IS WHERE IT GETS INTERESTING: PERSONALITY AND PERSONALITY DISORDERS

We all have personality traits, and many people have personality traits that interfere with their job effectiveness, achievement, success, and satisfaction. But simply interfering with performance and satisfaction does not equate to a personality disorder. A *personality disorder* (1) is a chronic pattern of feelings and behaviors that significantly deviate from the cultural expectations, is resistant to change, and causes significant impairment (job derailment is one example) and (2) meets a minimum number of very specific behavioral criteria.

For example, a narcissistic personality disorder (NPD) requires (1) a chronically inflated sense of importance, deep needs for admiration, and a lack of empathy for others. A presenting mask of high confidence is projected to protect fragile self-esteem that's vulnerable to the slightest criticism. *In addition*, (2) the person must have five or more of these behaviors (edited for brevity):

▶ Has a grandiose sense of self-importance

▶ Is preoccupied with ideas of unlimited success, power, brilliance, or ideal love

▶ Believes he or she is "special" and only understood by or associates with high-status people

▶ Requires excessive admiration

▶ Has a sense of entitlement: expects automatic compliance with his or her expectations

▶ Is interpersonally exploitative: takes advantage of others to achieve own ends

▶ Lacks empathy; unwilling to recognize the feelings and needs of others

▶ Is often envious of others or believes others are envious of him or her

▶ Exhibits arrogant behaviors and attitudes

People with NPD show intolerance for criticisms and disagreements, are easily triggered into emotional outbursts, belittle and disparage others, and make vicious comments. Situations that most people would view as "no big deal" can set NPDs off.

Clients often ask, "Did Steve Jobs have a narcissistic personality disorder?" Tina Redse, longtime girlfriend of Jobs, told biographer Walter Isaacson that she never fully understood Jobs until she read the DSM description of NPD: "It fits so well and explained so much . . . I realized expecting him to be nicer or less self-centered was like expecting a blind man to see."[5] Andy Hertzfeld described how Jobs "had the sense he was special, a chosen one, an enlightened one . . . there are a few people who are special—people like Einstein and Gandhi and the gurus he met in India—and he's one of them."[6]

People with some disorders, like dependent personality disorder characterized by a lifelong history of dysfunction related to "clinging behavior" and found in 1 percent of the population, don't generally aspire to or end up in a leadership role. But take NPD estimated at 6.2 percent, borderline PD at 5.9 percent, and obsessive-compulsive PD at 2 percent, and you have a lot of people.[7]

A 2005 study by British psychologists Belinda Board and Katarina Fritzon found three personality disorders more common in senior executives than "the criminally insane":

▶ Narcissistic personality disorder

▶ Histrionic PD (characterized by superficial charm, insincerity, egocentrism, and manipulation)

▶ Obsessive-compulsive PD (characterized by perfectionism, excessive devotion to work, rigidity and dictatorial tendencies, superficial charm, insincerity, egocentrism, and manipulation)[8]

THIS IS WHERE IT GETS VERY INTERESTING— THE FINE LINE

Okay, now putting aside whatever (small) percentage of full-blown personality disorders there are in the workplace—that number is *dwarfed* by the prevalence of professionals who have many but not all the required dysfunctional behaviors to fulfill the diagnostic criteria. As a clinician and as a personality psychologist for 30 years, I've meet *many* professionals who fall one or two DSM criteria short; yet their behaviors interfere with leadership, teamwork, and communications—what we call normal people.

"Normal" does *not* mean an absence of behavioral issues that impact work performance. Executive researchers David Dotlich and Peter Cairo say, "The average person has two or three derailers. While we've worked with people who have had many more and a few who seemed to lack any of them, the odds are that some will fit you perfectly."[9] Dotlich and Cairo also cite stress and its negative impact on behavior *as one of the great displacers of natural strengths*. As stress ratchets up, natural strengths can be overused or less reliable.

MORE WAKING HOURS THAN . . .

Think about it: professionals spend more waking hours with work associates than with family or friends. Interactions between coworkers can get highly charged and emotional.[10] At best, strong relationships are forged, and passion drives the work. At worst, coworker clashes create intense workplace stress—whether you're at the center of the conflict or you're collateral damage. The interaction of team members' personality styles—more even than business strategy, tactics, or technical skills—drives the culture and employees' experience of and engagement in work.

THE FINE LINES AND FRACTURES OF PERSONALITY

Over the last 20 years, I've spent half my time working in a clinical setting. For 8 years I directed a program for clients with a dual diagnosis: schizophrenia, bipolar disorder, or another serious mental illness *and* substance dependence or abuse (alcohol +/or crack +/or meth +/or downers +/or opiates . . .). Most were on disability payments from the government and had been homeless.

What I miss being reminded of on a daily basis is that life can be tough without psychiatric problems, but it is magnitudes more stressful with psychiatric problems. I got a daily dose of how fortunate I am with the cards I've been dealt. I felt more gratitude and a sense of doing obviously meaningful work helping patients who were dealt a lousy genetic hand . . . and I went to graduate school and had two years of APA internships to learn how to be a doctor for those in need. In my current role, built around LMAP, I spend most of my time with talented, successful senior executives, who also are fortunate with their cards—yet often are missing a sense of perspective and gratitude.

Deference: Derailers and Development

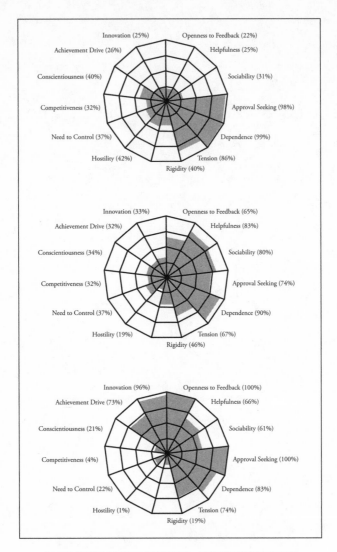

SAMPLE RIGHT-SIDER PROFILES—PROGRESSING FROM
LEAST TO MOST EFFECTIVE

CHAPTER 9

Deference—The Right-Sider

We all know a *Right-Sider*: a loyal team member with an agreeable, easygoing, and accommodating nature, a person who willingly follows the lead of others and who treats others with consideration and tact. Twenty percent of professionals have a profile combining prominent Deference and Teamwork traits. These individuals do their work without making waves, and they contribute to the overall effort without craving the spotlight or needing to be the center of attention. Their unassuming, modest, and other-centric style can be a refreshing change in an all-too-frequently narcissistic world.

Right-Siders, in general, are much more willing to make sacrifices for the collective good than Left-Siders, who are more independent-minded, self-serving, and self-absorbed. Right-Siders with prominent Social Intelligence and Teamwork traits have empathy, compassion, and interpersonal relationship skills. Their patience, listening skills, and willingness to take time to coach and mentor others are key leadership assets. In the book *TouchPoints*, Doug Conant and Mette Norgaard describe this kind of individual as having a natural affinity for being tenderhearted with people.

As leaders, Right-Siders often find the second part of Conant and Norgaard's prescription for effective leadership more challenging: being tough-minded around results. This is particularly true when getting those results involves confronting others and making tough decisions (e.g., holding others accountable, giving negative performance feedback, firing staff, etc.)—decisions that, by their very nature, involve displeasing others.

Right-Siders can be great leaders if their high EQ, teamwork, and interpersonal skills are combined with Grit—with one or two of the Task Mastery traits. These are the high-performance Right-Side Profiles. Right-Siders with average or above Task Mastery traits are highly effective as leaders: Their tenderhearted approach is complemented by the drive, action-orientation, and initiative required to get ahead and get results.

For Right-Siders *without* Grit—without at least one of the three Task Mastery traits—there is a void around initiative, results orientation, and urgency, the very behavioral styles that propel Left-Siders into leadership roles. Where Left-Siders are alert and angle to take the lead, this does not come naturally to the Right-Sider who is more the follower than leader—*unless that Right-Sider also has enough* Conscientiousness, Achievement Drive, or Innovation to take the initiative and drive great work. And even then Right-Siders may be seen as not urgent or driven enough.

Recall Steve Wozniak, a Right-Sider with Grit: Helpful, Deferential, and Tense with substantial Conscientiousness and Innovation. Though Woz, as we saw, rejected the corporate leadership path, he expressed his great ambitions in other ways. Besides cofounding Apple Computer, Woz founded or cofounded multiple companies and foundations, earned four sole patents, is a member of the National Inventors Hall of Fame, and was awarded numerous prestigious engineering awards including the 66th Hoover Medal for professional engineering achievements and personal endeavors that have advanced the well-being of humankind. People do not achieve this much without substantial Grit.

Like Woz, there are countless examples of deferential leaders who are founders, or have mission-critical technical skills, or gained seniority in a patronage system or through nepotism. When this occurs, they and their organization are challenged by their lack of assertiveness and their tendencies to be more reactive than proactive and to avoid the necessary confrontations that are a part of an effective work process and competitive work environment. They struggle in leadership roles.

THE EMOTIONAL EXPERIENCE OF WORK

For professionals with Right-Sider Profiles, their own accommodating and supportive nature can lull them into thinking that others are as patient, understanding, and encouraging as they are. As a result, they can end up feeling disappointed and hurt by coworkers who don't have the social skills to provide what Right-Siders look for from others—approval, encouragement, and regard. Teammates with Left-Side Dominant (or Bottom-Heavy) Profiles—roughly half the workforce—are so preoccupied with their own responsibilities, worries, and issues that they can be oblivious to the needs of others. In fact, Left-Siders can be so short on empathy that they *expect* everyone else to demonstrate the initiative, self-direction, and assertiveness that are natural to them.

As such, the Right-Sider who seeks approval, regard, and reinforcement from coworkers—all reasonable things to desire—may find it unavailable when it's needed the most. When this occurs, some Right-Siders withdraw, anticipating negative future interactions and stress. Right-Siders may be even more reluctant to inquire or advocate when teamed with others who are aggressive and hostile. But this strategy can backfire: Failure to inquire or advocate can lead to negative outcomes when open and direct communications are mission-critical. Crew errors in aviation illustrate this most dramatically.

LEADERSHIP EFFECTIVENESS

Twenty percent of the LMAP sample has a profile combining prominent Deference and Teamwork traits. For these professionals, their effectiveness in moving into leadership roles depends on two factors:

▶ The relative balance of Teamwork to Deference traits

▶ The relative balance of Deference to Task Mastery traits

Let's look at how this plays out in the wide array of Right-Side Profiles.

1. THE DEPENDENT PROFILE—LOW EFFECTIVENESS AND NOT A MATCH FOR LEADERSHIP

Those with only prominent Deference and *without* Teamwork traits (see Figure 9.1) are *very rare* in senior leadership. Individuals with this type of profile prefer to stay out of the leadership spotlight and to follow the lead of others. They are risk averse, prefer to play it safe, and want to follow others instead of creating rules and norms. They are most comfortable and effective applying their technical training, experiences, and smarts as an individual contributor to a team. With an "external locus of control," they believe that events happen to them rather than making events happen through their efficacy—essentially the opposite mindset of Grit.

2. DEFERENCE + SOCIAL INTELLIGENCE = MIXED EFFECTIVENESS

Far more common in sales professionals and managers are Deference traits combined with Teamwork traits (Figure 9.2). Openness to Feedback, Helpfulness, and Sociability project social and emotional intelligence and provide the base of relationship skills that results in a low-key, nonconfrontational style that can make them effective in their endeavor to *get along by going along*. Some excel as social leaders through networking and connecting others. They excel in networking because they do not come across as self-serving or overtly driven and ambitious for themselves. They will diligently follow up, not because they are conscientious, but because they want to please others, they have good man-

FIGURE 9.1 | HIGHLY DEPENDENT PROFILES WITHOUT TEAMWORK TRAITS

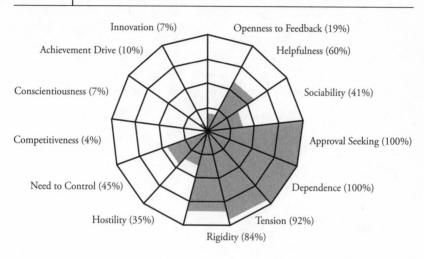

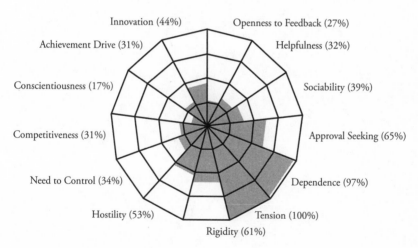

ners, and they want to do the right thing. An upside of their brand of relationship skills is that they build a network of people with whom they've earned trust and goodwill, as they are not seen as pushy and self-interested.

Because these Right-Siders are not overly ambitious or aggressive, they rarely ascend to the highest corporate ranks to become the leader of leaders. To be effective in team leadership roles, many Right-Siders need

FIGURE 9.2 | DEFERENCE + SOCIAL INTELLIGENCE/TEAMWORK TRAITS

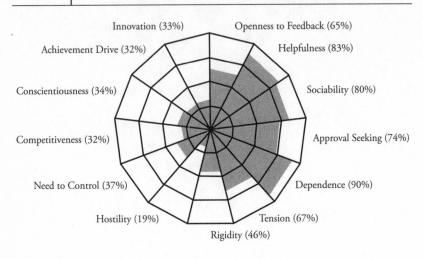

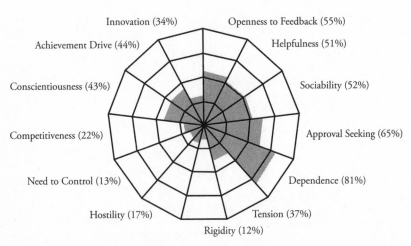

to worry less about what others of greater rank think, and they need to exercise their own independent authority and judgment when the situation demands and speak up.

We have seen how these behavioral characteristics play out in negative ways, particularly when it comes to aviation disasters. Recall the Alaska Airlines accident examined in Chapter 6. The captain's arrogance and unwillingness to listen were perhaps the most obvious behaviors

Introverted Right-Siders

Right-Siders with low Sociability (see Figure 9.3) are often quite shy and introverted. They are self-conscious and uncomfortable in a leadership role where attention is focused on them. Some, like Steve Wozniak in the early days of Apple, partner with a more dynamic, directive, and visible team leader, while they do their work in the background.

FIGURE 9.3 | INTROVERTED RIGHT-SIDER PROFILE

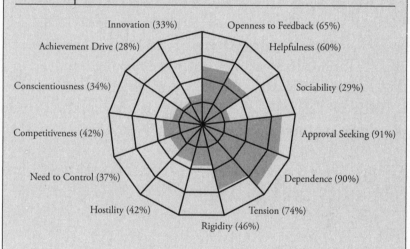

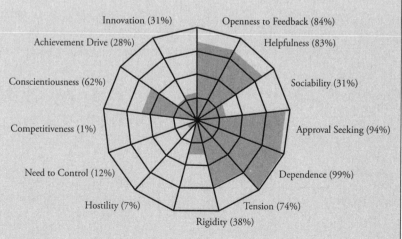

that contributed to that accident, but recall how the first officer's deferential and mitigated communications also significantly contributed to that awful outcome. Given the stakes involved, the magnitude of a first officer's inquiry and advocacy efforts must match the magnitude of the situation, but this is often not the case with unassertive, deferential individuals.[1] Indeed, assertiveness skills are of paramount importance, not just in aviation, but also in healthcare, energy services, and foreign policy where life-and-death decisions are made and catastrophic consequences can result.

Of course, speaking up is necessary in all organizations though, and this is why firms offer rewards and recognition for employee ideas and suggestions, reinforcing the notion that even less-assertive employees are needed to contribute to the organization's mission. To thrive, organizations depend on the next great idea or suggestion that someone advocates; a compelling observation or information left unspoken can bring down a project—or worse.

3. DEFERENCE + TEAMWORK + GRIT = HIGH PERFORMANCE

> *Perseverance is a great element of success. If you only knock long enough and loud enough at the gate, you are sure to wake up somebody.*
>
> —Henry Wadsworth Longfellow

Composing 5 percent of the LMAP sample are Right-Siders who also have prominent Grit—like Woz—and truly are high-performance profiles (see Figure 9.4).

These leaders have the two essential behavioral components of effective leadership: Teamwork and Task Mastery traits. They possess a unique blend of initiative, focus, flexibility, teamwork skills, and humility. These leaders think in terms of "we" rather than "I," and they share many of the behavioral attributes of the servant leader model and the

FIGURE 9.4 | DEFERENCE + SOCIAL INTELLIGENCE + GRIT

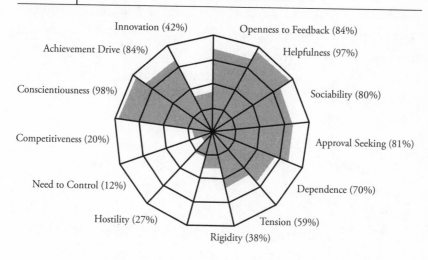

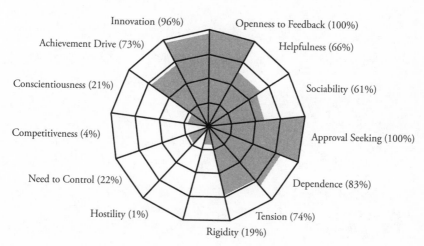

Level 5 leadership model that Jim Collins describes in his book *Good to GREAT.*

In addition to having a tenderhearted approach toward people, these leaders have a tough-minded approach to issues and results. Their initiative, persistence, and strong quality orientation make all the difference in the effectiveness of these Right-Siders. These leaders have extraordinarily high leadership effectiveness ratings, outstanding work relationships, and strong results. In part, they get strong results because they know how to bring out the best in people. While these leaders are clearly appreciated for their empowerment of others, their humility, and their low-drama team leadership skills, ironically they sometimes get feedback asking them to be more directive, assertive, and urgent—that is, to operate more like authoritarian, hierarchical leaders.

Damned If You Do, Damned If You Don't

I must admit, sometimes you can't win in a 360 profile. People are seen as either too urgent or not urgent enough . . . a workaholic or too leisurely . . . too quick to stir up conflict or not confrontational enough . . . too micromanaging or too *laissez-faire*.

This is reminiscent of research showing that the traits and behaviors that initially attract us in relationships are ultimately the very traits and behaviors that later come to annoy us.[2] The assertive person who says what is on his or her mind is later seen as pushy or self-centered. The easygoing person who starts as a low-maintenance teammate eventually is seen as too passive, too willing to compromise, and not assertive enough.

I am reminded of Gregory, a brilliant leader at a Singaporean investment firm with a strong investment management history and a stellar reputation. All agreed Greg was an emerging leader, had the intellect and presence and social skills to grow into a prominent leadership role, and was seen by all constituencies (managers, peers, direct reports) as a highly effective professional. Yet some feedback raters commented about his style being "too laid back" and "leisurely," and others said they would like to see "more fire in the belly" and "more intensity and passion."

I went looking for what might be underlying this impression in others that Greg needed more passion, intensity, and fire in the belly. One thing I noticed was that Greg scored himself below average on the Achievement Drive assessment item—"Likes to solve complex problems." *He'd scored* a 3—sometimes like me—compared with the sample average of 4.29 (see Exhibit 9.1).

EXHIBIT 9.1 | LIKES TO SOLVE COMPLEX PROBLEMS

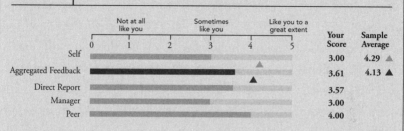

	Your Score	Sample Average
Self	3.00	4.29
Aggregated Feedback	3.61	4.13
Direct Report	3.57	
Manager	3.00	
Peer	4.00	

When we met, I asked him about this, and he told me, "I get enough complex problems thrown at me regularly. I'll sometimes take a few easy ones." To me, it seemed like a healthy perspective and the kind of emotional balance that his more driven, intense peers would do well to emulate. Not only did he find time to be a standout professional, but he was widely read and well informed, and he was a dedicated father who was taking karate lessons with his son. He knew how to keep what I considered to be a healthy perspective about work: he was working to live, not living to work. And he was doing a pretty good job at both.

If someone gets his or her work done well at a high level, leads the team effectively, and creates great morale—and appears to do so in a more leisurely manner—what's wrong with that? Why isn't this an asset? Does this simply reflect the rater's personal needs and biases? Or does it reflect a larger Western cultural bias that always demands more and where bigger, better, faster is the ever-sought-after goal?

THE PRESSURE TO MOVE UP IN ORGANIZATIONS

In our society, there is tremendous pressure to move up in the organization. In the first four years serving as an executive coach in Yale Executive Education programs, I met hundreds of senior managers. All had impressive professional skills and expertise built on educational training and work experience. *Every* one of them said they wanted to move up in the organization. They sought out new challenges, increased compensation, and the status and validation of career growth. Yet, in coaching sessions, I saw a pattern emerge for Right-Siders: even those who felt comfortable in their current role and believed that moving up into a higher leadership role would create unwanted additional stress and pressure also felt compelled to move up. Some organizations, in fact, demand this, with explicit or implicit up-or-out career models where partnership is the goal.[3]

TO LEAD OR NOT TO LEAD

Not only is it rare to receive honest, direct, useful feedback, but it is also rare to take time to reflect on our career development path. There are times in our coaching practices where this becomes a focus with a client. At such times, we ask some key questions:

▶ What is it that you really want, and what do you think you will achieve by rising in your organization?

▶ What drives this need?

▶ How will your life be substantially different if you continue to rise in the organization?

▶ Where do you derive your greatest satisfactions at work?

▶ What kind of life do you really want?

These are fair and important questions to ask, particularly, but not just, for Right-Siders. We believe it is important not to fall into the default position: moving up merely because it seems the next logical step in a career. As in life, satisfaction at work doesn't always lie in taking the next logical step, and fulfilling career paths are not always linear progressions. We agree with those who stress that leadership is not for everyone. It requires putting in hard work, managing difficult personalities, navigating company politics, and having a real passion for leadership. Conant and Norgaard ask:

> Is being a leader really worth the long hours, the endless meetings, the wrangling over forecasts and budgets, the reports, the grumbling, and the travel? Is it really worth devoting more of your waking hours to work, or to thinking about work, than to anything else? Is that really the way you want to spend your life?[4]

Professionals who are slotted toward a leadership role need to deeply and honestly consider if they really want to be a leader with formal authority. It is difficult in today's competitive world to not simply default into a leadership role both because it is the conventional route and because moving up is considered a sign of success.

But there are many other ways for professionals to have a powerful impact and to cultivate and leverage influence and contributions without being in a formal leadership role. Leaders are required to oversee and manage a range of other professionals—some who are difficult and require tremendous oversight and emotional investments. Many professionals, especially those who were star performers in their individual contributor roles, find that they enjoyed their work more and could contribute more without the additional leadership responsibilities. For some, *not* defaulting into a leadership role that does not match personal and professional preferences is a sign of courage and conviction, not a sign of weakness or lack of ambition.

In a related way, studies have shown that given the choice between money and time, a vast majority of people pick money. But follow-up studies with these individuals find that those who opted for more time were actually more satisfied. Whillans, Weidman, and Dunn published research in the March 2016 issue of *Social Psychological & Personality Science*, where they summarized their findings: "Across six studies ($N = 4,690$), we provide the first empirical evidence that prioritizing time over money is a stable preference related to greater subjective well-being."[5] Laszlo Bock reports similar findings in studies done at Google, where—given a choice—Googlers chose money over other types of rewards. But follow-up studies at Google showed that nonmonetary rewards (reservations for dinner or theater tickets on the company) had a longer-lasting positive impact on satisfaction than money.[6]

LEADERSHIP BY DEFAULT I— A CHOICE FOR PROFESSIONALS

Many ascend to leadership roles because it is the next logical step. These are leaders by default. Unfortunately, most people jump at an opportunity to move up to roles offering higher status and compensation, considering it a no-brainer. Few of us consider accepting a promotion as a conscious choice. Promotions into higher management and leadership roles are simply a natural and logical consequence of attaining tenure and doing good work.

But in terms of the match between one's personality and leadership, it is not so simple. Only about 20 percent of professionals are "naturals" with behavioral styles ready-made for effective leadership. The majority of us—the other 80 percent—find that to lead requires increased self-awareness and some behavior modification to be most effective.

Right-Siders with leadership aspirations do best by consciously making a personal choice: either develop the leadership tools necessary to step up into that role and those responsibilities or, as Woz decided, pursue a different course. Taking on a management (and leadership) role did not match the type of work Woz wanted to do, the tenor of interpersonal relationships he desired, or the lifestyle he wanted. "That's why I was sure, even at twenty-two, that I didn't want to go into management and have to fight political battles and takes sides and step on people's toes and all that stuff," he said.[7]

Recognizing his personality makeup and priorities, Woz made a choice: "In my head, the guy who'd rather laugh than control things is going to be the one who has the happier life. . . . I figure happiness is the most important thing in life, just how much you laugh. . . . That's who I am, who I want to be and have always wanted to be."[8]

Not everyone has Woz's self-awareness around these issues though. It often takes a stalled career, a demotion, or worse to make it clear to people that an organizational leadership role is not the best fit for them.

LEADERSHIP BY DEFAULT II— A CHOICE FOR ORGANIZATIONS

Leadership by default is by no means restricted to individuals. It's also an all-too-common practice (and source of woe) for organizations. A company takes its top salesperson or senior engineer and makes him or her manager, because it's the person's next step up the corporate ladder and the position must be filled. Sometimes in doing so, the organization loses its top salesperson or engineer and ends up with an underperforming manager. While such by-default leaders may have all the technical skills and experience necessary to be considered for promotion to a leadership role, if they do not have the behavioral styles needed to be effective, without good coaching and training, they are candidates for derailment. It becomes a lose-lose proposition.

There are powerful emotional and interpersonal consequences for both those who assume leadership positions and those who follow. Hiring a leader who either cannot or does not want to lead will negatively impact every aspect of the team. As we have seen, leaders have the power to create a culture that motivates or demotivates others. From employee engagement to retention to bottom-line results, the leader's attitudes and behaviors set the reference point—and other team members are watching. If the leader does not want to go above and beyond, how can we expect his or her team to do so? How does the Right-Sider with authentic leadership aspirations develop the leadership behaviors necessary to step up to be effective in that role? This is the focus of the next chapter.

Leading with Grit and Assertiveness

DERAILMENT

When we think of derailment, many envision someone's career rising to great heights and then crashing and burning—a trajectory true for some Left-Siders. This is not often the case for Right-Siders, however. Rather, their careers tend to plateau or peter out. Robert Hogan cites excessive caution, indecisiveness, reserve, and passivity as common derailers, and these behaviors are characteristic of the deferential leader.[1] These are deficits of passivity and reactivity—behaviors that impede and interfere with high performance. This is why Right-Siders do not as often end up in senior leadership roles, and when they do, these behavior patterns hold them back.

Their key to greater effectiveness is to reduce the impact of Deference behaviors (showing restraint, being reluctant, holding back) and create greater operating room for Grit and Task Mastery behaviors (being assertive, being proactive, taking risks). So what is it that holds a Deferential Right-Sider back?

THE PROBLEM OF DEFERENCE—FEAR

Fears are educated into us, and can, if we wish, be educated out.

—Karl Menninger

Behaviors that emanate from the Deference sector are behaviors of inhibition, indecision, and lack of confidence—all behaviors rooted in *fear*. There are many fears common to the Right-Side Deferential Profile. Fear of:

▶ Having interpersonal conflict

▶ Offending others

▶ Being embarrassed and humiliated

▶ Being rejected

▶ Displeasing or disappointing important people

▶ Being wrong or imperfect

▶ Being responsible for managing people and projects

▶ Being the "bad guy" for setting limits and holding others accountable

▶ Showing anger and other strong emotions—their own and others'

▶ Failing

Right-Siders derail due to errors of omission—of not speaking up or acting swiftly or decisively enough. Fear as a key force holding people back is a focus of the work of psychologists Karen Horney, Harry Stack Sullivan, and Erik Erikson, whose work had a large influence on Timothy Leary's thinking and is reflected in his Circumplex Profile design.

In discussing LMAP 360 results with deferent leaders, what emerges are their heightened sensitivity, anxiety, and concerns around displeasing others, not being good enough, offending others, being wrong, etc. So rather than taking the risk of acting on their own, they "wait for permission" from others to act. In this sense, Deference is all about insecurity with oneself and how this influences interactions with others.

LMAP 360 feedback raters comment that they'd like to see greater self-confidence in the deferential leader, as these team members trust and have greater confidence in the leader than the leader has in himself or herself. The crux of the matter for competent leaders with lagging self-confidence and chronic restraint is to believe their feedback results and act with the confidence that others have in them. We suggest that highly competent deferential leaders learn to act *despite* their anxiety and fear in part because of the irrationality of their fears. We remind them of their track record of successes and that others are asking them to act with authority. In fact, they have earned their leadership credibility and can behave accordingly. *Their biggest obstacle is not around the consequences of their actions, but in their reluctance to act.* Overcoming this obstacle may be easier said than done, but with deliberate practice, ongoing coaching, and a growing record of success, it gets easier and the anxieties dissipate.

SPEAK UP, STEP UP

LMAP 360 feedback raters provide comments about behaviors they would like their leader to change, to start, and to stop in order to raise their effectiveness. *What is it that team members say they need and want from Right-Side leaders?* Frequent suggestions for Right-Side leaders include:

▶ Be more assertive.

▶ Be more proactive.

▶ Hold people accountable.

▶ Do not avoid conflict.

▶ Act more decisively.

▶ Show more rigor around quality.

▶ Think more outside the box.

▶ Take more risks.

▶ Learn to say no.

▶ Authoritatively stand your ground.

▶ Stop trying to please everybody.

▶ Stop deferring to higher management.

▶ Be more confident.

While each of us retains the right to choose how assertive to be in our personal life, leaders have a professional obligation to ask the tough questions, to openly raise concerns, and to call out breaches in values and ethics when these arise. For those in leadership, holding back for fear that you would be "acting presumptuous" or that it is "not your place to speak up" when issues critical to the mission arise is counterproductive. Leaders bear a responsibility to subordinate personal preferences to avoid conflict and to simply conform—they must be willing to engage in open, honest, and direct conversations around the work.

COACHING CAROL, A DEFERENTIAL LEADER

Carol is a leader who completed an LMAP 360 and was by all accounts a very capable and competent manager. She was in her early forties, was well liked and respected, and had a strong IT and customer service background. Carol was described as trustworthy, humble, and considerate. Her team, which had the lowest turnover in the firm, had produced several years of strong results.

LMAP 360 Report on Assertiveness and Risk Taking

Your LMAP 360 feedback indicates that you are low on assertiveness and risk taking (see Figure 10.1). What can you do?

FIGURE 10.1 | LOW ASSERTIVE/LOW RISK PROFILE

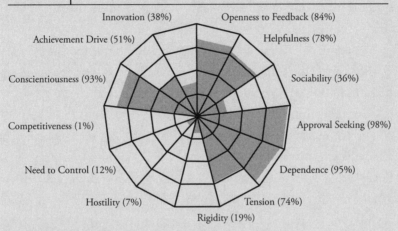

Innovation (38%)
Openness to Feedback (84%)
Achievement Drive (51%)
Helpfulness (78%)
Conscientiousness (93%)
Sociability (36%)
Competitiveness (1%)
Approval Seeking (98%)
Need to Control (12%)
Dependence (95%)
Hostility (7%)
Tension (74%)
Rigidity (19%)

Take more communication risks. Learn to contribute by asking tough questions that need to be asked to clarify situations that may be confusing or unclear (to you and to others). Further, by being assertive and speaking up, you will get information you may need in order to feel more secure, directed, and satisfied—you will have structure rather than confusion.

Your opportunity is to fully leverage your social skills and to cultivate greater self-confidence and the assertiveness required to fully express your knowledge and technical skills. Be assertive about what you know and your point of view. Be an active listener by soliciting information that is important but may have not been freely communicated by the other person.

Don't worry about being seen as aggressive or picky or not minding your own business—that is not how people see you. Your job is to think of and ask good questions. Asking questions is the only way to get answers, and most businesses have lots of needs for answers.

Carol seemed to have everything going for her—but was *too* reluctant to speak up. She told me she'd been this way her entire life. But Carol justified this in her own mind by telling me (and herself), "I don't want to be presumptuous and just take over . . . other people might see this as aggressive and egotistical. I was always taught 'now don't go getting a big head,' and I make every effort to stay humble and not presume too much."

I responded, "This may be a nice sentiment, but leaders must speak up, and you *are* the team leader. It's not presumptuous or wrong or egotistical to fulfill your work roles and responsibilities."

She said, "Yeah, that makes sense."

I continued, "Your raters specifically wrote comments asking you *to be more assertive*—not just your direct reports, but your peers, your manager, and even *you* say you are too reluctant to speak up. So for you to behaviorally respond to this stated need is *not* being presumptuous; it's your job."

Earlier we'd talked about her habit to wait for permission to speak up or act, and she connected this with the feedback.

"Yes, exactly," I said, "So if you were waiting for permission, consider it granted."

We went on to her effectiveness ratings. I noted, "Your organization selected you for this leadership role for good reason I see—your effectiveness ratings are strong, and people see you as very capable, clearly leadership material."

Carol responded modestly, "Yes, that was very nice of my team and peers to give me those high ratings. But I imagine everyone gets high ratings on these 360s like the LMAP effectiveness ratings." (This was her way to mitigate these results to "avoid getting a big head" but at the risk of discounting their relevance.)

I said, "No, Carol, that is absolutely not the case. Only a small percentage of leaders score in the top 5 percent on these effectiveness ratings. If your effectiveness ratings were just average, we'd be having a *very* different conversation."

SEVEN COMMON PATTERNS OF BEHAVIOR

In our decades of work with leaders, we have found that translating deference themes into concrete, common-language words and phrases is particularly helpful for Right-Siders like Carol. Phrases like "waiting for permission," "take the governor off,"[2] and "ready, aim, aim, aim . . ." strongly resonate and help them become aware that other, more effective choices are often readily available. Here are seven key learning points that ring true with deferential leaders.

1. STRENGTHEN INQUIRY AND ADVOCACY

Inquiry and advocacy are terms used in crew resource management training with commercial airline pilots. *Inquiry* means proactively asking questions to get information from all available resources. *Advocacy* means expressing your ideas, concerns, and perspectives allowing others to see a situation as you do. Both forms of communication raise the team's situational awareness. *All crew members* have the *professional obligation* to inquire and advocate even in interpersonally uncomfortable or difficult situations.

The Fischer and Orasanu pilot studies identified a continuum of communication from the least to the most direct and explicit: hints, preferences, queries, suggestions, obligation statements, and commands. Deferring leaders prefer the least direct, explicit forms of communication, mitigated speech found in hints, preferences, queries, and suggestions—the least effective communications.

In professional settings with complex tasks, the collective team intelligence is superior to individual intelligence and necessary for situational awareness. This is especially true when circumstances are uncertain or confusing. To the deferential leader we say, the information you have may be critical to the team's situational awareness. If you are not loud and assertive enough to get above the background noise, you won't be heard. When I suggested this to one such leader, he later informed me,

"I told my wife what you said. She said, 'I've been telling you that for the last 12 years, Arnold. How much are you paying this guy?'"

Not surprisingly, the same reluctance and restraint in inquiry holds true for advocacy as well. Deferent leaders are reluctant to push their ideas, concerns, and perspectives—to debate and argue their position persuasively.[3] When debates become emotionally charged or threaten to devolve into arguments, these leaders are reluctant to enter the fray. This leads to the second relevant learning point:

2. Master the Courage to Interrogate Reality

In her book *Fierce Conversations*, Susan Scott frames this issue elegantly. She calls it "mastering the courage to interrogate reality."[4] If an organization is to operate and execute effectively, all team members need to have a common understanding of the reality of the situation. Scott asks (the dependent leader) to consider this question: "How often do I find myself—just to be polite—saying things I don't mean."

Great leaders have to have the courage to ask the tough questions, to dig deep for straightforward, nonnuanced answers. Potential issues must be surfaced and thoroughly discussed; minimizing, ignoring, or denying problems does not cause them to go away. Unresolved problems and issues—aka reality—will inevitably resurface. Therefore, we encourage deferential leaders to *not hold back, not beat around the bush or dance around the subject, skirting the real issues.* Instead, we advise, *turn the dial up.* (Moreover, because Right-Siders tend to talk around the issues, beat around the bush, and find the exact mitigating, nonoffensive words to use when they speak, they are often seen as not being concise. They can unwittingly spend too much airtime trying to say what they mean instead of just saying it openly and honestly and concisely.)

3. Turn the Dial *Up*

Many deferential leaders are overly concerned with not offending others. Thus, they may avoid asking others tough questions; or they may soft-pedal and tiptoe around the issue when asking their questions or advocating an alternative point of view. Being polite to avoid offending others may be a pleasant social convention, but around important matters at work, it prevents the team from getting straight answers to important questions, in a timely manner.

> **Building Confidence and Competence Through Rehearsal**
> Practice makes perfect, and a test run of your ideas with a trusted friend or business associate prior to presenting them in public (meetings, one-on-ones, formal presentations, etc.) is a great way to hone your ideas and build your confidence. Ask your associate to be a critical listener and when appropriate to be a persistent "devil's advocate" and raise any objections he or she thinks (or you think) you might encounter in your actual presentation. Do a few practice runs until you feel comfortable with the words, pace, and tone of your presentation. If you find it difficult to comfortably respond to objections to your ideas, practice responding to the objections several times until you feel comfortable that your responses are grounded and that you are able to communicate your positions clearly and with confidence.

The Right-Siders' concerns about being perceived as pushy, adversarial, or overly aggressive are misplaced, because generally their feedback indicates that they have good teamwork skills. Their considerate demeanor has earned goodwill from others, and this banked goodwill allows them to be even more assertive and persistent in asking the tough questions without being seen as a bully. LMAP coaches suggest that deferential team members need to push the boundaries of their inquiry, persisting until a clear and sensible response to all their questions is provided.

4. WHEN IN DOUBT, SPEAK UP

If you are a leader who is reluctant to speak up, there is plenty of room for your contribution to the organization. Remember the Lovallo and Sibony studies from Chapter 4: less than one in three strategic decisions was seen as a good one. Of those surveyed, 60 percent thought that bad decisions were about as frequent as good decisions, and 12 percent thought that good decisions were altogether infrequent. If you are deferring because you think other people who act *as if* they understand it all *are* totally competent and informed, think again. Others also have their blind spots and cognitive biases and reach conclusions on faulty assumptions. So if you have questions about something going on, speak up—clearly your contributions are needed.

In her book *Lean In*, Sheryl Sandberg makes the point that, *by virtue of the fact that you are in a meeting, your perspective is of value.*[5] Part of a professional's job responsibilities is to think of and ask even the tough questions that perhaps others are afraid to ask—even when you fear that it is just you who is confused. Confusion is a symptom of *the team's decreased situational awareness.* Crew resource management teaches us that *when you sense that something may be wrong or does not make sense to you—even if you are not sure why—speak up.*

Even when you are not an authority, fully engage with others and critically listen to and inquire about issues where there is a need for clarity. When you are an authority, speak with authority; the information you provide is vital. As we saw so clearly in the aviation accidents, direct, unmitigated communication is essential for safe and effective *execution.*

5. Reframe Conflict

For Right-Siders, even those with good social skills, passivity and preference to avoid conflicts can lead them to be passive-aggressive and to not fully engage in the group process. They may not speak up, behaving *as if* they are with the plan when in fact they have unstated concerns and doubts. As Patrick Lencioni says:

> The reason that conflict is so important is that a team cannot achieve commitment without it. People will not actively commit to a decision if they have not had the opportunity to provide input, ask questions, and understand the rationale behind it. Another way to say this is, "If people don't weigh in, they can't buy in."[6]

One area that carries tremendous conflicted feelings for the deferential leader is the need to confront the underperforming team member. The leader may try to avoid it, but it inevitably creates morale problems for those team members who must shoulder the extra burden. A frequent comment from feedback raters to the deferential leader is to more assertively manage underperformers—either fix it or terminate the employee. Lencioni articulates this well:

> At its core accountability is about having the courage to confront someone about their deficiencies and then stand in the moment and deal with their reaction, which may not be pleasant. It is a selfless act . . . to hold someone accountable is to care about them enough to risk having them blame you for pointing out their deficiencies.[7]

This is particularly difficult when a deferential leader must confront a highly aggressive team member whose productivity may be adequate but whose abrasive or even hostile personality causes team morale problems. Here the fear and anxiety, the visceral dread that a leader has in even thinking about confronting the person, is a hard sign that the situation needs to be addressed and resolved, sooner rather than later.

The deferential leader—who is often quite tenderhearted with others—needs to reframe taking action as serving the organization, the team, and the problematic employee. Even in a termination. The reality is, sometimes people just need to be fired. One highly effective, tenderhearted healthcare leader described his mindset in this way: "I don't fire people; I help them move on."

6. Stay on Target: Ready, Set, *Action*

Heike Bruch and Sumantra Ghosal conducted a decade-long study titled, "Beware the Busy Manager."[8] Great management requires *focus* and *energy* properly applied to advancing the business, and this is in short supply. The study found that *only 10 percent of managers are highly efficient and purposeful*; the other 90 percent are time wasters. Many managers lose focus on bringing work to completion or get distracted and misspend energy on nonessential activity. Bruch and Ghosal describe this phenomenon as "unproductive busyness" and "active inaction."

Bruch and Ghosal found 40 percent of managers are "distracted," 30 percent are "procrastinators," and 20 percent are "disengaged."[9] Many deferential professionals are procrastinators due to a lack of Grit to start and drive high performance. They are activity- versus results-oriented. They are reactive and easily influenced to respond to the endless situations and crises that take their focus away from completing critical projects and tasks. They prefer doing routine tasks, like holding meetings and writing e-mails and memos, rather than breaking new ground.

For deferential leaders with very high Conscientiousness, *perfectionism* can result. These leaders may focus on getting all the little things right but lose sight of the key priorities. There is seemingly endless planning, countless new initiatives imposed from above, but nothing ever seems to get done (ready, aim, aim, aim. . .).

Jeffrey Pfeffer and Robert I. Sutton describe how some leaders think that talking about taking action is synonymous with taking action—but perhaps even a safer substitute than actually taking action.[10] This is the paralysis by analysis syndrome—inertia—driven by perfectionism and the fear of acting or, worse, acting wrongly. So every contingency is examined and reexamined. We all have seen this play out where a meeting that has been scheduled to discuss, say, what to do to fix something, ends with another meeting being scheduled to discuss it some more—and on it goes, meeting begetting meeting. Pfeffer and Sutton say this approach is appealing to some because it has the appearance of doing something productive—because talking carries less risk than actually doing—but can be paralyzing to a team or organization over time. This is what Patrick Lencioni calls "death by meeting": the dissipation of energy, morale, and productivity—a slow death.

Exercise: Review and Eliminate Time Wasters

There are just so many hours in a day and a limited number of productive things one can do in those hours. Many people get hooked into activities and events that are not critical to the success of the mission but that draw focus and energy.

We recommend leaders take a hard look at what they spend their time on, with an especially critical eye for any meetings and activities that are not essential to productivity. Be ruthless at eliminating any inefficient use of your time so more is available for the things that count. Don't attend optional meetings. Do not spend time on low-priority tasks when higher-priority projects *require* your time and focus.

Do this exercise independently and then meet with team members to share your analysis and to hear their recommendations to refine your priorities.

7. LEVERAGE EXISTING STRENGTHS

Finally, look for opportunities to leverage existing strengths in new ways. Since it is not uncommon for deferential leaders to get feedback that to be more effective they need to take more calculated risks or "be more creative." (Although some Right-Siders are extraordinarily innovative— Steve Wozniak, for instance—and because Task Mastery and Deference traits are negatively correlated, Right-Siders tend to have lower scores on Innovation.)

Rather than encourage a leader to be "more innovative," we suggest they work to consciously create an environment where very creative team members can flourish. We recommend that these leaders become *facilitators of innovation.* To do this, they will need to shift their attention from trying to be creative to using their social, listening, and critical thinking skills to facilitate a process where creative team members are encouraged to think out loud and collaborate. Don't become an idea generator; become an idea facilitator.

Less innovative leaders can listen, ask affirming follow-up questions to keep the conversation progressing, and facilitate an exchange of ideas that is itself an important aspect of the creative process. The leader can be alert to provide balanced positive and negative comments (per the Losada line) and solicit perspectives from outside resources (per Lovallo and Sibony) and thereby build excellence in becoming a *facilitator of innovation.*

LEVEL 5 LEADERSHIP

Perhaps no work has led to a greater appreciation of the effectiveness of the low-maintenance, high-humility leadership style than Jim Collins's book, *Good to Great: Why Some Companies Make the Leap . . . and Others Don't.* Collins did not go looking for these findings; in fact, he states that he had absolutely no interest in conducting yet another study of leadership style. But the results were so strong and provocative that his research assistants convinced him to report these findings in his book.

Collins looked at elite companies that made the leap from good to great financial results and sustained those results for at least 15 years. The research uncovered key leadership characteristics of what he calls a *Level 5 leader*: "They are ambitious to be sure, but ambitious first and foremost for the company, not themselves."[11] In contrast to the charismatic, arrogant, self-absorbed leaders that draw attention in the headlines, Collins found that *professional will* and *personal humility*, in combination, are the key characteristics that lead to enduring great performance.

Collins's research found that *every* good-to-great company had Level 5 leadership during pivotal transition years. Level 5 leaders display:

▶ "Compelling modesty" and are self-effacing and understated.

▶ Both the tendency to "look out the window" and to attribute success to factors other than themselves and the tendency to "look in the mirror" and take full responsibility when things go poorly. They take accountability for decisions and avoid blaming others, external factors, or luck.

▶ Unwavering resolve to produce sustained results—no matter how big or hard the decisions.

▶ Commitment to set up successors for even greater success in the future.

▶ Workmanlike diligence typified by a "*plow horse* more than *show horse*" mentality.

Clearly, the behaviors that Collins identified, like *diligence* and an *unwavering commitment to results*, show that Grit and the Task Mastery traits are essential for success. But these leaders are also humble and have no sense of entitlement, avoid any impression of presumption, and roll up their sleeves and do work below their pay grade—true to the *plow horse* mentality.[12]

In our work with leaders, some of the most compelling conversations around the links between behavior and values emerge when leaders reflect on the qualities of the Level 5 leadership. We ask, "Do you see yourself as more the plow horse or the show horse? What about others' perceptions? Do they see you as more the plow horse or the show horse? What do these attitudes and behaviors reflect about your core values and beliefs? What is the purpose of your work in your life?"

Level 5 leadership shares features with the servant leadership model. In servant leadership, deeply held beliefs around service and humility, and in inverting the traditional leadership hierarchy, stand in stark contrast to the values and operating principles of some of the more charismatic business leaders that occupy the headlines these last few years. The servant leadership approach breaks down traditional communication barriers and reinforces greater employee empowerment and engagement. These leaders see their job as providing leadership services to their team, and when accompanied by a tough-minded approach to results, this engenders strong followership.

Replicating Success

Over the years I've noticed that most people, in soliciting feedback from others, ask for examples of a behavioral deficit, what they don't do well. They say, "Can you give me an example of when I was not as assertive as I needed to be?" Not only does this put the other person on the spot, but giving an example of what did not work does not illuminate what does work.

Instead, as coaches, we recommend seeking affirmations—"Ask work associates to give you examples of times you *were* assertive, didn't mince words—examples of you communicating at your best." Learn from these examples, practice what others identify as effective, and seek opportunities to replicate this success. Focus on the solution, not just the problem.

Dominance: Derailers and Development

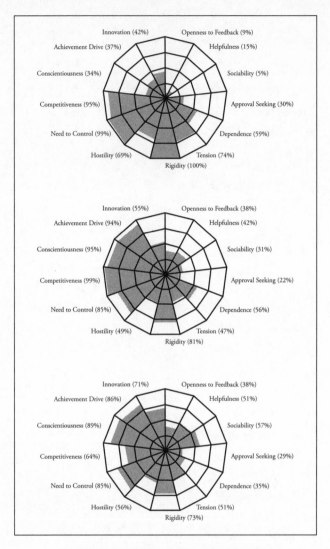

SAMPLE LEFT-SIDER PROFILES—PROGRESSING
FROM LEAST TO MOST EFFECTIVE

CHAPTER 11

The Dominant Personality of Our Time

THE ULTIMATE LEFT-SIDER

Ask anyone anywhere in the world to name the iconic business leader of our time, *and* Steve Jobs would top the list. His transformational impact on business, technology, and lifestyle ranks with that of Edison and Ford. Jobs is the modern standard to which business leaders in the future will long be compared.

As is true for most of us, Jobs's personality assets and liabilities shaped his work and life. More so since Jobs died, he has become a cultural hero—a great leader and role model to emulate. As such, this chapter profiles Steve Jobs so that emerging leaders do not confuse Jobs's extraordinary genius, Grit, and vision—the drivers of his effectiveness—with his hostile, domineering behaviors—forces of derailment in his work and life. Steve Jobs's success was *not due to* but *in spite of* his hostile and domineering personality. As Bill Gates astutely observed, "So many of the people who want to be like Steve have the asshole side down. What they're missing is the genius part."[1]

1984—SHINY ON THE OUTSIDE, DYSFUNCTIONAL ON THE INSIDE

With great PR, Apple looked shiny and successful on the outside: it debuted at #411 on the Fortune 500 in 1983, and Steve Jobs was on many magazine covers. The internal reality was that projects were behind schedule, Lisa sales were 90 percent below projection, IBM was readying the release of its PC, and the Apple Corporation needed real adult supervision. In a public bromance, Jobs recruited John Sculley from Pepsi to become Apple's CEO, which within a year degenerated into another internal Apple war.

It was during this time that I—the author—came into the picture.

THE APPLE ENGAGEMENT

In 1984, I cofounded Acumen (assessments) with John Thompson, who was the principal in a consulting boutique, Human Factors Inc. (HFI). Sculley had hired Thompson to consult to the Apple executive team layered in dysfunctional friction, mistrust, personal agendas, power plays, and hardened silos. HFI was to help build the teaming and collaboration necessary to execute in a complex organization.

The 360 personality assessment that I'd developed was used in the work at Apple, and I regularly met with Thompson to discuss the personality profiles and act as a sounding board on personality and team dynamics, drawing on my clinical psychology expertise. The intense adversarial relationships at Apple threatened the company with implosion. HFI had been brought in to fix the problems.

By all reports, a major problem was Steve Jobs. He had an uncontrolled temper and explosive, vitriolic style—beyond what the seasoned HFI consulting team had seen in any other corporate setting. Jobs was working in a separate building that flew a pirate flag, signaling that Apple rules did not apply in his domain. Worse, Jobs refused to participate in the executive team's team-building work and would not complete any assessments (the only executive team member to not participate).

Jobs was the company cofounder, visionary, and key executive team member, and he was creating havoc and ill will across the company, so his refusal to participate was not received well.

The young Steve Jobs refused to consider or understand that team process matters for an organization's success and effectiveness. He did not seem to understand or appreciate that a leader's interpersonal behaviors matter. His refusal to participate denied him insights into how his personality undermined his effectiveness as a leader and a person. He believed his gifts were so special that he was not accountable to behave and operate as a member of the executive team. This further isolated him from the team. Unchecked by Sculley, Jobs's arrogance and hostility went unmitigated at Apple. He continued to be a destructive force from within, and his behavior became even more unstable with intense mood swings. When Jobs heard that Mac team members had approached senior management about his behavior, he ironically denounced the "management by character assassination" without realizing that in fact his behavioral character *was the issue.*

Isolated, self-absorbed, and without the empathy needed to accurately assess the situation, Jobs misread his reputation and his power. On May 24, Jobs tried to convince the board to fire Sculley (behind his back, as Sculley planned a trip to Asia). But Jobs had burned so many bridges and made so many enemies that on Memorial Day 1985, Jobs was out at Apple.

THE 1986–1996 FORMATIVE YEARS

Some aspiring leaders look to Jobs and see his success and wonder, *if it worked for him, why can't it work for me?* It might—if you are a genius with tremendous Grit and fortunate to be in the right place at the right time. And if you also have Jobs's hostility and domineering baggage, you may need the hundreds of millions of dollars Jobs had by age 26 to fund your work after you derail.

After Apple, Jobs invested some of his money by funding NeXT and buying Pixar from George Lucas. These two ventures provided him with fertile experimental environments to heal, learn, and grow. These were second chances in his professional life, and fortunately, Jobs also had a positive second chance in his personal life.

SECOND CHANCES

Jobs was fortunate for his second chances. His relationship with his first daughter, Lisa—borne by Chrisann Brennan in his first serious relationship—was ugly. It began with Jobs's denying paternity, progressed to a settlement just prior to the Apple public offering (on advice of counsel), led to his exerting heavy-handed control over child support payments—even when Chrisann was on welfare—and eventually, over many years, evolved into a less toxic relationship with Lisa.

His second chance at parenting went far better.[2] With his marriage to Laurene Powell in 1991, Jobs began to settle into a family. He and Laurene quietly raised their children in a nice, (but) unpretentious, ungated house with a white picket fence. They gardened, showed up at community BBQs, and made extraordinary efforts to raise their children with normal values, without feelings of entitlement, and to avoid ostentatious public examples of wealth.[3] This was the one environment where Jobs made the effort to *be normal*, to fit in, to be a good husband and father and *not be special*. The family took vacations twice a year and avoided the limelight. Lisa was eventually warmly welcomed into this family system.

NEXT AND PIXAR—DIFFERENT ENVIRONMENTS, DIFFERENT LESSONS

In his work, a unique situation unfolded: Jobs exerted absolute and total control over all decisions and operations at NeXT. His role at Pixar was hands-off. He was the largest investor, but he had no operational control and spent years watching and learning from Pixar leaders John Lasseter and Ed Catmull. "At Pixar, Steve couldn't shape the corporate culture. He wasn't the founder. . . . It already had a culture. It already had a leader. Its cohesive and collaborative team knew exactly what it wanted to do. And Catmull was not about to let his young new owner mess things up."[4]

Catmull said, "Steve actually didn't know anything about our business and he didn't even know how to run a small business. He knew something about running a consumer products company, but early on he actually had nothing of value to say."[5]

Lasseter and Catmull kept Jobs at a distance—literally. Pixar offices were across the bay—a different world from NeXT. Yet aside from pure work, Lasseter and Catmull became close friends with Jobs. Lasseter's and Jobs's young families clicked and had a lot of fun together.

At Pixar, Jobs was not part of the "Brain Trust"—writers, directors, and animators who critiqued the director of every movie. Catmull kept Jobs out of those discussions, knowing Steve's big personality would skew the process. So Jobs literally spent years watching and learning from a crack team—witnessing creative thinking and teamwork at its best—including inevitable failures and dead ends.[6]

Pixar was a healthy, creative environment with strong, supportive, emotionally mature leadership: "Pixar is warmer than Apple or NeXT. We're not about technology, we're about stories and the characters and human warmth," said Lasseter.[7] Catmull was "the most masterful of the many people who had figured out ways to manage Steve's idiosyncratic excesses." Lasseter was Jobs's intellectual equal and "a confident grown-up and not persnickety in any way."[8]

The behaviors that Jobs got away with at Apple and NeXT were not acceptable at Pixar, and both Catmull and Lasseter were secure enough to call Jobs out and influence his thinking. Pixar was a healthy environment with "no bozos. . . . Watching our collaboration, seeing us make ourselves better by working together, I think that fueled Steve," said Lasseter. "I think that was one of the key changes when he went back to

Apple. He was more open to the talent of others, to be inspired by and challenged by that talent, but also to the idea of inspiring them to do amazing things he knew he could not do himself."[9]

THE RIGHT SITUATION AT THE RIGHT PLACE AT THE RIGHT TIME

Pixar was exactly the right company environment, with the right leaders and the right operational boundaries, that Steve Jobs needed at that time in his life. It was the perfect learning lab for the control freak Jobs; it was a lab where he could not exercise power and control—and (ironically) therefore was more able to relax, not be the center of attention, and learn from absorbing the teamwork and leadership. Ed Catmull observed, "Steve was more relaxed at Pixar than he was at Apple. He never tried to make us like Apple or run us in the same way." Andy Dreyfus, who worked with Jobs at Apple and at Pixar, said that if you wanted to catch Jobs in a good mood, you would meet on a Friday because "Friday was the day he was at Pixar, and he was always in a good mood there."

NeXT—with Jobs in control—was failing under his leadership. Products were years late and far more expensive than projected. Decisions were made on technology that crippled the firm, and the emotional chaos and tensions took a toll. Ross Perot, who invested $20 million in 1986, called the experience "one of my biggest mistakes." NeXT cofounders left the firm in a steady drain: Dan'l Lewin left in 1990, Susan Barnes in 1991, and Bud Tribble in 1992; Rich Page and George Crow—the last of the founders aside from Jobs—resigned in 1993. Also in 1993, Jobs laid off 280 of the 530 NeXT employees on "Black Tuesday" and sold the proprietary hardware to Canon so that NeXT could focus on software.

The mess at NeXT was only superseded by the mess at Apple, which was losing money and had lost its way. As a near-desperate move, Apple bought NeXT for $430 million in December 1996, and Jobs returned to Apple as an advisor in January 1997. He became the de facto head in

August and the interim CEO in September, and soon he was given the titles of CEO and chairman.

RETURNING TO APPLE

Jobs returned as a hero to a lost, broken Apple Computer more than a decade after he left. He was now 42, was solidly rooted in a family, had broadened his technology and operational skills, and had dramatically diversified his work experiences. Jobs returned a leader who had been humbled, yet was not short of Grit and the need to achieve, and he had learned a decade's worth of lessons at Pixar on effective leadership and teamwork. At his best, Jobs demonstrated a new respect for empowerment, positive persuasion, and partnership. But Jobs was not always at his best (who is?) and was a complicated person (who isn't?), and neither time nor circumstance fundamentally tempered his characteristic brutality. This was a shame, as Walter Isaacson speaks to:

> Family members wondered whether he simply lacked the filter that restrains people from venting their wounding thoughts or willfully bypassed it. Jobs claimed it was the former. "This is who I am, and you can't expect me to be someone I'm not." . . . But I think he actually could have controlled himself, if he had wanted. . . . The nasty edge to his personality was not necessary.[10]

ENDING THE WAR WITH
BILL GATES AND MICROSOFT

Back in the early 1980s when Jobs learned that Microsoft was developing its own mouse and graphic interface for navigation, Jobs was *furious* with Gates and insisted Apple sue Microsoft (and HP). Jobs said, "You're ripping us off! I trusted you, and now you're stealing from us!" Gates remained cool and in a classic response told Jobs, "Well, Steve, I think there's more than one way of looking at it. I think it's more like we both had this rich neighbor named Xerox and I broke into his house to steal the TV set and found out that you had already stolen it."[11]

The lawsuits and vindictive press caused grief for Gates and was expensive for Microsoft. Jobs was fortunate that Gates did not hold a grudge. On his return to Apple in 1997, after massive layoffs and with Apple inching toward bankruptcy, Jobs now needed Gates. Gates invested $150 million in Apple and committed to develop and ship future versions of MS Office and Internet Explorer for the Macintosh. Apple CFO Fred Anderson said at the time, "This deal strengthens Apple's viability. It's a new era in terms of Apple and Microsoft working together."[12] The announcement pushed Apple stock up more than 40 percent. At the Macworld Expo trade show, Steve Jobs called a truce with Gates and Microsoft, insightfully saying, "We have to let go of a few things here. We have to let go of the notion that for Apple to win, Microsoft has to lose."

Was this grudging admission by Jobs a statement of gratitude or new appreciation of partnering or just a practical necessity? Though Gates had the power to destroy his decades-long nasty rival and critic, he chose to save both Apple and Steve Jobs.[13] Had the circumstances been reversed, would Jobs have done the same? Gratitude, like gracefulness in interpersonal relations, sadly, seemed foreign to his character.

Of course, Gates was not just being altruistic; he had assessed the situation and saw talent and opportunity at Apple. He observed that the team at Apple was more mature than those on the Mac team years before or at NeXT, who had been afraid to confront and manage Jobs. This Apple team was stronger and together could push back and manage Jobs's volatile personality. "When Steve would pull any one individual out of the pack and say, 'Your work is suck shit and you're such an idiot,' the pack . . . could go to Steve afterwards and say, 'Hey come on, there aren't that many people we can hire that are near as good as that guy, go back and apologize.'"[14] Jobs had assembled a team strong enough to deal with who he was, and like at Pixar, the team had developed its own tactics for managing Jobs.

THE WONDER YEARS

It took several years to turn around Apple, and 2001 was the breakout year with the introduction of iTunes, the new operating system OS X, the titanium MacBooks, the first Apple Store, and the iPod—the first product that transformed Apple's business.

In 2003, Steve Jobs was CEO and chairman of the board. Macintosh computers, previously used mainly by desktop publishers, now had a healthy consumer market share. iTunes in combination with the iPod revolutionized both the music distribution and music player businesses and expanded dramatically Apple's customer base (iPod sales hit 400 million in 2015).

Glamorous Apple retail stores opened in fashionable locations and became a destination in each city in which they opened. Sales at the Apple stores were several multiples higher per square foot than any retail store in history. Jobs had had his hand in every detail of the store design. Jobs was listed first on the U.S. patent for the glass stairwell, now emblematic for Apple stores. Apple fans loyally wait in long lines to buy the newest Apple products, whose releases make headlines in national and international news. Apple products became even more beloved in Asia than the United States. Steve Jobs was the most admired business leader in the world.

CANCER WAR I

In October 2003 Jobs was diagnosed with a form of pancreatic cancer that fortunately was treatable with surgery. Despite the unanimous advice of doctors, friends, and cancer survivors that he submit to Western medical treatment, Jobs stubbornly refused and instead used natural remedies, vitamins, foods, and juice. Jobs's need to be in total control, to defy conventional wisdom, and to *think different* had no impact on the cancer. It spread, and nine months later Jobs underwent surgery and chemotherapy. He responded well and months later returned to work, but the delay in aggressive treatment gave the cancer a foothold that overwhelmed Jobs eight years later.

The iPhone

> *Who sells a half billion of anything costing hundreds of dollars?*
> —Schlender and Tetzeli, *Becoming Steve Jobs*[15]

In 2007, Apple introduced the iPhone; within a few years, over a billion units were sold. The iPhone became a true global event—a happening—*the* product that everyone wanted. Consumers and corporate professionals wanted it, expanding Apple's revenues, including royalties on AT&T contracts (AT&T was given an exclusive on the iPhone for which the company paid Apple a [still unprecedented] royalty on the AT&T services that went with the phone). Clearly Jobs was doing a lot right to lead a product team to do this level of work.

We see times where Jobs is at his best, motivating and empowering Apple's veteran talent that he learned to trust and appreciate. Tony Fadell did not hear that his work was shit. Instead Jobs told him, "You've figured out how to blend music and a phone; now go figure out how to add this multi-touch interface to the screen of a phone. A *really* cool, *really* small, *really* thin phone."[16] By some reports (Tim Cook, Jony Ive, and other team members), Jobs led with more positive Grit, encouragement, recognition, and praise and with less of the negative, controlling, and competitive style.

But at other times, Jobs was his old prickly self—no doubt, sometimes amplified by poor health. Designer Jony Ive, who was Jobs's key collaborator on all key Apple 2.0 products, describes Jobs's reaction to an early version of the touch screen: "He was very, very dismissive." Ive hung in there and became Jobs's closest collaborator over the last 10 years of his life, and touch screens were transformational to Apple's technology and reach.

During these times Jobs still had his share of bad press. In 2011, Ryan Tate, who wrote "What Everyone Is Too Polite to Say About Steve Jobs," describes how Jobs "regularly belittled people, swore at them, and pressured them until they reached their breaking point. In the pursuit of greatness he cast aside politeness and empathy. His verbal abuse never stopped."[17]

CANCER WAR II

Jobs's cancer returned in 2008. In 2009 Jobs underwent a liver transplant and took a six-month medical leave of absence,[18] returning to Apple in September to oversee the release of the iPad in early 2010. At this point, Apple is the most admired company in the world, and Jobs's legacy as a great leader is secure. Even with all the amazing events of the previous decade, Jobs never learned to keep things in perspective and to not sweat the small stuff; he remained an angry, volatile man.

THE GOOGLE WAR

When Apple released the iPhone in 2007, it was going after BlackBerry's lucrative stranglehold on the growing global smartphone market. Google, already the major player in search, wanted in and was rapidly expanding its footprint into areas that Jobs considered Apple's turf. In 2010, Google released the Android—a touch-screen smartphone with many of the features the iPhone had pioneered. Now Apple's lucrative hold on the smartphone market was threatened, and Jobs was furious. Apple filed a lawsuit, charging copyright infringement of 20 of its patents. Jobs told Isaacson:

> Our lawsuit is saying, "Google, you fucking ripped off the iPhone, wholesale ripped us off." Grand theft. I will spend my last dying breath if I need to, and I will spend every penny of Apple's $40 billion in the bank, to right this wrong. I'm going to

destroy Android, because it's a stolen product. I'm willing to go to thermonuclear war on this. They are scared to death, because they know they are guilty. Outside of Search, Google's products—Android, Google Docs—are shit.[19]

The intensity of Jobs's feelings and his commitment to Apple's vision were—some assert—an intrinsic part of what inspired others. Yet words that threaten to start a thermonuclear war, vow to spend Apple's banked dollars to "right this wrong," and characterize Google's work outside of search as "shit" reveal the dark side of Jobs's personality—a hostile, arrogant, contemptuous style that was his trademark to the end. And ineffective leadership: after Apple spent over $60 million on legal fees and countless hours of internal executive staff time, on the distractions created by the lawsuit, Apple dropped the suit.

In addition to the Google war, there were a series of sorry episodes including the illegal backdating of employee stock options (Fred Anderson sadly was the fall guy), the Foxconn suicide scandal, the federal lawsuit on e-book price-fixing (Apple lost), and an unending filing of lawsuits on IP and infringements too long to list. It was as if Jobs believed that Apple was entitled to exclusivity in the key technology and market domains in which Apple operated. Did he also believe Apple was entitled to exclusivity in people?

THE TALENT WAR

Witness the class-action lawsuit filed on behalf of 64,613 software engineers against Adobe, Apple, Google, Intel, Intuit, Lucasfilm, and Pixar. The court ruled that the companies colluded in preventing "their employees" from being hired by other Silicon Valley firms. The indictment and agreement identified Jobs's e-mails as key incriminating evidence. One e-mail to Google read, "If you hire a single one of these people that means war."

Contrast Jobs's history of generously appropriating employees inappropriately (Xerox employees to Apple, Apple employees to NeXT). Legal deterrents mattered little to Jobs when he implemented secret "employee noncompete" agreements with other employers—not with Apple employees. Jobs exercised control over Apple employees' careers for years, preventing their right to pursue lucrative opportunities elsewhere. In 2015, the court approved a settlement of $415 million.[20]

RELATIONSHIPS AND LOYALTY

Jobs had better relationships on his return to Apple. Current Apple CEO Tim Cook is a big fan and says Jobs was not the harsh, dysfunctional leader that others portray. There is truth in both portrayals.

Jobs's relationships *were* strong with the core team at Apple that together turned Apple around. But these close, decades-long relationships abruptly transformed into *estranged relationships* when team members wanted to move on and leave Apple. If you left Apple, you left Steve, and you became a traitor, disloyal, lazy, and "less than." This happened with CFO Fred Anderson, Avie Tevanian, Jon Rubinstein, and Tony Fadell. When Rubinstein left Apple to join Palm—an exciting opportunity for the then bored Rubinstein—Jobs was furious, viewing it as "akin to treason,"[21] and after 16 years of closely working together, the two never spoke again. Andy Hertzfeld described Jobs as "the opposite of loyal. He's antiloyal. He has to abandon the people he is close to."[22] *Clearly* Jobs maintained different rules and expectations for others than he had for himself.

THE LAST WAR

Unfortunately, Jobs never learned to manage his anger and hostility. While Jobs applied his Zen training to hone his incredible focus and to create simply elegant products, he never cultivated a Zen disposition around emotions to achieve inner serenity and calm.

In April 2010, a new iPhone prototype was accidently left by an Apple employee at a bar. The patron who found the phone sold it for $5,000 to *Gizmodo*, which saw a hot story about the new, never-before-seen iPhone model. *Gizmodo* ran the story and pictures of the iPhone, and *Gizmodo* editor Jason Chen promptly reached out to Apple to return the phone. Jobs was furious, and Chen was astounded to find that Steve Jobs personally was in charge of overseeing the return of the iPhone.

Days after the iPhone was returned, Apple used its influence with local police, who proceeded to kick in the front door of Jason Chen's home and aggressively search it, supposedly looking for additional illegally garnered Apple gear![23] As Chen later said, "The sad thing is how many months did he have after that . . . this was a guy who knew, who knew at the time, that he was dying and he dedicated . . . 10 minutes of his life to argue about how I got a phone in a bar and posted a story about it. . . . isn't that a little strange."

PROFILING STEVE JOBS

My missed opportunity to have 360 data about Steve Jobs's Personality Profile in 1984 was a blessing in disguise, because if I had the actual data, I could not write about it. Fortunately, Jobs did interviews with media and discussed his personality and leadership beliefs, and much has been written about his personality at work.

Back in 1984, at age 26, Steve Jobs derailed. His dominating behavior—characterized by Tension, Rigidity, Hostility, Need to Control, and Competitiveness—was so prominent and extreme that even with Jobs's 200 IQ, company founder status, extensive industry knowledge, and experience, his services were no longer wanted (Figure 11.1).

At that time, Jobs no longer had the level of self-control, interpersonal flexibility, and insight required to maintain his job at Apple, much less serve as a role model for leadership. At age 26, Steve Jobs had several hundred million dollars in the bank and was financially able to take big risks. But he paid the price of public humiliation, and he had to

FIGURE 11.1 | REPRESENTATION OF STEVE JOBS PROFILE BY AUTHOR

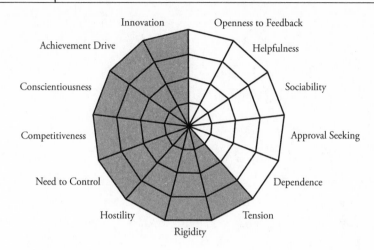

fund his next 10 years of work. He came back to Apple a more capable, mature, seasoned leader.

In 1997 Jobs returned to Apple as an "advisor," a role that the Steve Jobs of 1985 was not temperamentally or behaviorally equipped for. Now 42 years old, he had matured as a responsible father and husband and had accumulated an additional decade of work experiences and life lessons. *From this time forward, Jobs seemed to (mostly) develop the self-control, interpersonal flexibility, and insight required to lead and empower teams of talented professionals at Apple, and this Steve Jobs does indeed serve as a capable role model for leadership.*

The decade from 1986 to 1996 provided Jobs with two distinctive work experiences that led to radically divergent outcomes that reflected key dynamics of Jobs's personality at work. Jobs could not have missed seeing some patterns:

▶ From 1986 to 1996 Jobs funded NeXT with total control over every aspect of the work.

• He invested tens of millions of dollars and ten years' work at NeXT.

- NeXT sold for $420 million in 1996.

▶ From 1986 to 1996 Jobs funded Pixar with virtually no control over the work.

- He invested tens of millions of dollars and years observing teamwork at Pixar.

- Pixar sold for $7.4 billion in 2006.

When Jobs returned to Apple in 1997, did he bring lessons learned from these patterns and facts? Did Jobs learn from a decade of observing different processes and outcomes in one environment where he exercised total control and one environment where he did not? Could Jobs have overlooked or discounted that he was demonstrably happier and in a better mood at Pixar than at NeXT? By almost every measure from mood to money, there was just no comparison between Pixar and NeXT.

As Jobs told Isaacson and others throughout his life, "This is who I am, and you can't expect me to be someone I'm not," abdicating accountability by conflating his uncivil behavior with his authenticity.

Jobs is not alone. Many difficult personalities resist taking responsibility for their offensive behavior by claiming "that wouldn't be the authentic me." (I am not the first or last executive coach who's suggested to difficult personalities *to not be their authentic unpleasant self,* but instead to behave with respect and civility toward others. Authenticity can be overrated.)

Steve Jobs career offers an illuminating contrast of a brash, young leader who dominates team process and business operations to the more mature leader who learned to (sometimes) manage his intense needs to dominate and control in order to effectively leverage the team's collective creativity, intelligence and specialized talents.

CHAPTER 12

The Toll of Hostility

BRUTES, BULLIES, AND JERKS

While it would be reassuring to believe that actively hostile, aggressive behaviors are relatively rare, survey research, in both U.S. organizations and those worldwide, indicates otherwise. Hostility is not only well represented in leadership positions—it runs rampant.

There is a large body of literature on leaders variously described as *aggressive, abusive, brutal, bullying, jerks,* and *narcissists* . . . a list of synonyms that goes on and on. A web search of the term *brutal boss* yielded 44 million hits. Much of the research focuses on how the behaviors generated by these personalities create toxic work environments. Because leaders set the behavioral norms for a culture, their behaviors have a contagious quality. Bullying begets bullying, down the line. Although almost every organization promotes *treating others with respect and consideration* as a core value, the research shows that hostile, abusive workplace behavior is common throughout the Westernized world.[1]

In a 2007 a Zogby national survey of 8,000 Americans, 37 percent reported being bullied by others, and yet only 0.05 percent self-reported behaving like a bully. This reveals that the vast majority of bullies are oblivious to the toxic impact of their behavior on others.[2]

Harvey Hornstein, a psychology professor at Columbia University, surveyed 1,000 people and found that 90 percent claimed that, at some point in their career, they had worked for a "brutal boss" who publicly humiliated them or blamed them for his or her own failures.[3] Hornstein estimates that at least 20 percent of employees currently report to a manager who is a brutal boss. David Campbell, a senior fellow at the Center for Creative Leadership, said, "We've had managers come to our center who actually defined leadership as the ability to inflict pain."[4]

Loraleigh Keashly, Joel Neuman, and Karen Jagatic's well-respected research on workplace and school bullying shows that 25 to 35 percent of U.S. employees report being bullied, abused, and mistreated in the workplace, with roughly equal injustice for men and women.[5] Men are more likely to be bullied by men (62 percent), and women are more likely to be bullied by women (63 percent).[6] Keashly's 2000 study at the U.S. Veterans Administration Hospital system found that 36 percent of the employees experienced persistent hostility on a weekly basis.[7] After fourteen years and two wars (Afghanistan and Iraq), the 2014 congressional investigations into the VA uncovered widespread fraud, abuse, and cultural pathology at the VA.

Few workplaces are as stressful as hospitals, where life-and-death decisions are being made 24/7/365. Just as in the aviation accident findings, 75 percent of medical errors are due to breakdowns in leadership, teamwork, and communications. (I was consulting to a hospital a few years ago and was told that a few weeks prior, an anesthesiologist had fallen asleep in an early-morning surgery and the other members of the surgical team were afraid to wake him. Nonverbal signals and communications passed between the medical team—eye rolls, nods, a "not me" signal with hands up—until the surgeon gently intervened and woke the anesthesiologist.)

A 1997 study of U.S. nurses in the *Journal of Professional Nursing* showed that 90 percent of nurses reported episodes of verbal abuse where they felt attacked, devalued, or humiliated by a physician in the last year. A 2003 study with 461 nurses in *Orthopedic Nursing* showed that 91 percent had been verbally abused in the past month! Physicians were the most common—pardon the expression—provider. As a result of the research on healthcare cultures and medical errors, medicine has been adopting aviation's crew resource management's best practices and providing fertile new research on the emerging field of *teaming*. Teaming is work that depends on collaboration and communications in high-risk environments "that require a level of staffing flexibility that makes stable team composition rare. . . . You could be working on one team right now, but in a few days, or even a few minutes, you may be working on another team."[8]

In 2010, Robert Sutton, a Stanford Business School professor, wrote his bestselling book, *The No Asshole Rule*. Sutton says that while "it isn't fair to call someone a certified asshole based on a single episode . . . a persistent pattern of certain behaviors does."[9] Sutton provides a two-part test for "spotting whether a person is acting like an asshole." First, does the target or victim of the abuse "feel oppressed, humiliated, de-energized or belittled or diminished?" Second, does the "alleged asshole" target those who have less power and rank rather than those of equal or greater power? Sutton delineates the "dirty dozen" of interpersonal behaviors that demean and undermine others:

1. Personal insults

2. Invading one's personal territory

3. Uninvited physical contact

4. Threats and intimidation, both verbal and nonverbal

5. "Sarcastic jokes" and "teasing" used as insult delivery systems

6. Withering e-mail flames

7. Status slaps intended to humiliate their victims

8. Public shaming or "status degradation" rituals

9. Rude interruptions

10. Two-faced attacks

11. Dirty looks

12. Treating people as if they are invisible[10]

THE ROLE OF HOSTILITY IN
LEFT-SIDE LMAP 360 PROFILES

Highly hostile individuals are intolerant of people or situations that do not match their wants and expectations (see Figure 12.1). When things are not going their way, these are the leaders who yell and shout at others, criticizing and belittling them. They lead through fear and intimidation; they are big on raising their voice to blame and short on humility, empathy, and listening. When disagreed with, they easily feel offended and antagonized, and they therefore feel justified to react to "provocations" by acting even more forcefully and aggressively. Rather than finding ways to reduce conflict, people with a hostile personality escalate the confrontation; they *go on the offensive*. Emotional arguments and heated confrontations follow, which takes the focus off doing the work and finding solutions and puts it on managing emotions. We all have had the unfortunate experience of being subjected to a rant by a teacher,

FIGURE 12.1 | LEFT-SIDE HIGH HOSTILITY PROFILE

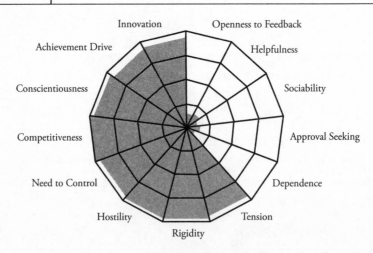

boss, colleague, friend, or family member and can recall how unpleasant and unproductive that experience was.

Fortunately, most LMAP Left-Siders are not overtly hostile, but when an individual is perceived by others as hostile, it is always accompanied by prominent Tension, Rigidity, and Need to Control.

HOSTILE LEFT-SIDERS IN ACTION AND INTERACTION

Domineering individuals with prominent hostility do not so much *respond* as *react*. They do not do well with uncertainty or ambiguity, becoming anxious and agitated. As a result, they can be impulsive in making decisions, seeking to reduce the anxiety quickly rather than patiently and rationally seeking the best solution. At those very times when Hostile Left-Siders feel the urge to act, they need to slow down and create the emotional distance needed for effective decision making.

Yelling and Learning

Jim was a Hostile Left-Side leader—a screamer who invariably blamed others when he didn't get what he wanted, when he wanted. His initial reaction to the feedback report was no different: "I wouldn't have to yell and scream if they did things right the first time. But they didn't learn, they don't listen, so I yell." I pointed out that when he yelled and screamed at others, he was *creating exactly the wrong conditions for learning*. His raised voice and threatening emotional style automatically activated other team members' sympathetic nervous systems. Now they were adrenalized and in fight-or-flight mode—*a biological mode effective for fighting or fleeing, but not for learning*. So if his goal was to simply vent and express his irritation, his method was fine. But *if* his goal was to coach the people on his team to help them learn and to improve operations, his emotional style simply would not work. He was very quiet as he pondered this, and then he said, "I've never thought about it that way before."

THE IMPACT

Hostile leaders not only negatively impact those who work for and with them; they hurt their organizations. Hostile behaviors impact not only the target of abuse but also the observers, which raises stress and turnover and lowers engagement and the willingness of employees to put forth discretionary efforts.[11]

In contrast to a national average of 5 percent annual turnover rate, Keashly and Raynor found that organizations with bullies have much higher turnover rates: 25 percent of those bullied and 20 percent of witnesses leave (this is exactly what Steve Wozniak described observing and disliking about Steve Jobs's behavior at Apple). Robert Sutton calculated that the annual cost to a Silicon Valley firm for just one abusive salesperson was $160,000 (in 2006)—a figure that does not include the costs associated with less motivated and productive employees working for abusive bosses.[12] Costs vary by industry and other factors—especially if those abused litigate—and replacing trained employees who leave because of bullying is an expensive and recurring cost if the abusive behavior does not change.

Beyond the impacts on fellow team members and the organization, there is a high cost to the quality of the individual's personal life and that of his or her family. The famous 1950s type A personality studies by cardiologists Meyer Friedman and Ray Rosenman initially linked an individual's driven, impatient, competitive, aggressive behaviors to cardiovascular disease and increased mortality. Updated research in 2001, by Redford Williams at Duke University (and others), shows that, in fact, only hostile and irritable behaviors are tied to higher mortality.[13]

Given the costs to their personal and professional relationships and their health, leaders who even slightly suspect they have an irritable streak must be strong and vulnerable enough to ask others for their honest feedback about their behavior—recall that 0.05 percent surveyed say they bully others, and yet 37 percent report being bullied. If you have heard from others that they see you as having a bad temper, ask them if they see you as easily crossing the line from civil to uncivil behavior. Many controlling leaders unknowingly do—and can experience deadly consequences.

The following chapters provide insights and suggestions for the domineering personality—good to know and even better to put into use. And again, if reading through this chapter, *you* recognized that you too are someone who gets easily irritated and you express it in your leadership with others, seek out coaching or psychotherapy to understand and *learn to identify your emotions and better manage your temper.* Hostility is a significant liability in work and in life that deserves your inquiry and attention.

> *Anyone can become angry.*
> *But to become angry with the right person, to the right degree,*
> *at the right time for the right purpose and in the right way—*
> *this is not easy.*
>
> —Aristotle

13

Dominance Is Not Leadership

Everybody knows a Left-Sider. At their best, they are results-oriented, driven to succeed, confident, and assertive. Some are more creative, others more exacting and precise—or, like Steve Jobs, both. Some are quietly capable, and others are promoters, exude charisma, and put on a show. They focus on projects and tasks, on getting the job done. Their Grit and their drive are compromised by inflexibility and the need to dominate, control, and compete. They can be self-absorbed, self-centered. and interpersonally insensitive. And while most are not overtly hostile, their rigid, controlling, and competitive behaviors interfere with team processes and productivity.

Left-Siders have a natural affinity for being tough-minded around results but are challenged in being tenderhearted with people. Yet one out of four Left-Side leaders also has average or better social intelligence—soft skills that temper the person's hard edge. These Left-Siders are consistently perceived by their teams as more effective leaders than those without social skills.

This is consistent with the Bell Labs studies of engineers published decades ago in a classic article in the *Harvard Business Review*.[1] The most productive and valued engineers were not those who had the highest IQ or achievement test scores, but those who excelled in teamwork, cooperation, and rapport. The engineers who formed alliances with other workers and used positive persuasion (versus authority or rank) and consensus building were the most successful.

Left-Siders make up 30 percent of the LMAP sample, with a range of profiles of varying degrees of Rigidity, Hostility, Need to Control, Competitiveness, Conscientiousness, Achievement Drive, and Innovation. The author is a Left-Sider, and what we Left-Siders have in common are shortcomings in patience, listening, cooperating, playing nicely with others, and team leadership. This chapter explores Left-Sider attitudes and behaviors and why so many Left-Siders are in leadership roles.

INDEPENDENCE AND ISOLATION

Left-Siders habitually chart their own course, follow their internal compass, and are driven by strong internal feelings of urgency. Often they appear oblivious to, impatient with, and uncaring of others. In their intense focus on project mastery and their own needs, many do not bother to cooperate and collaborate, to play and work well with others. In their 1997 study of 511 company leaders, Linda Grant and Richard Hagberg found that 70 percent are "loners," dangerously insulated from other team members.[2] These leaders were intellectually and technically skilled, but also self-absorbed, impatient, impulsive, manipulative, dominating, and critical of others. They lacked insight into their strengths and weaknesses and were abusive to others in the workplace.

When motivated to do so, many Left-Siders can and will make the effort to focus on others and can be empathic and engaging, even charming.[3] This ability to *turn on the charm*, combined with an aura of self-confidence and assertiveness, shows well in job interviews. But as the Left-Sider gains tenure and status within the organization, the empathy and charm are left behind. Some may modify their aggressive style when dealing with those of higher status or with customers or situations they deem important. The silver lining to this is that the neural pathways for collaborating and playing nicely are already established. To raise their effectiveness, these leaders have to consciously decide to act on and practice more collaborative, collegial, and congenial behavior, which they often know how to turn on but aren't usually motivated to do so.

Even though most Left-Siders do not demonstrate the EQ required for excellent team management and leadership, they are ambitious and show Grit, which helps them produce results and rise in organizations— *despite* their lack of interpersonal skills. These emerging leaders, because of their Herculean work ethic, assertiveness, and confident personality, are sometimes fast-tracked to the top of the organizational chart. But if Domineering traits go unchecked, with promotions and greater status, these traits can become more prominent and problematic over time.

These Left-Siders are the people that others say have the potential to be great leaders—*if only* they had better teamwork skills. The LMAP 360 data show clearly that Left-Siders who have average or better teamwork skills are perceived as much more effective as leaders than those who don't. Yet even these Left-Siders must work to consciously minimize their rigid and controlling behaviors and grow their teamwork and communication skills.

This means not just listening better to others, but also communicating with greater care and consideration. Left-Siders often believe their unvarnished communications are simply in the service of being honest and direct, but their careless comments can be hurtful and damage relationships. Especially when disagreements arise, others can feel unheard or even attacked. The tendency of Left-Siders to focus on problems and to do so with urgency comes across as abrupt and pushy, which creates interactions that feel negative to others. Without a conscious effort to empathize, engage, and collaborate with others, they leave a trail of damaged relationships and people who feel unappreciated, undervalued, and abused.

This lack of interpersonal skills is an Achilles heel that can ultimately derail those who were formerly fast-tracked. The earlier in their career that shortcomings in their EQ and social intelligence are addressed, the more likely it is that they will have enough runway to develop, practice, and hone collaboration and team leadership skills. The common practice of providing leadership assessment, training, and coaching only to senior leaders is puzzling. Industrial and organizational psychologist Vergil Metts points out that "providing leadership training *only after* someone is in a leadership position is akin to giving your child the keys to the car, then teaching them to drive sometime later. Perhaps if we focus on providing people the skills they will need *before* they need them, we will get much better outcomes."[4]

LEFT-SIDE PROFILES AND LEADERSHIP EFFECTIVENESS

1. DOMINEERING PROFILE = LOW EFFECTIVENESS

Domineering leaders are inflexible, critical of others, and egocentric, and they try to dominate and control both people and processes. Figure 13.1 shows two examples of the Domineering Profile without the high-performance driver of Grit or EQ. These are leaders who are anxious, easily distracted, and impulsive. Domineering traits are home to most of the derailers that Robert Hogan identifies: *emotional explosiveness, suspiciousness, insensitivity, overbearing/manipulative, reckless and deceitful, impulsive and distractible, and micromanaging.*[5] This common toxic mix of traits *actively interferes* with and detracts from teamwork and communications. Remember, from Chapter 4, that this is what happened to the people on Joe Cassano's team, who learned that "not upsetting Joe" was critical for avoiding emotional volatility and, as a result, focused on that rather than doing their best work.

Across industries, cultures, and gender, these traits are consistently negatively correlated with leadership effectiveness.[6] Without prominent Grit and Task Mastery traits, domineering leaders' anxieties and worries interfere with their ability to channel their energies into productive work and feelings of satisfaction. They try to manage their tension by controlling events and other workers—they externalize.

FIGURE 13.1 | DOMINEERING PROFILES

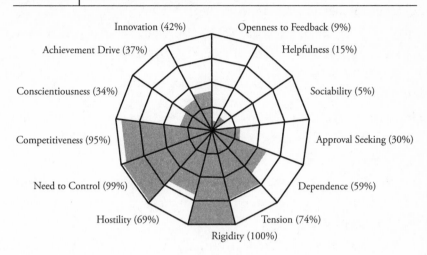

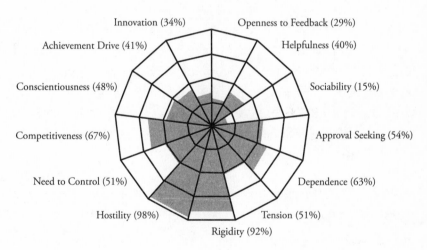

Domineering leaders spend precious time and energy being upset with others, finding fault, and assigning blame. All too often they focus on problems—real or construed—rather than finding solutions and moving the ball forward. This creates unnecessary destructive tensions and adversarial dynamics. It has a negative impact on the leader and on the team, depleting trust, focus, and productivity.

For the team, the drama it creates can be exhausting and makes it difficult to operate and cooperate. It destabilizes team dynamics and fuels team dysfunction at the expense of time and energy better spent on meeting customer needs and advancing the business.

ON THE OFFENSE, YET QUICKLY DEFENSIVE

Interpersonally, these leaders are impatient and emotionally labile, hypercritical of others, inflexible, and dogmatic—often refusing to seriously engage around alternative points of view. They love to debate, argue, and contest others. Yet they are quick to become defensive and interpret being questioned as a personal attack on their intelligence, knowledge, or integrity.

Even without prominent hostility, the combination of urgency and tendency to blame comes across as negative and annoyed. Without the trait of Grit that drives curiosity and a desire to learn, domineering leaders reject contrary opinions, alternative hypotheses, and candid feedback. This creates a team environment where fear, negativity, and criticism are abundant; trust, positive reinforcement, and praise are in short supply. With the domineering leader's tendency to *kill the messenger*, team members may suppress bad news, fearing repercussions. Team members come to feel psychologically "at risk," leading them to focus less on doing great work and more on efforts not to displease the boss.

MAYBE SMART BUT NOT WISE

Domineering leaders may be smart, but as Stanford Business School professor Robert Sutton writes, they are not flexible and adaptable enough to be "wise." A wise leader may have strong opinions, but only if weakly held, to allow room for better ideas and actions to be adopted, as warranted.[7] Constructive confrontation—a good argument—in the words of Karl Weick is to "fight as if you are right, listen as if you are wrong."

Domineering Left-Siders instead hold steadfast to opinions and beliefs and are vulnerable to confirmation biases in selectively seeking and interpreting information that confirms their preexisting ideas—all too often, they are *strong but wrong*. This is a career-limiting dynamic, and the reason that most who have these traits are able to ascend to senior leadership roles is that they also have prominent Task Mastery traits.

2. Domineering + Task Mastery Traits = Mixed Effectiveness

The addition of Task Mastery traits (Grit), as shown in Figure 13.2, makes a significant difference in the experience and effectiveness of Left-Siders at work. A half century of studies on conscientousness, competence, and achievement drives—Grit—have demonstrated the tremendous impact of these traits on performance. These are people who get emotionally charged in their work and seek out challenging projects. When able to override internal and external distractions created by their Domineering traits, these professionals can enjoy tremendous focus and *flow* experiences around their work—flow being a focused state of concentration and absorption in the work, where one's full capabilities are put forth and challenged.[8]

Grit and Task Mastery traits bring enhanced abilities to focus on projects and enjoy work, and this helps in team management and leadership roles. Individuals with these traits are more organized, resilient, and driven to get results and are respected for their strong work ethic. They too are assertive, but at their best, they think before they speak and communicate joy in doing work and solving problems. They love figuring things out, engaging their intellect, and stretching their capabilities. They are intrinsically motivated and have strong internal standards for performance. In psychodynamic terms, they sublimate and channel *some* of their anxiety and intensity into their work.

But *some* is not all, and even Left-Siders with substantial Grit *and* Domineering traits have serious challenges with empathy, patience, listening, and collaboration. They remain self-centered and self-absorbed and they like being the center of attention, which for leaders whose

FIGURE 13.2 | DOMINEERING + GRIT PROFILE

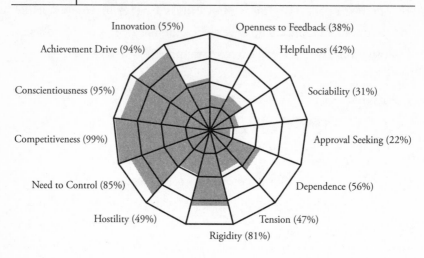

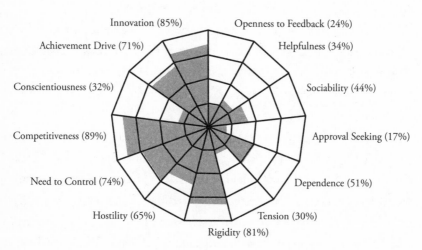

critical mission is to work with and through their teams—versus doing it independently—presents difficulties.

Those with Grit bring high energy, focus, and motivation to their work such that *even without teamwork skills*, they can be highly productive and deliver results. They can be great individual contributors. They seek situations where they can have influence and impact—so many seek leadership roles. But *without at least average (aka good-enough) teamwork skills to complement their immense results orientation*, they face significant challenges in team leadership roles. And because they naturally seem to pay greater attention to data, projects, and facts than people and team processes, they have difficulty empathizing, collaborating, and cooperating with others—which are all essential if one wants to be a highly effective leader.

A SHIFT IN FOCUS

One method for Left-Siders who do not have strong Teamwork traits is to channel their curiosity and focus—normally dedicated to projects— on to others, interpersonal processes, and teamwork. For some Left-Siders, it is not a matter of capability; it is a matter of committing to a conscious effort to *focus more on the interests and ideas of others*. The key leadership challenge for many Left-Siders is to channel well-honed self-efficacy into facilitating others' efficacy, to help others achieve results. Rather than be great at doing the work themselves, they must want to become great by helping others do the work—achieving more through being a force multiplier.

Just as a shift in focus from self-efficacy to team leadership is required, so is a shift in focus on interpersonal relationships. Psychologist Simon Baron-Cohen says that the ability to shift from "sole focus" to "dual focus" is what underlies empathy and concern for others.[9] So if, as a Left-Sider, you *consciously make the deliberate effort* to shift from sole to dual focus, you can radically change the quality of your interactions with others and their perceptions of you and your effectiveness as a leader. Some even find special appeal in mastering skills that do not come naturally but are essential to be effective as a leader. I've known psychologists and psychiatrists who are Left-Siders and yet are great therapists or coaches; because it is required in their professional role, *they conscientiously channel their focus, curiosity, and thinking on the patient, family, client, or team.*

3. Domineering + Task Mastery + Teamwork Traits = High Effectiveness

About one out of four Left-Siders is perceived as having about-average or higher Teamwork traits (see Figures 13.3). For these leaders, their development is focused on building on their base of listening, empathy, and collaboration skills. These are strong leaders who retain their asser-

FIGURE 13.3 | DOMINEERING + TASK MASTERY + TEAMWORK PROFILES

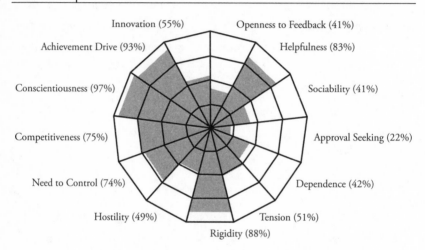

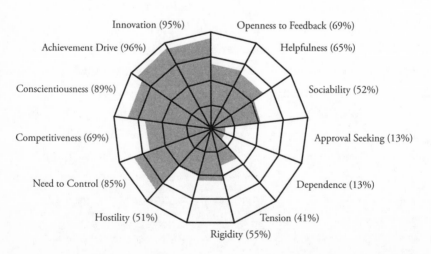

tive, decisive, and urgent style. Yet they also understand that the unique opportunity for a leader is to be a force multiplier—which can only be achieved through facilitating team processes that leverage collective intelligence, not by going it alone.

CHAPTER 14

Leadership EQ and Teamwork Behaviors

In May 2014, after 11 years as managing editor and then executive editor of the *New York Times*, Jill Abramson was fired by *Times* publisher Arthur Ochs Sulzberger Jr. Abramson was surprised by being fired,[1] but trouble had been brewing for a while. A year prior, "Turbulence at the *Times*" had been published in *Politico*, detailing the leadership problems.

Jill Abramson was no ordinary leader—she was a superstar. In 2012, *Foreign Policy* cited her as one of the 500 most powerful people in the world, and she ranked fifth on *Forbes*'s list of most powerful women leaders. Moreover, she succeeded in guiding the *New York Times* through tough changes in print journalism and in transforming the company's business. Sulzberger said, "She helped a great deal in moving *The Times* further into our digital future." Nor was her termination about the quality of the news reporting, "Jill did an outstanding job in preserving and extending the level of excellence of our news report during her time as executive editor."[2]

SO WHAT HAPPENED?

The public statement stated that the problem was "an issue with management in the newsroom." Another source said, "Abramson lost the confidence of her staff and could not regain it."

The problems first became public in 2013 when *Politico* wrote: "Just a year and a half into her tenure as executive editor, Abramson is already on the verge of losing the support of the newsroom. Staffers commend her skills and her experience but question whether she has the temperament to lead the paper. At times, they say, her attitude toward editors and reporters leaves everyone feeling demoralized; on other occasions, she can seem disengaged or uncaring."[3]

Her coworkers described Jill as difficult, impossible, unreasonable, stubborn, condescending, temperamental . . . "every editor has a story about how she's blown up in a meeting." When she independently appointed a co-managing editor without first discussing or then informing the existing managing editor, it was the last straw.

Ironically, Abramson had just hired an executive coach to help with these issues—but it was too little, too late. Despite her demonstrating incredible Grit in successfully leading the publication into the digital age, transforming its business model, and maintaining top journalistic standards, Abramson's stellar career derailed—*because of* her domineering personality. She's not the only one.

Let's take a look at some recent statistics to get a better idea of how serious this can be:

▶ *Chief Executive* reported the results of a 2012 survey conducted by executive recruitment firm Egon Zehnder International. EZI reviewed the success of years of CEO placements. It found that CEOs are hired primarily based on IQ, results drive, and business expertise; they were fired because they lacked emotional intelligence.[4]

▶ A 2015 *Harvard Business Review* article reported on the results of an Interact/Harris Poll of employees on what prevented their bosses from being effective. Fully 91 percent of the 1,000 respondents said that communications issues dragged down their bosses' performance. The research revealed "a striking lack of emotional intelligence among business leaders, including micromanaging, bullying, narcissism, indecisiveness, and more."[5]

▶ A 2015 Gallup study found that half the surveyed 7,200 respondents had left a job to "get away from their manager."[6] Only about half considered themselves currently engaged in their work. A previous Gallup study with nearly 2 million respondents found that 40 percent of employees who rate their boss's performance as "poor" seek employment elsewhere (usually at a competitor).

At a 2016 London Business School roundtable, hosted by Nigel Nicholson, men and women leaders from across government, industry, sports, finance, commerce, diversified services, and education met to discuss and identify the key reasons that leaders fail. Leading the list is the *pathological leader*: "There is a disturbing tendency for us to elevate narcissists, bullies, and psychopaths to lead us . . . [that] leave us a tattered legacy."[7] Next on the list are the *inflexible leader*, the *overreaching leader*, the *lopsided leader*, and finally the *unlucky leader*—unfortunate timing.

We consistently see professionals with high intelligence, technical skills, experience, competence, and Grit traits that are ineffective and do not succeed as they move into top leadership roles. This is because leadership roles require a different skill set *in addition to* those required of individual contributors. As an employee begins to move up, self-management and interpersonal skills become increasingly necessary to be effective. These self-management and interpersonal competencies—collaboration skills, social intelligence, EQ—are independent from IQ and technical expertise.

NECESSARY BUT NOT SUFFICIENT

Second class intellect; first class temperament.
—Supreme Court Justice Oliver Wendell Holmes
on meeting Franklin Delano Roosevelt

Intelligence and technical competencies are necessary for success but are not sufficient for leadership. Students who enroll in MBA programs often have strong technical and analytic skills. Schools are now recognizing how important it is to provide students with experiences, assessments, and ongoing feedback to develop the self-awareness and teamwork behaviors that are essential to leadership.

In the Leadership Fundamentals course attended by MBA students at the Yale School of Management (SOM), students use assessments, learn about emotional intelligence, and receive ongoing formal coaching. "The course is designed to give students knowledge that in concert with their experiences and reflection will increase their capacity to lead," says Tom Kolditz, former director of the Yale SOM program and recent Founding Director, Ann and John Doerr Institute for New Leaders at Rice University.[8] Class projects are assigned to teams, not individuals, just as most work in organizations is accomplished by teams and requires social and emotional intelligence in team members and especially team leaders.

Australia's highest-ranked MBA program—Macquarie Graduate School of Management (MGSM)—uses the educational version of LMAP 360 with executive MBA students.[9] Professor Richard Badham introduced LMAP 360 in the Managing Change course so students—many already managers—would develop a deeper understanding of themselves, leadership development, and organizational change. Students collect 360 rater feedback where they are currently employed, discuss the results with peers in class, and identify and practice their target development behavior in intensive role plays with professional facilitator actors. Students increase competence to manage counterproductive behaviors and to lead with Grit and EQ. Badham believes that addressing behavioral issues early in a career minimizes risks of derailment and focuses on building behaviors required for extended career advancement.

Unfortunately, leadership assessments and development programs don't work like a vaccine—get inoculated against Rigidity and Need to Control and off you go to the future as a flexible and empowering leader. Where behavior change is involved, development is a long-term, ongoing process. An individual may take two steps forward, then with new responsibilities and stresses fall back into old habits. Because the behaviors that underlie derailers are deeply rooted, they require ongoing care and attention over the course of a career.

ARROGANCE AND LEFT-SIDERS

> *It is well to remember that the entire population of the universe, with one trifling exception, is composed of others.*
> —John Andrew Holmes

Arrogance is a behavior frequently cited as a liability in aggressive, Grit-driven leaders and is expressed in an array of unappealing and ineffective attitudes and behaviors. Arrogance is associated with difficulties delegating and empowering, failure to build a cohesive team, emotions clouding judgment, low empathy, failures in relationships, and isolation, to name the most prominent.

One common expression of arrogance in a Left-Sider is to think and feel that because "I am so capable and so good at my job, all the 'rules' don't apply to me." The rebelliousness and sense of entitlement of the Left-Sider lowers the threshold for breaking rules and social conventions. Assuming privileges for oneself creates resentment and alienates others. The self-focused and imperial style of Left-Siders has costs that they do not count in their tally of the assets and liabilities they bring to an organization. These are individuals who will say, "I'm not paid to be nice," conveniently overlooking the fact that in most cases that is incorrect, and that the costs of "not playing well with others" are excessive in eroding the trust of team members.

At their best, they are "demanding" bosses and "difficult" team members; at their worst, they feel entitled to criticize and demean others. There are countless examples of Left-Side leaders who deliver superior products, sales, and services but leave behind a trail of damaged working relationships, poor morale, and high turnover. At the personal

---

The Gorilla of Wall Street

When we think of arrogance, many of us associate the Wall Street personalities, lifestyle, and salaries that seem wildly out of proportion to their relative value to society—characters like Richard Fuld, the former chairman and CEO of Lehman Brothers who was nicknamed the "Gorilla of Wall Street." Fuld had his own set of rules and privileges including a private elevator secured for him when his limo approached headquarters. He literally did not want to rub shoulders with Lehman colleagues he considered less consequential.

Fuld was very highly compensated and successful. He led Lehman Brothers to 14 consecutive years of profits, including in 2007 a $4.2 billion profit. Fuld sarcastically joked about his ruthlessness: "I am soft, I'm lovable, but what I really want to do is reach in, rip out their heart and eat it before they die."

He made many enemies on Wall Street—including those who had migrated to top positions in the U.S. Treasury Department. This is the same U.S. Treasury that helped work out quick acquisitions or bailouts for Bear Stearns, Washington Mutual, Wachovia, Merrill Lynch, and other financial firms that were deemed *too big to fail* and were saved from bankruptcy. Lehman Brothers was not. Instead, Fuld and Lehman went bankrupt in 2008 with a debt of $619 billion. A Condé Nast Portfolio survey named Fuld *the worst CEO of all time.*

and professional level, they are seldom, if ever, satisfied, and despite their accomplishments, many are unhappy and unfulfilled.

HUMILITY—THE OPPOSITE OF ARROGANCE

The opposite of arrogance is humility—a key attitude and behavior in the servant leadership model. Servant leaders invert the traditional leadership power-distance hierarchy and bring an attitude of service to their team and the organization. This approach stresses greater employee empowerment and engagement—as a component of effective leadership.

Domineering leaders worry that being tenderhearted with people is mutually exclusive of being tough-minded with results. This is *not* the case. A large body of evidence shows clearly that being tenderhearted with people is complementary to being tough-minded with results. We see this in the research reported in *Good to GREAT*—humility and consideration are leadership drivers when complemented by *diligence* and an *unwavering commitment to results*—especially over the long term.

In the last decade, the Arrogance–Humility continuum has become more recognized as an important aspect of personality and of leadership effectiveness. There are now revised versions of the Big Five personality model (see Chapter 3, with five behavior dimensions: Openness to Experience, Conscientiousness, Extraversion, Agreeableness, and Neuroticism) with an added sixth dimension: Humility ⟶ Arrogance, to become the Big Six:

Humility	⟷	**Arrogance**
(sincere, honest,		(sly, deceitful, greedy,
faithful, humble, loyal		pompous, pretentious,
unassuming, modest)		hypocritical, boastful)

Laszlo Bock, SVP of People Operations at Google and author of *Work Rules!,* speaks to the link between intellectual humility and learning: "Without intellectual humility, you are unable to learn . . . your end goal is what can we do together to problem-solve. I've contributed my piece, and then I step back."[10]

THE SWEET 16

In Chapter 12 we introduced Professor Sutton's *dirty dozen*—behaviors that hostile, aggressive, low-empathy leaders demonstrate. This chapter closes with the *sweet 16*: 16 straightforward, evidence-based (or at least evidence-inspired) methods to minimize domineering behaviors and maximize teamwork behaviors. Frankly the bar is not very high for improvement, because the goal is not mastery or perfection. *The goal is in making continuous improvement efforts away from negative, uncivil, and de-motivating behaviors and toward more positive, collaborative, effective behaviors*—efforts fueled by your conscious strivings to develop—nothing more, nothing less. As one client said, it is his commitment to that effort *each day, every day, forever.*

1. More Inquiry, Less Advocacy

> *Smug scientists congratulating themselves on "inventing" new drugs led the anthropologist Robert de Ropp to wryly observe that "some chemists, having synthesized a few compounds, believe themselves to be better chemists than nature, which in addition to synthesizing compounds too numerous to mention, synthesized those chemists as well."*
>
> —Mark J. Plotkin[11]

Recall that the research both by Losada and by Lovallo and Sibony identified that the highest-performing teams asked questions to better understand and explore alternative ideas rather than promoting their own. The lowest-performing teams asked fewer questions and instead spent more time advocating their own ideas and solutions, behaviors common to Left-Siders. We recommend instead to:

▶ Raise questions that show you genuinely seek to understand others' views—you are not just "reloading" to take another shot at advocating your position.

▶ Ask follow-up questions to express your interest to dig even deeper to better understand others' thinking.

▶ Stretch your empathy: focus on what the team members are saying and address *their* insights and ideas rather than your own.

2. Listen, Listen, Listen

Self-sufficient leaders must not only seek cognitive diversity; they must listen with 100 percent focused attention.

Assertive, aggressive leaders naturally focus on persuading others to buy in to their thinking. They lose opportunities to hear alternatives and to explore and leverage these alternatives with their own creativity and wisdom.

Great leaders get very curious and listen carefully to alternative views. Alternative ideas provide rich data to nurture to generate new ideas and improvements to products and processes. Even when someone suggests a new idea that does not work for a specific situation, this cognitive diversity can trigger your—or the team's—next great idea. Steve Jobs was a keen observer and idea borrower (often without giving due credit to others). Thomas Edison surrounded himself with smart engineers and advised: "Make it a practice to keep on the lookout for novel and interesting ideas that others have used successfully. Your idea has to be original only in its adaptation to the problem you are working on."

Do not let arrogance interfere with intellectual humility by relying only on your own ideas—it deprives you and your team of the cognitive diversity that's needed for higher performance. Thinking independently, in isolation, without seeking more grist for the mill, is not effective, particularly in our quickly and ever-changing environment.

3. *WE* NOT ME

Peter Drucker observed: "The leaders who work most effectively, it seems to me, never say 'I.' And that's not because they have trained themselves not to say 'I.' They don't think 'I.' They think 'we,' they think 'team.' They understand their job to be to make the team function. They accept responsibility and don't sidestep it, but 'we' gets the credit. This is what creates trust, what enables you to get the task done."

Domineering behaviors are all about *me*, not *we*. Even the most disengaged employee is alert to how leaders refer to *me*, *my team*, *my people* rather than *us*, *we*, *our team*. The former communicates self-focus and a narcissistic style; the latter clearly communicates that something larger than oneself is the mission. Everyone picks up on this language, so if you are *in the habit* of using self-referential pronouns (*I*, *me*) or refer to the team as *my people*, *my team*, break that habit now. Instead use this opportunity to start to use words like *our*, *we*, and *us* that communicate teaming. Words are important.

4. BE ACCOUNTABLE FOR YOUR BEHAVIOR

Some Left-Siders resist, debate, and argue that teamwork-oriented behaviors are not the authentic me—"That's not who I am." Authenticity, however, does not necessarily equate to effective or professional behaviors, which leaders are handsomely paid to demonstrate. Moreover, leaders routinely hold others accountable for behaviors and results that may not come naturally to them or express their authentic self! They expect others to stretch to do the work, but do not seem to apply the same stretch rule to their own behaviors around respect and consideration.

Marshall Goldsmith describes this lack of accountability as an "excessive need to be me": where leaders use their power to reframe faults as virtues because they are who they are.[12] Steve Jobs did by conflating his dysfunctional, hostile, domineering behaviors with his more effective gritty behaviors that actually drove his productivity.

Leaders must be aware that just like in other primate groups, it is the leader whom other team or troop members watch. This is why *even a whisper can be a roar* when a leader speaks. Team members carefully monitor and interpret what leaders say and do. What seems like an unvarnished, off-the-cuff remark or an offhand gesture by an aggressive leader can cause turmoil in others. Leaders who want followers must understand that this is *their problem*. Some leaders argue (of course) that "people are just too sensitive . . . half the time they know I don't mean comments made in the heat of the moment." I'll often ask if it is possible that others are *not too sensitive*, but *you are insensitive*? Susan Scott, in *Fierce Conversations*, says a leader must *take responsibility for his or her emotional wake*:

> For a leader, there is no trivial comment. Something you don't remember saying may have had a devastating impact on someone who looked to you for guidance and approval. The conversation is not about the relationship; the conversation *is* the relationship. Learning to deliver the message without the load allows you to speak with clarity, conviction, and compassion.[13]

5. GET CURIOUS, NOT FURIOUS

To aggressive, domineering leaders, we suggest you *get curious, not furious* about why others disagree with you or hold different opinions from yours. Use your gritty inquisitiveness to focus on learning what others think and to ask follow-up questions in a way that communicates curiosity and real interest in understanding their point of view. In your questions, avoid any hint of interrogation, as if others are not to be believed. You will learn much in listening—about yourself, others, and the world.

6. Fake It Until You Make It

When teamwork and other-focused behaviors are not in your sweet spot, do as Harvard Business School professor Amy Cuddy suggests for practicing *Presence*: fake it till you make it.[14]

Cuddy's thesis is consistent with findings from research in cognitive behavioral therapy, where interventions at the level of cognitions (thoughts), emotions (feelings), and behaviors (actions) are targeted. For a better presence, Cuddy suggests beginning with behaviors: she stresses power postures and gestures, combined with scripted, affirming words and thoughts supported by "breathe and focus." Practice and repeat; practice more and fake it till you make it . . . with 10,000 hours required to attain mastery. Fortunately, the mastery literature suggests that *progress from low to average skills is quick*—the slope toward mastery slows in later stages of the progression from great to grand master. Cuddy and others have observed that with time and practice the behaviors come to feel more natural and authentic. Moreover, if a leader's development effort is to better manage aversive behaviors, he or she can absolutely count on willing audience support!

Harvard Business School professor Joseph Nye describes how President Ronald Reagan and General George Patton both practiced presence and presentation: "Successful management of personal impressions requires some of the same discipline and skill possessed by good actors." Reagan portrayed a warm, friendly, accessible manner despite actually being distant and hard to know even for his own children. Like Reagan, FDR too was a "master at projected confidence and optimism. Despite FDR's pain and difficulty in moving on his polio-crippled legs, he maintained a smiling exterior."[15]

7. Be the Facilitator

One way to maintain greater outward focus and be fully engaged in the process is to assume the role of *facilitator*: reaching out and soliciting different points of view, period. Your only role as facilitator is to create opportunities for team members to contribute, to encourage dialogue and constructive debate, and to *help others explore their ideas*. Only at the end of the discussions does the leader step back into a participant role to contribute to the collective intelligence.

Independent-minded leaders do well to consider: "How can I encourage more cognitive diversity and more complete information to assure good decision making?" One way is to empower each team member with the responsibility to maintain *situational awareness* of the meeting process and business operations and to speak up. Leaders must explicitly communicate to the members of the team that their input is welcome and essential. Learn from Qantas airline pilot Captain de Crespigny's command to Second Officer Mark Johnson, "If we are all looking down, then you look up. If we are all looking up, then you look down" (more about this in Chapter 15).[16]

There are many ways for even introverts to engage more with their team. Ask questions about their work passions; inquire around an outside activity or family or book or music . . . they'd mentioned at work. Simple efforts to connect and support others does not mean acting super-social, chummy, or gregarious. Left-Siders with just-average EQ are described by raters as strong, positive role models, as individuals who are driven to get results, who don't suffer fools, but who collaborate, respect, and care about others. Even average social intelligence expressed in being more open-minded, helpful, and collaborative will smooth the rough edges off an aggressive leader.

8. PUT THE CELL PHONE AWAY

Using a cell phone in a meeting is not just poor etiquette; it sends a strong, negative leadership message: nothing very important is going on now. Leaders using their cell phones in meetings is a common complaint in 360 feedback. We too easily rationalize the necessity for multitasking and too easily discount its disruptive and distracting impact on team process.

Remember that Alan Mulally implemented a no–cell phone rule in executive meetings at Ford. He "showed up" 100 percent, and he expected the same of others. It helped transform the meeting and the culture.

Because smartphones are so commonly used in meetings, leaders have the opportunity to send a positive—all too rare—message to others: in putting aside my phone, I am devoting 100 percent of my attention and focus to *our* meeting and to you.

9. Teamwork Is Not (Just) About Being Nice

Leaders need to remember that the use of teamwork and social intelligence skills is not just about *being nice*—it is also to *shift the entire interpersonal dynamic of the team in a direction that consistently leads to better outcomes.* Lovallo and Sibony's studies showed that team process has a huge impact on productivity and results. The team leader's personality sets the tone, is a behavioral role model, and has a decisive influence on team process. This is true on the flight deck, in the operating theater, and in most organizational settings—as a leader's personality goes, so goes the team.

Strong decision making depends on fully leveraging the team's collective intelligence so that biases and assumptions are surfaced, examined, and overcome. This does not come naturally to aggressive, confident, independent leaders that are self-focused. Unless conscious efforts are made, domineering leaders miss opportunities to leverage collective intelligence. Lovallo and Sibony found that explicitly including perspectives that contradicted the senior executive's point of view and input from a range of people who had different views on the issues helped to drive quality decisions.

Losada's studies reinforced the idea that high-performing teams demonstrate a balance of inward and outward focus—on others, vendors, customers, smart competitors, business factors, work climate. This is not easy for urgent, aggressive leaders. But as Professors Richard Hackman and Ruth Wageman say, "The impulse to get things taken care of sooner rather than later (for example, when conflicts about how to best proceed with the work become intense) can be almost irresistible. It takes a good measure of emotional maturity to resist such impulses."[17]

10. THE LOSADA LINE

The Losada line provides Domineering leaders with insights and guidelines on how to use positive and negative communications to impact team process and ultimately results—which Left-Siders are most concerned about. The highest-performing teams showed a ratio of more than five positives for each negative comment; the lowest-performing teams communicated three negatives for each positive comment. Left-Siders focus on problems, shortcomings, and errors—and do not acknowledge others' ideas, contributions, and successes enough.

▶ Since team success is partly a function of this ratio, leaders have to step up and ask themselves, "How do I stack up in my communications?" Leaders must seek honest feedback and inquire about their ratios: "What do others say? Do they see me as more critical and negative or positive and encouraging?"

To raise effectiveness, Left-Side leaders can consciously practice generating four or five neutral or positive comments for each critical comment. *Pay attention and literally keep score.* Keep in mind that:

▶ It takes just a moment to think through how to restate a critical comment into a more open question that suggests interest, encouragement, and support. For instance, rather than saying, "That's another screw-up on that project"— which communicates blame—try saying, "Sounds like we still have difficulties on that project. What are your thoughts? How can I help?" Think with the mindset of a team leader before you speak and offer your services.

▶ If you have nothing positive to say, apply discipline and listen patiently for the opportunity to arise—*it will*.

Left-Siders will debate that accentuating the positive *devalues* praise and reinforcement; it lowers the bar and becomes gratuitous. Yet on reflection, most acknowledge that they are just too skimpy with praise that is well deserved.

Negativity Versus Positivity

The faultfinder will find faults even in paradise.

—Henry David Thoreau

A key drawback of the Domineering style is the ready tendency toward faultfinding and criticism. Without reciprocal praise, positive reinforcement, and recognition, the feedback experience is *all negative*. In behavioral conditioning terms, the whole reinforcement schedule is punishment—not a reinforcement schedule where people learn quickly, engage easily, or perform at their best.

Moreover, because of the negativity bias, negative events are more potent and have a greater impact on people than positive events.[18] Even a one-to-one ratio of positive to negative comments will not create the supportive team environment that employees need to be motivated to be at their best.

---

11. Be Generous with Praise and Reinforcement

Self-sufficient leaders—with more Grit than Dominance traits—may not be as negative as those with less Grit, but they still may not readily demonstrate enough positivity, reinforcement, and praise. Some are so focused on work, goals, and activities that they do not focus enough on positively managing relationships and processes. Some high-Grit leaders are introverted or shy and uncomfortable initiating interactions. But by minimizing communications, they limit leading others to higher levels of performance (a challenge that is easily coached). Some high-Grit leaders simply assume that others are like them: having abundant initiative, possessing the ability to plan and think things out, and being intrinsically motivated to stay the course—which is obviously not the case.

Many independent-minded leaders need to reframe their work. They must change from working as a hands-on individual contributor to leading others to do great hands-on individual contributor work. This requires providing encouragement, support, and praise and communicating that your job is to help make their work great—*how can I help?* Learning more about the servant leadership model helps some self-reliant, competitive leaders reframe their service role to the team.

12. WATCH YOUR WORDS

A core driver of positive or negative comments is the communicator's *personality.* Leaders with prominent Teamwork traits have *dual focus* and are naturally empathetic and interested in what others think and want. By contrast, Domineering leaders are predisposed to *sole focus*: being cognitively and emotionally independent—the opposite of empathy. This difference influences how a leader conducts meetings, delegates and empowers, develops and mentors staff, and is continuously encoded in his or her communications.

Like Steve Jobs, many Left-Siders use a critical-negative style that feels aggressive and argumentative. Harsh, critical, demeaning words target others. For such leaders, "Watch your words" is an absolute starting point if you are genuinely interested in smarter, faster, better. Negative emotional behaviors trigger the *fight-or-flight* response in others—a response that is physiologically hardwired. *Fight* and *flight* was primitive survival reaction for a dangerous, predatory, pre–knowledge-worker world.

But neither teams nor organizations should be hostile environments, where predatory behaviors elicit prey reactions. In modern workplaces, adrenalized *fight-or-flight* reactions are the exact opposite of what is required for collaboration, learning, and clear thinking—all optimized by calm, lower-stimulus, positively reinforcing environments where emotional distractions and interpersonal drama are minimized.[19]

13. Watch Your Nonverbal Communications

"Watch your words" is a good start, but not a negative word need be said to generate tense reactions or interactions. Negative emotions are literally hardwired into facial expressions: fear, anger, disgust, contempt— and each has very specific microexpressions. Emotionally expressive, aggressive leaders are easy to read. We communicate negativity and disengagement with crossed arms, steely stares, eye rolls, exaggerated "hrumph" exhales, and other dismissive gestures. Not only words but also nonverbal expressions can be monitored and managed—by consciously committing to do so. There is no other way.

14. Pay Attention to Self-Talk

> There is nothing good or bad, but thinking makes it so.
> —*Hamlet*, Act 2, scene ii

It's not only our words *to others* that are impactful, but our words *to ourselves* as well. In her book *Positivity*, Barbara Fredrickson reviews a series of studies on the impact of positive or negative self-talk.[20] Self-talk is the mental messages we give ourselves: from "This is an unfamiliar, uncomfortable situation, and I have to get out of here" to "This is new and interesting . . . hmm, what's that; I'm going to check that out now." Studies estimate we spend 60 percent of our time awake in self-talk and preoccupation with our personal and interpersonal issues and concerns. Fredrickson's research demonstrates the strong relationship between our self-talk (and for most of us, the internal dialogue seldom rests) and a range of outcome measures, including mood and mental health, healthy relationships, and job performance.

Left-Siders are not only tough on others; they are very tough on themselves. Many a Left-Sider has told me, "I'm my own worst critic," and when we explore their self-talk, it becomes apparent that they are driven by a harsh internal critical voice that is focused on what is wrong rather than what is going well. This unrelenting critic in our head creates stress and damages self-esteem, mood, and work results. Moreover, research in cognitive-behavioral psychology shows that "cognitive distortions" commonly drive such self-talk even though it is irrational. Do a web search for "cognitive distortions" and see which of the cognitive distortions feel familiar to you, and then practice the suggested methods to modify your self-talk.

Depending on its nature, frequency, and intensity, our self-talk can provide us with either wisdom and perspective ("I'm angry but need to cool off rather than blow up") or relentless criticism and self-abuse ("I'll never get this right"). And we can program this self-talk with a conscientious effort to do so.

15. Lean Back: Positivity, Appreciation, and Gratitude

In my coaching, I see many Left-Siders who feel *compelled* to work hard, seeing it as both *a requirement of the job* and the pathway to be *even more successful*. There *is* a correlation between a work ethic and productivity, so there is some reality to this thinking. But even while they complain about it, many Left-Siders become addicted to the adrenaline-fueled rush of *all work, all the time*. Some lose touch with how to do anything other than work. They have trouble disengaging from work even when engaged in nonwork activities. So they are distracted and unavailable and not present.[21]

Regrettably, some of us only know how to *lean in* (to use Sheryl Sandberg's phrase) and find it very difficult to *lean back*. Many have great difficulty leaning back to take stock and reflect on their accomplishments. Instead, they focus on past work that fell short of their lofty standards or more work that has to get done. Some of us become so preoccupied by our unrelenting efforts that we lose touch with any sense of gratitude for what we—and the others around us—*have achieved*. We can easily lose perspective, forgetting how fortunate we truly are.

16. FIND YOUR FALLUJAH

I'll never forget how I almost lost perspective on my first trip from San Francisco to New Haven, Connecticut, to present LMAP 360 in a Yale program. It took me nine hours to get from home to JFK, and then I was to take a van "limo" for the two-hour ride from JFK to Yale. The van worked its way through heavy New York City traffic, then made four stops in four different Connecticut towns, leaving me as the last passenger in a three-hour-and-counting van ride. About five miles from New Haven, our van collided with a passing car. No one was hurt, but I was now late and anxious and thinking to myself, "It really can't get any worse." I slumped deflated and exhausted until I realized, of course, it could be *a lot* worse. Rather than visiting Yale, I could be in Fallujah, Iraq, or an outpost in Afghanistan . . . in a vehicle damaged by an IED and getting shot at. *That* would be a lot worse. I began to be more mindful of how fortunate I was to be traveling to Yale and to have my work featured in a program. Since that time—and unfortunately nearly 10 years later, it is still a hotspot of war—Fallujah remains my touchstone for how fortunate I am.

"Find your Fallujah" and similar gratitude exercises help us Left-Siders remember that all the things that irritate and aggravate us are usually little things or mild annoyances that 99.99 percent of people would be delighted to deal with if they could simply trade places with us. Only if and when we stop, breathe deep, and become mindful of our own, and our team's, efforts and results, can we fully appreciate our successes and enjoy them. We see many individuals that need time to get out of the daily grind to reflect on and feel gratitude for what they have, something that Left-Siders are not predisposed to and are often ill-equipped to do.

A humble man can do great things with an uncommon perfection because he is no longer concerned about accidentals like his own interests and his own reputation, and therefore he no longer needs to waste his efforts in defending them.

—Thomas Merton

Fredrick Herzberg, probably one of the most incisive writers on the topic of motivation theory . . . was writing for a business audience, but what he discovered about motivation applies equally to all of us.

Herzberg notes the common assumption that job satisfaction is one big continuous spectrum—starting with very happy on one end and reaching all the way down to the absolutely miserable on the other—is not actually the way the mind works. Instead, satisfaction and dissatisfaction are separate independent measures. This means, for example, that it's possible to love your job and hate it at the same time.

—Clayton M. Christensen,
How Will You Measure Your Life[22]

PART IV

Leadership Drivers and Development

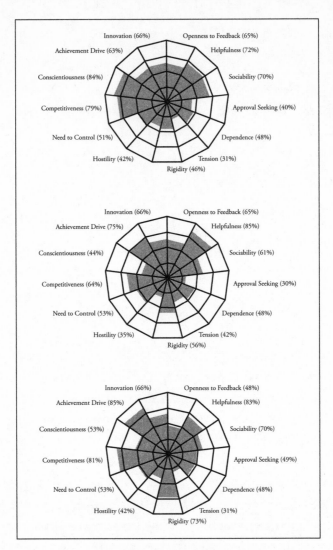

HIGH-PERFORMANCE PROFILES

CHAPTER 15

Leadership in Action—Qantas Flight 32

Richard Champion de Crespigny, captain at Qantas Airlines, is as celebrated in Australia as Captain Chesley Burnett "Sully" Sullenberger is here in the United States. Captain de Crespigny knows what it's like to be in Sully's shoes in a way that very few others can.

On the morning of November 4, 2010, de Crespigny was in command of a catastrophically disabled aircraft, Qantas Flight 32, going from Singapore to Sydney with 469 on board the Airbus A380. Compared with Sully's twin-engine Airbus 320 carrying 155 passengers, the A380 is a behemoth. The world's largest commercial airliner, it is a superjumbo jet with a tail eight stories tall and maximum seating of 853 passengers. The saga of QF32 lasted four hours and required far more sustained problem solving, decision making, delegation, and communication skills than U.S. Air Flight 1549. With an expanded flight crew of five, including three captains, a cabin crew of 24, and 440 passengers, de Crespigny would be called upon to stretch his leadership skills to a new level.

RICHARD DE CRESPIGNY: PERSONALITY IN ACTION

A professional pilot for more than 35 years at the time, de Crespigny had an impressive résumé: 11 years in the Royal Australian Air Force and 24 years at Qantas. Like Sully, de Crespigny spent a lifetime developing both technical skills and psychological tools that prepared him to successfully confront the challenges of QF32.

At Qantas, de Crespigny flew the Boeing 747 Classic and then the newer, next-gen Boeing and Airbus electronic, automated aircraft. De Crespigny, a self-professed computer geek, was hooked on this new technology, but he was also worried and warned that highly automated aircraft could lead pilots to "complacency and ignorance."[1] Years later, symptoms of crew complacency and reduced flying skills were highlighted in a 2013 FAA report.[2]

In 2004, de Crespigny completed the conversion training from Boeing to the Airbus 330. He was promoted to captain and, in 2008, traveled to Airbus headquarters in Toulouse, France, as part of the first crews certified to fly the A380.

Airbus 380

Today's newest-generation jets are so complex that they rely on advanced technological innovations and an intricate network of computer systems serving all three major functions of flight: aviation, navigation, and communication. The skill set necessary to manage these technologies requires much more than still-essential stick-and-rudder piloting skills. To be effective, the captain and crew of a modern commercial aircraft need the personality characteristics and leadership and communication skills far different from the old-school "top gun" image.

The A380 elevates "fly-by-wire" technology to a new level from what was first used in the Apollo spaceflight program and F-16 and F-18 fighter jets. It replaced large, heavy mechanical hydraulic systems in planes with lighter materials that can withstand heat extremes and allow manufacturers to build multiple redundant backup systems that make modern avionics so incredibly reliable and safe. The A380 fly-by-wire design features systems that sound like science fiction:

▶ More than 200 computers continually monitor more than 250,000 sensors and parameters and make subtle adjustments for a notably smooth flight, with no direct input or actions by crew and, for the most part, without the crew's awareness.

▶ Fully 85 percent of the monitoring data is never displayed to the crew on the flight deck's 10 computer screens. Only the information the computers deem relevant for the crew to fly the aircraft safely and to navigate a course is provided through the electronic centralized aircraft monitor (ECAM).

A380 deliveries were delayed. Qantas had trained 84 crews on the A380, so de Crespigny was not flying much and did not like it. He missed regular flying and regretted the loss of that feeling, like muscle memory, when the "aircraft fits like a glove," and to fight this he worked twice as hard to stay current by practicing on flight simulators and by studying manuals.[3] Because he had the time and passion, de Crespigny visited Airbus in France for four days to interview test pilots, design engineers, and the A380 aerodynamics team; and then he went on to the United Kingdom to tour the Roll-Royce engine production line and later said the visit "helped me understand the Airbus systems and gave me confidence when flying—something I was about to need on QF32."[4]

SINGAPORE: THE TEAM TAKES FORM

On November 2, 2010, de Crespigny traveled from Sydney to Singapore. Although he was not originally scheduled to fly QF32, his annual check flight was due and had been set up for the Singapore-to-Sydney return the following day.

Once settled into the Fairmont Hotel in Singapore, de Crespigny telephoned First Officer (FO) Matt Hicks and Second Officer (SO) Mark Johnson to arrange to meet in the lobby the next morning. De Crespigny had flown with Hicks but had never met Johnson.

De Crespigny knew that it was critically important to become familiar with the experiences and communication style of each of the other crew members in the fast-moving cockpit environment; in 44 percent of commercial aviation accidents, the pilots had not flown together previously. De Crespigny approached this preflight meeting required of all flight crews with characteristic conscientiousness to ensure that the QF32 flight crew was on the same page. "Since captains fly with so many different crews it's important to the team dynamics that the captain be proactive. . . . This is not about egos; it's about organized people who hold great responsibility on their shoulders to quickly get focused into their roles within the team. I was forming the QF32 team and the crew needed clear instructions on what to expect."[5]

This was de Crespigny's standard operating procedure (SOP). He wanted to create a sense of teamwork and communications on the crew's ride to the airport from the hotel and in preflight briefings. Though nothing extraordinary, it is an example of how simple, ordinary behavior can reinforce or discourage teamwork and communications that ultimately create for extraordinary outcomes.

With crews who have not worked together previously, these seemingly insignificant interactions allow crew members to learn about one another's background, training, experience, and technical strengths and to get a feel for one another's thinking and speaking styles in interaction. Building a team is an important part of the work. When a problem arises, the early foundation of teamwork makes discussion around problems more efficient and effective—a critical factor in potentially dangerous situations.

For de Crespigny there was an additional important reason to spend time with Hicks and Johnson prior to the preflight briefing: Because he was having his annual check flight, two very senior captains would join them on the flight deck. De Crespigny wanted things in order. He needed to be sure that the crew was aware that it had to follow SOPs, but to not be self-conscious and do things differently because of the two observers. De Crespigny says: "The two inspecting pilots would only observe the flight, playing no part in the operation of the aircraft, but there would still be five pilots on the flight deck where there would usually be three. I wanted to ensure the three of us were a tight and effective crew."[6]

PREFLIGHT BRIEFING

De Crespigny, Hicks, and Johnson conducted their preflight briefing to review the safety heights and altitude minimums, discuss a volcano ash cloud they'd need to fly around, check the history of the aircraft's problems, and finalize the fuel and weight calculations for takeoff. Additionally, because the flight crew was joined that day by two of Qantas's most senior captains, Dave Evans and Harry Wubben, for de Crespigny's annual check ride,[7] de Crespigny wanted to address seating and operations as Wubben, the check captain, sat in the seat normally occupied by the crew's second officer. De Crespigny did not want the flight crew's SO displaced to an observer's seat at the rear of the flight deck, and he asked Wubben to move. But Wubben said it was important he be in that particular seat with an unobstructed view to check de Crespigny. After some discussion, Wubben offered to serve as the SO should a situation arise. This worked for de Crespigny, who told Hicks, "Let's go." Hicks requested pushback clearance, and QF32 made its way to the runway. As Dave Evans said afterward, "It would be hard to find a more experienced A380 crew on the planet."[8]

TAKEOFF

Singapore tower gave QF32 clearance for takeoff. De Crespigny pushed the thrust levers forward, and the giant superjumbo, with 469 people on board, rolled down the runway and took off into the sky at 9:57 a.m.

At 10:02 a.m., the A380 was at 7,400 feet and climbing after a routine takeoff. The quiet, smooth ride was suddenly shattered by a series of booms. The A380 shuddered, and the flight became unstable. Alarm bells and horns sounded in the cockpit. Passengers looked around nervously, and those near the window above Engine 2 immediately could see something was very wrong. Engine 2, mounted under the giant wing and closest to the fuselage, had exploded. Huge engine parts ripped through the wing at twice the speed of sound, creating wing shrapnel that tore the fuselage as far as the tail, causing widespread damage:

▶ Over 600 wires in the main and backup electrical trunks—the central nervous system of the fly-by-wire electronics plane—were cut, degrading 21 of the 22 systems in the plane.

▶ Hydraulics, electrics, brakes, flight controls, and landing gear systems were all compromised.

▶ Two fuel tanks in the left wing were punctured in at least ten spots, and for the duration of the flight the crew was unable to transfer fuel between the fuel tanks, creating dangerous weight imbalances that grew as fuel was used.

▶ Fifty percent of the system networks and sixty-five percent of the aircraft's roll control were compromised.

▶ Wing slats, which allow a plane to fly slower during an approach, were lost.

No Airbus aircraft had ever sustained such widespread and catastrophic damages—damages so severe that ECAM was not programmed to assess and manage so many simultaneous system problems, and this made things much tougher for the crew.[9]

The plane was shaking violently. De Crespigny pressed the "altitude hold" button to stop the climb and reduce the stress and strain on the engines and airframe. The engines did not respond. Realizing that the autothrust system had failed, de Crespigny manually reduced the thrust levers and leveled the plane at 7,400 feet and held it at a constant speed. No one said a word on the flight deck. The explosion, the bells sounding, the red lights flashing, and the realization that they were in a dangerous situation, the extent of which was still undefined, had shocked the crew.

De Crespigny broke the silence by commanding "ECAM actions" of FO Hicks, who went to work through the checklists. ECAM was generating a constant flow of damage assessments, each with a checklist to work through to attempt to resolve or mediate the damage. Hicks said, "The system prioritises the messages as best it can. We had 50 something, 58 messages or something individual ECAMs and there was way more subsystem faults that weren't displayed. It just felt like it wouldn't end you know, you know, it just kept going and going and going."

ECAM presented a wave of gruesome checklists. De Crespigny recalled that there was "checklist after checklist, so we had engine and then we had fuel system and flight controls and electrics, hydraulics, pneumatics, landing gear, breaks, auto-thrust, air-conditioning." Second Officer Johnson said," Matt Hicks is a very competent operator with 15 or so years in . . . and I would not have liked to have seen someone with very low hours trying to do that job on that day."[10]

Meanwhile, de Crespigny communicated with air traffic control (ATC) and relayed what damages the plane had sustained and his intentions to communicate with ATC as he saw necessary. De Crespigny was aware that many accidents had communication breakdowns, so he actively managed and limited potential interruptions from ATC that would pull focus from flying the plane. The flight crew needed undistracted time to assess the crisis and their options.

DAMAGE ASSESSMENTS

ECAM provided the crew with assessments on the extent of the damages: The explosion in Engine 2 had critically damaged virtually every other system of the aircraft; the extent of the damage was catastrophic. Not only were the catastrophic damages to the airplane nearly overwhelming; so were the volume of information and checklists being continuously generated by the ECAM. Hicks later said, "You know, in that scenario, I mean I thought we could end up in the water."[11]

Organizing the Crew

Although de Crespigny was worried that "something as basic as a turn might cause something else to break,"[12] he said, "There was good news— we were still flying."[13] He set the tone for the crew, who could have easily panicked and made a very bad situation worse.

De Crespigny took responsibility to:

1. Physically fly the plane and to take all hands-on, action decisions

2. Exclusively communicate with air traffic control

3. Be the leader in managing the crew resources and assignments

He assigned FO Hicks to manage the constant stream of ECAM messages. In the preflight briefing, de Crespigny had stressed the need for himself, Hicks, and Johnson to operate as a team of three. The explosion changed the situation, and now they needed the expertise of the two noncrew captains who were assigned to monitor the situation, make calculations, and serve as on-call consultants.

To combat the dangers of groupthink,[14] de Crespigny instructed SO Johnson, "'If we are all looking down, then you look up. If we are all looking up, then you look down.' Harry and Dave were monitoring us, Mark was supporting us, and we were working together."[15]

Stabilizing the Situation

As the extent of the damages became clear, de Crespigny grew concerned that more systems might shut down and that they could lose the power required to fly the plane back to Singapore. He wanted to gain sufficient altitude so that if the engines failed completely, he could, as a last resort, glide the plane into Singapore with no power. When de Crespigny called ATC and explained that he wanted to climb to 10,000 feet, however, everyone on the flight deck shouted, "No!!!"

De Crespigny recognized he'd not shared his thinking with the crew members, who roundly discouraged his plan, and so de Crespigny, the pilot-in-command, deferred to their input. He did so, not because he believed his plan was faulty, but because he was unwilling to get caught up in being "right" or to exercise his authority. He similarly decided that his explanation to the crew that a safe, slow climb was what he'd had in mind could also wait.

De Crespigny's deferral to crew feedback communicated that no one had exclusive ownership of being right. It communicated that when the crew spoke up, it could have a decisive impact. For the moment, the priorities were maintaining a safe flight, keeping up with the endless ECAM checklists, and building teamwork and efficacy in the problem solving and decision making that would be essential for landing the plane.

The crew members by now had developed an overview of the plane's system failures and were working their way through mitigating damages with work-arounds or shutting down systems that were beyond recovery.

In the Cabin

Anxiety and concern were naturally very high in the cabin. All the passengers heard and felt the explosion. Many saw the explosion and debris on the SkyCam in-flight entertainment screens in the cabin that provided a live video feed of the exterior of the plane from a camera mounted on the tail fin. At the time of the explosion, passengers seated on the left side of the plane could see a flash, sparks, and material flying as the engine blew apart. After the explosion, they could see the wing with holes and gashes, fuel gushing from the wing.

Dave Evans announced to the passengers that the aircraft was secure and now flying safely. Later, de Crespigny told the passengers that Qantas pilots spend many hours training in simulators for situations just like this—though, in fact, crews never actually train for such widespread, catastrophic damages.

The passengers did not panic. As a group, they managed as well as can be expected when strapped in a seat, helplessly waiting to see if they would live or die.

QUESTIONING ECAM

Some of the ECAM recommendations bewildered the crew members, and they suspected that ECAM had not been programmed for so many concurrent system failures and that the system now was suggesting incorrect or even dangerous actions. At one point the "Fuel: Wings Not Balanced" checklist appeared, and Hicks was reaching to implement it when de Crespigny yelled, "Stop!" and questioned the crew on the wisdom of transferring fuel from the right wing to the damaged left wing. A critical error was avoided, but it raised very serious questions about ECAM data and recommendations. The crew members could no longer count on ECAM; instead, they had to rely on their collective understanding of the A380 systems, the damage assessments, and their decades of flight experience to problem-solve and make decisions.[16] De Crespigny said the crew "subconsciously recalled"* relevant past accidents, aircraft damages, decisions made, and lessons learned. The crew developed a plan to validate all ECAM checklists before any further action was taken.

In overruling the ECAM, the members of the crew showed great confidence in their ability to draw from their knowledge of accidents and systems and factor in the many variables in a nonstandard situa-

---

* Personal communication from de Crespigny to author.

tion simultaneously—a sophisticated, uniquely human collective intelligence that the ECAM system could not duplicate.[17]

NO MARGIN FOR ERROR

For ninety minutes the situation was tenuous but stable while the crew, with ground support, figured out how to fly an approach and land the plane.[18] De Crespigny assigned Evans to figure the landing solution using the Java program LanDing Performance Application (LDPA). This would be challenging with damaged engines, airframe, and landing control surfaces (spoilers, leading-edge slats), as the plane would be landing with more than 50 tons over the maximum landing weight, going 23 knots too fast with 10 tons more fuel in the right wing than left. The plane would land with 48 percent more kinetic energy and only 64 percent of normal braking and compromised antiskid braking.

Initially, the LDPA was unable to calculate any landing solution, but Evans and Wubben modified inputs to coax a landing requiring 3,900 meters to land and stop (compared with the 1,800 meters normally required). Changi Airport's 4,000-meter runway offered 100 meters margin. The plane's rate of descent exceeded the maximum for the A380 landing gear, 10 tons of fuel was stuck in the horizontal stabilizer, and there were a few other problems to deal with, but it was the best alternative. "Dave and Harry's calculations were a great relief," said de Crespigny. "We had a 100-meter margin on Changi runway. It wasn't much, but it was sufficient."[19]

Despite that relief, de Crespigny had lingering concerns about landing calculations based on data provided by ECAM. The crew had now uncovered multiple instances where ECAM was just plain wrong. He was convinced that the only way he could have full faith in the landing plan was to simulate a landing. He decided to do a flight control check that, because of the risks involved, some pilots regard as "cowboy behavior," though de Crespigny had practiced control checks in the RAAF where they were common. Nonetheless, when he told the crew his plan, he was met with silence.

De Crespigny wanted to check that the LDPA calculations were correct and test them with 4,000 feet between the crippled plane and the ground. If the computer calculations were wrong and the plane started to destabilize or stall, there was the time and altitude to allow de Crespigny to recalculate the landing with a higher approach speed. The heavy, unstable airframe and degraded engines would not allow a *go-around* and a second chance at landing.

APPROACH AND CONTROL CHECK

There was silence on the flight deck as de Crespigny put the plane through a complete dress rehearsal for a landing. Although the plane was not in good shape, it did not stall. This boosted his confidence in the plan, and he made the final turn in to a final approach to land.

As the plane passed below 1,000 feet, de Crespigny had to work using nonstandard methods to maintain the speed at 166 knots. The silence in the cockpit was broken by a flight warning call of "Speed! Speed!"—the warning call for dangerously low speed: 165 knots. De Crespigny added thrust.

FO Hicks monitored the approach, making callouts on the rate of descent, speed, flight path, and thrust. At 500 feet above the ground, Hicks called out, "Stable," signaling "all the flight parameters were within tolerances to continue and land." The flight deck filled with computer-generated callouts of altitude every 10 feet: 50, 40, 30, 20, and then suddenly, "Stall! Stall!"

Although de Crespigny had never heard a "Stall!" warning in the air before, he kept calm and focused, feeling assured from what he'd learned in the flight control checks and confident that they would land safely. At 11:46 a.m., the plane touched down near the exact spot targeted. De Crespigny said, "I had to get the nose wheel down as quickly as possible, because if I put the brakes on with the aircraft nose up, the wheels that didn't have anti-skid would explode in about half a second." Hicks: "The auto-brake system had malfunctioned. So he had his feet on the brakes manually braking the airplane."[20]

De Crespigny pumped the brakes, but the plane was fast and heavy. The flight crew grew alarmed, as the brakes seemed to have little effect on the massive plane speeding down the runway full of fuel. Finally, as the plane rolled past the halfway mark on the runway, it began to slow. Relief spread throughout the flight deck and cabin as the plane stopped with less than a hundred feet left of the runway. The passengers broke out in applause.

When the plane stopped on the runway, Hicks immediately went to work on the ECAM checklists, and de Crespigny warned the tower to be on alert for the dangerous combination of hot brakes and leaking fuel. The plane still held 72 tons of fuel, and the crew was concerned that the superheated brakes would ignite the flammable kerosene that continued to gush from the plane's wing. Inside the plane's cockpit and in the cabin, lights were flashing on and off and bells and sirens were sounding.

The fire trucks did not approach the plane, and QF32's crew did not understand why. Although the flight crew believed it had shut down the engines, the fire crew indicated that Engine 1—next to the engine that blew up—was still running. The flight crew ran checklists, accessed backup systems, and manually selected the emergency fire switch and extinguishers, and yet the engine still was running.

Fire crews sprayed water on the hot brakes and fire-retardant foam on the large puddles of fuel under the plane. The brakes began to cool, and the fire risk decreased. Hicks asked the fire crews to blast the high-power water hoses directly into the still-running engine to try to shut it down. It would take another 3½ hours to finally shut down Engine 1. A passenger, Carolyn Jones, said, "It didn't take much imagination at all to work out that one spark and we were cinders."[21]

De Crespigny weighed the risks of effecting an immediate evacuation or waiting until the situation stabilized, and he decided it was safer for the passengers to stay on the plane. At 12:40 p.m., after nearly an hour on the ground, passengers deplaned down a flight of stairs attached to the right side of the airplane (the fuselage between passengers and the still-running engine). At 1:40 the last passenger deplaned.

Just short of 2 p.m., de Crespigny departed down the stairs, 3 hours and 45 minutes after the engine explosion. Qantas's unblemished record of no fatalities on its aircraft remained intact.

AFTER THE FLIGHT

De Crespigny went to the terminal to meet in private lounges with the passengers, many of whom were still quite shaken. Throughout the lounges, TV monitors set to CNN showed QF32 as "breaking news." Gathering the passengers together, de Crespigny explained that engine failures are very rare—occurring only about every 300,000 hours—so they and their friends wouldn't have to worry about experiencing that again.[22] He explained how the explosion had destroyed several critical flight systems, which was why the engine would not shut down after landing. He answered questions and told passengers, "If you think Qantas is not looking after you, or if you think Qantas doesn't *care*, then call me on this number," and he gave his personal mobile phone number.

THE FAIRMONT HOTEL

Upon his return to the Fairmont, de Crespigny asked the hotel manager to set aside a private section in the bar with security staff outside so that he could gather the cabin and flight crews together in privacy. The 29 crew members who lived through the saga of QF32 stayed past midnight, debriefing and decompressing while watching CNN reconstructions of the disaster on enormous wall-mounted screens. Mindful and thankful for their contributions, de Crespigny gladly picked up the bar bill. When he left that evening, his wallet was $4,000 lighter.

Post-Traumatic Stress Disorder

In the days following QF32, de Crespigny and his family moved in with friends to get privacy from the media that had besieged their house. De Crespigny's normally optimistic mood plummeted. Recognizing that he was having a "post-stress reaction," he called Qantas to report he was too stressed to fly. He was interviewed by the Australian Transportation Safety Bureau and at one point began to cry. For the alpha male de Crespigny, these emotions were unknown territory for him, and he took note and sought a referral to a psychologist experienced in treating pilots with stress-related disorders.

De Crespigny says it took two months (his wife says four months) to get back to his normal self after the trauma of QF32. It would take another 25 months for the ATSB accident investigators to publish their report detailing what happened on board QF32 that day, including how the QF32 technical, flight, and cabin crews acted as one competent team.

The actions and interactions of de Crespigny and the crew of QF32 no doubt prevented one of the largest and worst disasters in commercial aviation history. Cited as "one of the finest examples of airmanship in the history of aviation,"[23] the actions of the captain and crew offer *key lessons about the leadership, teamwork, and communications skills necessary for effective outcomes that are now studied in CRM courses worldwide. These lessons relate to the personality and character of the individuals and the team as much as to their exceptional piloting skills.*

· · · · · · ·

Note of appreciation to Captain Richard de Crespigny of Qantas Airlines and Captain Allan Goldstein of UPS Airlines for their reviews and suggestions on the aviation chapters.

Your Best Self—the LMAP Method

Over the last 10 years, LMAP has been fortunate to partner with executive education programs,[1] global leader programs,[2] and organizational development experts[3] to develop a set of best practices for using LMAP in executive development. We are grateful to the thousands of leaders who have completed the LMAP 360 and trusted us to engage in an open, honest, and direct conversation to understand their feedback and how to use it constructively. For many, this conversation assumed deep meaning, not only as leaders, but also as people, parents, and members of a community.

Professionals spend more hours with work associates than with family or friends. Although many of us readily see how a coworker's personality influences his or her productivity and satisfaction, we typically find it difficult to objectively reflect on our own personality—on its impact on others and on our work experience. Coworkers see your preferences, aversions, strengths, weaknesses, and sweet spots, and they have a valuable perspective on how your personality affects your work experience.

But open, honest, and frank conversations about these issues are rare. Professionals are paid to look competent, not to share vulnerabilities and shortcomings. And consciously or unconsciously, many people respond to feedback by getting defensive. Giving feedback can be risky. So in many organizations, people learn to *not* have open, honest, direct, and frank conversations while interacting at work. Communications can be difficult and frank feedback rare.

However, most leaders are hungry for honest, direct, intelligent feedback stated in plain English. Unfortunately, most 360s provide the "feedback" mainly in the form of bar charts and numbers that often do not move and motivate people in their head and their heart ("Bummer, I got a 4.1 on People Skills, and a 4.3 is the average." "Great I think. I received a 4.4 on Confidence, and the norm is 3.9." *What does this mean?*)

People think in words: in narratives and stories. We use language to think about complicated matters—especially emotionally loaded, historically referenced, self-management and interpersonal dynamics—not numbers and bar charts. So LMAP Reports are written as plain-English narratives that emulate a coaching conversation to help leaders think about and better understand their behavior. This is helpful, not just for individuals, but also for teams and cohorts to have a language to talk about behavior, effectiveness, and accountability.[4]

THE LMAP REPORT

In a conversational narrative, the LMAP Report explores the leader's self-assessment and feedback from others. The focus is on feedback and how feedback results compare with research on leadership effectiveness. LMAP Reports are frank and do not shy away from difficult topics that others might be uncomfortable discussing face-to-face or that some leaders might dismiss or feel defensive hearing in conversation. LMAP begins that conversation.

It is an in-depth conversation—an LMAP Report averages 85 pages in length, and almost without exception, leaders read the report several times. LMAP provides an open, honest, and frank analysis of how the people you work with perceive your most prominent behavioral styles. It is not about how good or bad or right or wrong you are. It is about "the lay of the land" of your personality; it explains the research specifically relevant to a leader's feedback, makes personalized recommendations for looking at the behavior from other perspectives, tells how to modify behaviors, and suggests specific readings and other resources.[5] The intention is to identify both where the rough spots are and where you are at your best—so you better understand how to more often be your *best self.*

BEHAVIOR CHANGE

Richard Carter describes LMAP Report narratives "as first a story about you by you and then a story about you by others." The stories and narratives that we tell ourselves and that others tell about us are powerful. Defining the core of reputation and legacy, LMAP Reports act like a catalyst for some leaders to want to change the story.[6] Carter says, "The report is like a trigger for many people—it actually motivates them to do something of their own volition to address the shortcomings. Otherwise they experience cognitive dissonance and discomfort" (cognitive dissonance here meaning dissonance between the character you are and the character you want to be).

Carter sees the process matching Kurt Lewin's three-stage model of behavior change: *unfreeze, transition, freeze.*[7] The first stage uses narratives as a catalyst to *unfreeze counterproductive behaviors—aka ineffective habits and mindsets. Unfreezing requires overcoming defenses, established habits, and mindsets.*

The second stage uses peer—or professional—coaching to structure and reinforce transitioning behaviors. Lewin describes the transition as confusing—where old habits with deep roots are replaced by behaviors not yet established enough to feel comfortable (the beginning of the 10,000 hours to mastery).

The third stage is to *freeze in new behaviors* that feel increasingly comfortable and natural.

How It Works

Leaders complete the LMAP 360 as part of a leadership, team development, or coaching program.

▶ LMAP 360 is web based, and ratings are collected over two or three weeks.

▶ Each leader has a 60- to 90-minute *debrief* with an LMAP 360 certified coach.

▶ A week prior to the scheduled debrief, the leader receives his or her LMAP 360 Report and a worksheet.[8] The worksheet helps leaders think through their feedback and prepare for the debrief session.

Even if we take issue with what others say about us, most of us are deeply curious about how other people see us. Even when we get defensive around what others perceive as our shortcomings, we realize that we have a *vested interest in* and *need to know about* others' perceptions of us—our reputation. Leaders who believe in personal accountability *own their behavior* and are motivated to make changes in order to express their *best self*.

IDENTIFY ONE LEADERSHIP DEVELOPMENT GOAL

The goal of the LMAP exercise is not to *transform* your personality, but to *smooth the rough edges*—to raise your effectiveness as a leader. While a considerable effort is required to break longtime patterns, becoming more conscious of how your personality affects your work and others, you take a giant step toward accessing more of your *best self*. Much as a conductor uses a baton to quiet the horn section and bring up the strings, we can learn to consciously orchestrate our behavior.

We ask leaders to identify just *one* behavior that they will start, stop, or improve that will raise their effectiveness as a leader. *The behavior does not have to sound transformational to have a dramatic impact on work performance*, as these examples illustrate:

▶ I will stop interrupting others and listen so that others have their full say.

▶ I will start to ask the tough questions that I feel uncomfortable asking because I want to be "nice" to everyone.

▶ To be more helpful to my direct reports, I will ask them weekly how their projects are progressing and ask if they need my additional support.

▶ I won't yell at work. I will speak to others with respect and consideration.

▶ I will stop overanalyzing things and start taking more calculated risks.

▶ I will be more tolerant of others and really listen to others while they speak in a way that will make people feel valued rather than diminished.

After reading their LMAP Report and prior to the debrief session with a coach, most leaders have ideas for their Leadership Development Goal (LDG). Many leave with the same LDG, but some do not. The coach helps leaders think and talk through their feedback.[9] LMAP coaches are practiced and agile in identifying patterns across personality measures, effectiveness ratings, and rater comments that may not be apparent to leaders. We remind leaders and accentuate the idea that feedback is *about the upside*—use the feedback constructively to express more of your *best self*.

PROUD TO HAVE A LEADERSHIP
DEVELOPMENT GOAL

An LDG often requires developing behaviors that are outside a leader's natural comfort zone. Historically—in many management and leadership development programs—these were positioned as deficits, reflecting a *less-than* mindset. But leaders actually select goals that any person can rightly *feel proud of*: to be a great listener; to mentor and empower others, to be more assertive because people think you have something to contribute, etc. It is important to reinforce a *greater-than* mindset: to focus on how to raise your game, gain upside, be greater than before the feedback, and proudly share goals with others on the team.

Dirty Laundry

A management consultant from Germany asked me, "Why must we share this leadership goal? You know we are not all like you Americans—sharing everything with everyone. We don't share our dirty laundry so easily. Why is this sharing necessary?"

I clarified that in a 360, it is the raters who are sharing their perceptions of you with you—letting you in on the confidential information. It is not really confidential if they already know.

What is important is to acknowledge you heard their feedback. After all, they spent 30 minutes providing it, and when you multiply that by 15 or 16 raters, you have a whole workday. So it isn't really asking much for you to, at a minimum, thank them for their time and confirm that you received their feedback.

We don't position suboptimal behaviors as dirty laundry . . . just common, simple, human imperfections. And these behaviors impact your performance whether you acknowledge it or not. Life is short. Get curious about who you are and want to be. Do you have other priorities and more important *things to do*?

WHAT TO SHARE WITH YOUR RATERS: 3-3-1

We recommend that a leader's LMAP Report be treated as confidential, but an LDG is best attained by making it public and sharing it with other team members. By sharing their LDG with feedback raters, leaders create goodwill with their raters and communicate openness to hear and use feedback wisely. Amazingly, less than 10 percent of 360 feedback raters hear anything at all back from the leader they rated. The typical response is *nothing, nada, zip*. Not even a minimal thank you, which is sadly ironic for a feedback process.

Some leaders aren't sure what to say or how much to share with raters, so we recommend a simple formula we call *3-3-1*:

▶ 3 leadership behaviors where your LMAP feedback indicates you excel

▶ 3 leadership behaviors where your feedback indicates you can improve

▶ 1 behavior to start, to stop, or to improve that will be the focus of your leadership development efforts in the next 12 months—your LDG

This seems the right amount of information to initiate a conversation, to convey to raters that their feedback was understood and used constructively. Ask others for their support and ideas and listen. Humbly listen with no defensiveness, justifications, or rationalizations. Ask questions that show you are curious about really understanding how others see your behaviors.

Since this is not a conversation that we are all agile at having, in training programs we have the leaders practice with one another. The goal is to:

▶ Thank all your raters for taking the time to provide the feedback.

▶ Share your 3-3-1: what others said are behaviors where you excel, behaviors that you can improve, and your LDG. Welcome any input, feedback, and suggestions about your LDG.

▶ Ask for examples of when your raters observed you demonstrating the behavior in your LDG effectively—so that if you were simply to replicate those exact behaviors more, you'd be more effective.

▶ Tell your raters you want to continue the conversation with them about your leadership development. To assist in this, in the coming months, you will invite their feedback on your progress using LMAP Pulse.

Some leaders tell their team, "I'd appreciate if you would acknowledge my improvements over time. I also give permission to call me out (nicely) when you see me 'slip' into counterproductive behaviors." Accountability partners and peer coaching are powerful tools for behavior change, and they work particularly well with intact teams.

FOLLOW-UP—LMAP PULSE

Three to six months after leaders share their LDG, they and raters complete LMAP Pulse.

Pulse collects web-based ratings of leaders' efforts to implement their LDG. Pulse *requires* sharing an LDG; raters cannot comment on your progress if they don't know your goal. Sharing a goal opens up opportunities for leaders to more broadly practice and master new behaviors. When teams and cohorts go through the Pulse process together, there is an even greater shared positive energy as the whole team works to raise its game and to coach, mentor, and share stories, struggles, and best practices with one another. Pulse is a quick-and-easy survey that takes only five minutes. LMAP Pulse is included with LMAP 360.

Remember that the development of new behavioral skills—*more* than any other kind of skill development—requires practice, practice, ongoing feedback, and more practice. We know and clearly state to clients that even the best 360 Report is only the beginning—not the end—of a successful leadership development process.

ORGANIZATIONAL DEVELOPMENT

For the process to work, the organization and leaders have to be committed and accountable and put forth an honest effort. When peers and teams buy in to the process together, raising effectiveness and improving satisfaction become a part of the culture. If you want a 360 to drive *serious* leadership *development*, it must go beyond a one-time 360 event.[10]

It's What You Do After a 360 That Counts

Marshall Goldsmith completed a study of 8,000+ managers at a Fortune 100 company.[11] Leaders received 360-degree feedback, identified a leadership goal, and were instructed to spend 5 to 15 minutes dialoguing with direct reports around their leadership goal. Quarterly follow-ups consisted of spending 5 to 15 minutes talking with direct reports about the leadership goals and progress.

Eighteen months later, Goldsmith surveyed direct reports and found that the more a leader followed up, the greater the person's improvement—*if leaders did "a lot of follow-up," 95 percent of them dramatically improved*. In contrast, leaders who did not follow up were rated unchanged or less effective. The research and common sense both suggest that the efficacy of using a 360 for leadership development is determined by what a leader does after reading a 360 Report.

LEADERSHIP DEVELOPMENT AT CLAYTON HOMES

This process can and does work, and no one does it better than Clayton Homes, the largest manufactured home builder in North America, based in Knoxville, Tennessee.[12] Because of strong leadership from the CEO, the senior leaders, and organizational development teams at Clayton Homes, over 95 percent of leaders complete Pulse follow-ups. (It also helps to have a great consultant. Some of the Clayton Homes success is due to the impressive leadership development work of industrial-organizational psychologist Vergil Metts and the superb team at Impact Associates.)

As a practice, leaders at Clayton Homes have their LMAP LDG posted in their work area. Everyone is engaged in leadership development and wants to help each other and the organization reach their goals. A manager might ask, "Where's your leadership goal? What are you working on to raise your game?" Clayton Homes now posts its "Plant 3-3-1" that highlights three manufacturing plant strengths, three areas for improvement, and one plant goal.

Clayton Homes has also created best practices in using LMAP Pulse as a powerful, positive feedback mechanism to support a serious ongoing leadership development program.[13] LMAP Pulse provides leaders with the structure and feedback to support ongoing conversations around their leadership behaviors and effectiveness.

CHAPTER 17

Red Teams and WRAP

Previous chapters have examined how the habits of Deferential and Domineering (Right- and Left-Side) personality types influence confidence, teamwork, conflict, communications, and leadership . . . and methods to raise effectiveness. This chapter addresses how a leader's personality drives judgment and decision making (JDM) on teams and presents two methods to support sound JDM: Red Teams and the WRAP model developed by Chip Heath and Dan Heath.[1] Regardless of one's personality, these two methods help individuals and teams exercise strong JDM by combating common JDM errors.

RED TEAMS

> Red Teaming is a structured, iterative process, executed by highly trained, educated, and practiced team members that provides commanders an independent capability to fully explore alternatives to plans, operations, concepts, organizations, and capabilities in the context of the operational environment and from our partners' and adversaries' perspectives.[2]

Red Teaming is used by organizations to respond to the tendency of plan advocates (the Blue Team) to seek to persuade others to adopt their plan, rather than to seek out and listen to constructive criticism. Smart organizations know that many professionals do not seek out nor are open to feedback. Red Teaming forces cross-checks on decision-making assumptions and biases. The Red Team process surfaces factors overlooked in the proposed plan, questions assumptions, asks the tough questions, and forces critical thinking around potential unintended consequences (think G. W. Bush and the Iraq War).

The U.S. Army built Red Team University "to avoid overconfidence, strategic brittleness, and groupthink," retired colonel Greg Fontenot says. "Our underlying assumption is not that people are evil, lazy or incapable but it's just hard to critique your own work when you're doing it. . . . People reason by analogy, and it's hard to recognize your own untested hypotheses. If someone doesn't challenge them, hubris can set it, bred of custom and complacency."[3] The goal is cognitive diversity, says Scott Page,[4] who studies Red Teaming.

Not all leaders can appoint a formal Red Team, but Red Team tactics can often be applied—sometimes with little sunk cost: technology companies pay hackers to expose security weaknesses. Some of the best practices of Red Teaming are ensured with the use of the WRAP model.

THE WRAP MODEL

Dan Heath is a senior fellow at Duke University Center for the Advancement of Social Entrepreneurship. His brother Chip Heath is a professor at the Graduate School of Business at Stanford University. For years they have studied the impact of judgment and decision making on organizational strategy and process. They say, "The discipline exhibited by good corporate decision makers—exploring alternative points of view, recognizing uncertainty, searching for evidence that contradicts their beliefs—can help us in our families and our friendships as well. A solid process isn't just good for business; it's good for our lives."[5] On the basis of decades of experience in clinical, developmental, and industrial-organizational psychology, I could not agree more.

The Four Villains of JDM

The Heaths say, "Research in psychology over the last 40 years has identified a set of biases in our thinking that doom the pros-and-cons model of decision making. If we aspire to make better choices, then we must learn how these biases work and how to fight . . . the four most pernicious villains of decision making."[6] Those "four pernicious villains" include:

1. **Narrow framing.** We limit our options and therefore outcomes by framing decisions as "do I do either this or that" rather than "how can we do this *and* that."

2. **Confirmation bias.** We tend to seek out and find data to support our beliefs—a bias so strong that some argue it is hardwired in our brain.

3. **Short-term emotions.** Our thinking is swayed by our emotions in the moment.

4. **Overconfidence.** While leaders must make predictions and demonstrate confidence in the decisions they make, they cannot become overconfident.

The four-step WRAP model is a process to counteract these four insidious villains. Moreover, WRAP works to counteract leader personality biases that interfere with effective team decision-making processes. Strong JDM skills pervade every aspect of the work that leaders do—interacting with others, assigning work, thinking through issues, motivating others, motivating oneself. *It's all judgment. It's all decision-making.*

WRAP is an acronym for these four steps:

1. **W**iden options.

2. **R**eality-test assumptions.

3. **A**ttain emotional distance.

4. **P**repare to be wrong.

All teams benefit from using the WRAP process. Below are specific suggestions for Right- and Left-Side leaders.

W—WIDEN YOUR OPTIONS TO AVOID THE NARROW FRAMING

Explore how to *do both this and that.*

Left-Siders tend toward black-and-white, either-or, all-or-nothing thinking that does not accurately match reality with its gray areas and black swans. We coach Left-Siders to actively solicit and encourage alternative perspectives and maintain an open mindset. Prompt your team to widen options and to use inclusive, *both* this *and* that thinking.[7]

Right-Siders let others frame the reality and options and are bound by convention, rules, "how things are done." With their low-risk threshold, they prefer the tried and true and are resistant to change. This limits their ability to see how things *can be done*—widening their perspective to elicit options and innovations. Widening options helps to generate ideas, so don't censor your thoughts, ideas, or concerns; be willing to float even unformed ideas for you and others to build upon. Even bad ideas are sometimes the catalyst to explore a new direction. The only stupid question is the one unasked, and answers may trigger previously unseen options and opportunities. Don't assume that others know what you know or what you are thinking—speak up. Ask questions and prompt your team: how can we widen our options—do this better, different, faster; raise quality; lower costs?

R—REALITY-TEST ASSUMPTIONS

Seek contrary opinions and data to fight the confirmation bias, a powerful JDM pitfall. Collective, team intelligence is required to overcome biases and assumptions . . . and bad decisions are routine.

Each of us can learn to do this more effectively. Use your team as a Red Team, remembering that a primary function of a *team's intelligence and cognitive diversity* is to ferret out faulty assumptions and JDM biases.

Left-Siders are opinioned, assertive advocates. They focus more on persuading others than on listening to disconfirming and alternative points of view. Some get competitive and *want to win*—seeing it as an adversarial struggle around *who is right* rather than *let's get it right*.

Yet the research shows that the highest-performing teams spend time asking questions to understand and explore alternative ideas. The lowest-performing teams ask few questions. Instead most time is spent advocating ideas and solutions—a behavior common to Left-Siders.

▶ Ask questions that show that you really do seek to understand others' views and then ask follow-up questions to dig deeper to understand their thinking.

▶ While others talk, think about what they are saying—resist the urge to use this time to reposition and "reload" your own ideas so you can take another shot at advocating your position.

▶ Do not let your sense of urgency define the timeline and rush you to premature closure.

▶ Ask team members to Red-Team your favored approach. Don't interrupt and don't just listen passively—be an active, interested, open-minded idea facilitator. Probe to *understand people's thinking*, not to debunk it.

▶ Be very generous acknowledging others' good observations and ideas. Whenever possible, build on *their* ideas and always generously give credit to contributors.

Right-Siders too readily buy in and subscribe to the opinions of aggressive advocates. They dislike heated debates and arguments and so avoid them. Their need to please others can cause them to acquiesce even when they harbor doubts and concerns. With big decisions or high-risk situations, speak up.

▶ Have the courage to interrogate reality. Use inquiry skills. If you have questions, ask. If the plan is unclear to you, it may be unclear to others. This especially happens when the plan advocate is aggressive and intimidating.

▶ Ask the tough questions that need answers for the team to execute successfully. Inquire further with follow-up questions if the answers provided do not directly satisfy concerns. When mission-critical questions persist, suggest, "Let's Red-Team this issue and get the answers we need to get it right."

▶ Do not employ the above to reinforce excessive caution, paralysis by analysis, or procrastination—potential Right-Side derailers.

▶ Remember that Left-Siders are wired for the confirmation bias and will try to persuade others. They get competitive and adversarial, focusing on *who is right* rather than *getting it right*. Don't take it personally; say, "I want to examine ideas, the situation, not *who* is right, but the right idea. Constructive conflict is about ideas."

A—ATTAIN EMOTIONAL DISTANCE

Take time away from the issues before reaching a decision. The adage "Sleep on it" reflects the wisdom of keeping short-term emotions from swaying our thinking.

The Heaths suggest depersonalizing the analysis and provide a great example of how this worked for Intel's Andy Grove and Gordon Moore after months of agonizing over how to respond to Japanese competition in memory chips where Intel could not match the quality or price. "Then Grove had an inspiration and asked Moore, 'If we got kicked out and the board brought in a new CEO, what do you think he would do?' Gordon answered without hesitation, 'He would get us out of memories.'"[8] Asking themselves the question "What do you think he would do?" helped Moore and Grove depersonalize the issue. An outside, unemotional perspective can make things clearer.

Left-Siders with a *ready, fire, aim* urgency are vulnerable to giving in to their passions, impatience, and need for action. They can quickly shift from assertive to aggressive, picking heated battles and confrontations. This aggressive, emotional display triggers others to either engage in a fight or to withdraw into flight. While this approach works for many primates, in the modern human workplace, it is ineffective and impairs the team's judgment and decision-making abilities and processes.

Since the tendency of Left-Siders is to be emotionally volatile and aggressive, it is a priority for them to learn how to depersonalize debate. Constructive conflict is not a fight. Treat other team members (or vendors, customers, stakeholders, friends, family) as your ally, and they more likely will be.

▶ Should nerves get frayed, take a break and remember that surfacing differences helps ferret out JDM biases and errors. *Get curious, not furious.*

Right-Siders avoid emotional situations and shut down when things heat up. With a rush of emotions—particularly fear—they become anxious, feel unsafe, and look for the exit.

Call a time-out if you need to regain your cognitive clarity and emotional balance. Don't get overwhelmed by the emotional intensity of Left-Siders. When they *push* their ideas, this is just *their* aggressive style; it is not about you. Depersonalize the situation by understanding that this is how cognitive diversity operates. Remember that it is precisely at these times that your input, intelligence, and teamwork skills are critical; master the courage to interrogate reality.

P—PREPARE TO BE WRONG

Avoid overconfidence so you are prepared to respond to changing conditions in an ever-evolving environment. Even good decisions are made based on predictions of the future, which often do not come to be as envisioned.

Left-Side leaders with ample self-confidence and an action orientation can be overconfident, dismiss concerns raised by others, seek closure, and want to move on. A sure sign of impending trouble is when a Left-Sider positions complex problems as "simple" or "easy," dismissing objections or concerns out of hand.

These leaders must listen, and even when they move forward, they must be humble enough to acknowledge that their predictions may be wrong (think Iraq War). This is especially critical when there is a lack of consensus yet the situation requires action. In these situations, it is important to acknowledge others' concerns and—if mission-critical—empower them with contingency plans. If conditions change, those contingency plans may prove vital. Better to be humble than humbled.

Right-Siders' caution and indecisiveness become derailers when they stop action. Act and be prepared for contingencies, but if the situation requires action, act. Cautious leaders tend to regret having hesitated, not trusted their gut, not acted sooner, and then made adjustments. It is their *inaction* that they regret.

One advantage for (some) deferential individuals is their willingness to listen, take input, and consider options. Yet they also need to be prepared with contingency plans if the plan deviates. This is tough for Right-Siders whose loyal, nonconfrontational, sometimes Pollyannaish tendencies make it more comfortable to ignore than confront problems.

• • • • • • •

Personality imposes biases that we are often unaware of, that influence our own thinking process and experience *and* our team's thinking process. Chip Heath and Dan Heath wrote *Decisive* and introduced WRAP because judgment and decision making are hard to get right anyway—aside from personality-based biases and challenges. WRAP is precisely what many leaders need to more effectively leverage the team's cognitive diversity and intelligence.

18

Insight in Action

*P*ersonality at Work has introduced broad research showing strong links between a leader's personality and outcomes—sometimes, extraordinary. We've seen the impacts on performance in a cross-section of industries and professions. We've shown how normal, ordinary behaviors drive or derail teamwork, communications, decision making, safety . . . for better or for worse.

Personality at Work has also introduced the notion that each of us has choices: we can turn off our "behavioral autopilot" and make conscious choices to raise our effectiveness and satisfaction at work. Many methods have been provided to help readers move from "thinking about change" to implementing behavioral changes in their life. Insight is great, but putting *insight into action* is where much development and change lie.

PUT INSIGHT INTO ACTION → PERMISSION GRANTED

BIAS FOR ACTION

Don't just think about something—*do* something; *act*. It is very common to think about things we want to change in our life, but those who actually make the choice to act on their thoughts will change and evolve their life.

Design Thinking

Bias for action, anchoring, reframing, prototyping, team building, latent wonderfulness, and *flow*—this is the language of *design thinking.* The design thinking movement is based at the d.school (otherwise known as the Hasso Plattner Institute of Design) at Stanford University. The *Wall Street Journal* recently named the d.school the "hottest graduate program" in the world, and I strongly recommend readers become familiar with the model. Below I weave in some of the concepts from Bernard Roth, professor of engineering and cofounder of the d.school, that he articulates in his book, *The Achievement Habit.*[1] Equally appealing is the work by d.school professors Bill Burnett and David Evans, whose course, "Designing Your Life," is the most popular class at Stanford University.

ANCHORING

Evans and Burnett discuss how "*'anchor problems'* seen in being over-committed to life choices . . . keep people stuck and unhappy . . . assuming that there's only one right solution or optimal version of your life, and that if you choose wrong, you've blown it."[2] An example: the 18-year-old who goes to college with the anchor thinking that he or she wants to be a physician but actually has little interest or talent in biology or chemistry; yet the anchor goal to become a doctor trumps all other factors. (Many believe that when they become a doctor or lawyer, or get their PhD, or own their business . . . *then* they will finally "be happy," only to find they are the same unhappy person as a doctor, or lawyer, or PhD, or business owner . . . This too is a result of faulty anchoring.)

Anchors that operate as counterproductive habits and beliefs particularly relevant to personality and work include:

▶ Personality and behavior are static and unchangeable (so why bother).

▶ I need to look invulnerable and ever-competent (or I look incompetent).

▶ One *ought to (should)* move up in leadership (or it signifies a lack of ambition).

▶ Money has greater value than time, and increased compensation will bring greater satisfaction and happiness (or I need to figure out what I value and how to be more satisfied with my life time).

Irrational anchors keep us locked in place and need to be reframed and released to allow us to grow and develop.

REFRAMING

I particularly like how Burnett and Evans use reframing around the whole big concept of learning and development. They suggest reframing the idea of *assuming one knows the answers* (what do I want to do with my life, what profession is most appealing, how can I best motivate and engage my team at work?), changing it to making your life about actually trying to figure out the best answers—learning and development. Burnett said that as a faculty member, he's observed college and graduate students that reflect our cultural belief that we "should" have our career choices figured out "by 25, or maybe it's 27 now . . . the permission we give people is: Reframe this. You're not supposed to have it figured out."[3]

In a similar way, many professionals carry the faulty assumption and limiting belief that you *should* already have figured out how to self-manage and work well with others, and therefore they do not feel permission to admit the need to work on developing their self-management and interpersonal skills. We suggest reframing this proposition this way: most of us are a work in progress, and we do better to think before we act and to utilize a whole range of behavioral choices to raise our own effectiveness and satisfaction. So start prototyping new behaviors to learn how to raise your effectiveness. Failure is fine as long as you learn something that helps your next prototype behavior, incrementally increasing your effectiveness and comfort with new, more effective behaviors.

Ironically, in our culture, many of us are taught to act and look ever-competent and invulnerable, while the most highly aware people accept that they do not have all the answers and are willing to be honest and vulnerable with others. Others, far more often than not, respond well to vulnerability and are delighted to help those who ask for input, advice, suggestions, and support.

PROTOTYPING

Reframe your behavioral goals from achieving instant mastery to creating a series of low-risk, low-pressure prototypes that allow practice, testing, fine-tuning, and learning. Just as when you prototype new designs to create products or services or to improve quality, adopt a mindset of testing to learn what works and does not; the goal isn't to accomplish or finish the job right off but to get on the often-bumpy road to success.

Prototyping is where you spend the 10,000 hours of practice that lead to mastery. Development is difficult and the path littered with sub-optimal efforts—which are great because these efforts are necessary to provide critical insights to learn from and improve the next prototype. (Remember, developing good-enough rather than mastery-level skills is a far more rapid process than 10,000 hours.)

TEAM BUILDING

Not surprisingly, team building is a tool in design thinking—and is absolutely essential for empathy (understanding what *others* think and feel and need). Empathy is at the core, as design is all about providing something that our fellow humans need or want. Teaming provides a check and balance on egocentric thinking through collective intelligence, sharing of ideas, know-how, and perspectives—all with dynamic energy, fun, and a sense of engagement. (And was also our focus in Chapter 4, "Team Process and Personality.")

LATENT WONDERFULNESS

We all want to be alert for new stimulation, situations, ideas, relationships, projects, interesting phenomenon, etc., that trigger flow experiences. In this case, being alert simply means being more open, because we can't know where or when or how serendipity will strike. This is what Evans and Burnett call "latent wonderfulness." Evans described how he passed on a job interview offered by Apple Computer in the 1970s because he thought he "was bored by computers." In passing up this opportunity, rather than remaining open to possibilities, opportunities, and latent wonderfulness, he missed out. Had he interviewed and confirmed *he was indeed bored by computers*, he could make an informed pass and do something else. But Apple Computer in the mid-1970s was *a once-in-a-lifetime opportunity*—and potentially a source of latent wonderfulness for Evans, who now regrets the decision.

My own career in computer-based assessment is the result of latent wonderfulness. I was in a clinical psychology fellowship, and another intern had a scheduling conflict and asked me to swap times and supervisors. I did, and that supervisor recruited me into the field of computer-based assessment—and out of cold inner-city Chicago to a warm, countryside in northern California.

Susan Scott in her fine book, *Fierce Conversations*, takes this down to a more micro level—conversations:

> Our work, our relationships, and our lives succeed or fail one conversation at a time. While no single conversation is guaranteed to transform a company, a relationship, or a life, any single conversation can. Speak and listen as if this is the most important conversation you will ever have with this person. It could be.[4]

Latent wonderfulness begins with being open to serendipity—in every conversation.

FLOW

Design thinking advocates that you discover what you are best suited to do in a profession, or in other domains of life, by being aware of "when you seem the most animated, the most present." In what circumstances do you *flow*—yep, the same *flow experiences* that Csikszentmihalyi's research identified as situations where your attention, abilities, and interests are fully engaged and challenged.

Within the LMAP model, *flow is experienced and expressed in project results and productivity* and is rooted in the traits of Grit: passion, persistence, and intrinsic drives for task mastery. *Flow is experienced and expressed in interpersonal relationships* through curiosity, empathy, vulnerability, and a sense of being present and in the moment—largely rooted in social and emotional intelligence and intrinsic drives to relate to and team with others.

Find your flow . . . follow it.

Get Real—Situational Limitations and Opportunities

Evans, Burnett, and Roth are aware that some of these career and life choices (prototyping, reframing, flow, latent wonderfulness) are uniquely *first-world phenomena*—for us very fortunate professionals. Some of these topics and tools would be luxuries so out of context for unfortunate souls in Aleppo or Fallujah or Sanaa as to be irrelevant and tone-deaf.

But perhaps there is even an upside in realizing this: many of us first-worlders take so much for granted that we do best when we cultivate our appreciation and a sense of gratitude for our first-world choices—many of these choices do not exist for most people.[5]

YOUR BEST SELF

One LMAP feedback rater wrote it out perfectly: "I would like to see more of her best moments." This rater then described how these best moments were "too often compromised by . . . ." This rings so true and is the central question of this book: How can you be your best self more often and consciously avoid slipping into behaviors that are not you at your best.

FINDING YOUR BEST SELF

As we demonstrate throughout this book, there is important information about your behavior that can only be elicited with a quality 360 feedback assessment. The 360 method provides leaders with unique insights into how others view their personality—pluses, minuses, downsides, and upsides that are not apparent through self-reflection.

But no matter how much quality feedback we receive, ultimately only *you* are responsible for becoming your best self and creating your character and destiny. Twenty-five hundred years ago the Buddha spoke to this, saying:

Watch your thoughts; they become your words.

Watch your words; they become your actions.

Watch your actions; they become your habits.

Watch your habits; they become your character.

Watch your character; it becomes your destiny.

—Buddha Shakyamuni

LMAP

If you are interested in completing an LMAP 360 for yourself or your team, visit our website at www.lmapinc.com/personalityatwork.

Learn about our LMAP 360 corporate programs, the MMAP 360 (for professionals not in a leadership role), and coaching firms from across the world certified in LMAP assessments.

Please do check our website for updated books and articles to help fuel your thinking and development. We also appreciate any great books, development exercises, or suggestions you want to share with us.

A

Timothy Leary

Timothy Leary lived on the extremes: he was recruited to Harvard University by David McClelland in the late 1950s and later derailed and was fired by Harvard around an LSD study scandal in the early 1960s.

Leary took a rocky path from Middle America to the American intellectual elite. He attended West Point at his father's urging, but constant rule infractions led to his exit. He enrolled at the University of Alabama but was soon expelled for spending the night in a woman's room. He lost his draft deferment and conscripted into the Army toward the end of World War II. It was in the army that Leary developed interests in psychology and a fascination with combat soldiers returning with "shell shock." With a few years of behavioral restraint, he gained reinstatement at the University of Alabama, where he completed his BS via correspondence courses.

In 1946, Leary went to Washington State University and honed his methodology skills under Lee Cronbach (*the* Cronbach alpha). In 1947, he enrolled in the Clinical Psychology program at the University of California, Berkeley, to study with psychology heavyweight Erik Erikson[1] and write his dissertation, "The Social Dimensions of Personality: Group Structure and Process."

By 1950 Leary was an assistant professor of medical psychology at the University of California, San Francisco; cofounded the psychology department at Kaiser Hospital; and was well known for his brilliance, martini-making skills, and wild parties in the Berkeley Hills. At Kaiser, Leary published a landmark study of psychotherapy with World War II veterans with shell shock, aka post-traumatic stress.[2] One-third of patients improved with psychotherapy, a third did worse, and a third remained the same—the same as control groups with no psychotherapy and no treatment.

Life got tough: in 1955 his wife, Marianne, committed suicide and Leary became the single father of a daughter eight years old and son six. He described himself in these years as "an anonymous institutional employee who drove to work each morning in a long line of commuter cars and drove home each night and drank martinis . . . like several million middle-class, liberal, intellectual robots."[3]

Leary had continued to refine his dissertation ideas, and with his 1957 publication, *The Interpersonal Diagnosis of Personality*, he was recognized as a thought leader in the field. Recruited to Harvard, Leary partnered with David McClelland and Richard Alpert, who'd been recruited from Stanford University.

An elite crowd soon formed around Leary, including Huston Smith, the MIT philosophy professor, author of *The Religions of Man*, and television celebrity. Smith introduced Leary to Aldous Huxley (author of *The Doors of Perception*), and sharing interests in psychology, philosophy, consciousness, and altered states of consciousness, Leary, Smith, Huxley, and Alpert began dabbling in mind-altering substances. Leary and Alpert started the Harvard Psilocybin Project (psilocybin and LSD were legal at the time), and their research and personal interests shifted from personality to altered states of consciousness.

Their work at the Harvard Psilocybin Project ultimately led to Leary and Alpert being dismissed from Harvard in 1963. But Huston Smith later recounted, "During the three years I was involved with that Harvard study, LSD was not only legal but respectable. Before Tim went on his unfortunate careening course, it was a legitimate research project."

Their research assistant at the Harvard Psilocybin Project was Andrew Weil, now a famous doctor and author of three *New York Times* bestsellers, who runs the popular Ask Dr Weil website and a conglomerate of alternative-health, vitamin, and natural cosmetics companies.

Richard Alpert went off to India to study, became Baba Ram Dass, and authored a bestselling book, *Be Here Now*—now part of common language, more than a half century later.

Leary became a leading 1960s counterculture spokesperson and created such iconic phrases as "Think for yourself and question authority," "Set and setting," and "Turn on, tune in, drop out"—this last gem was wordsmithed with his close friend Marshall McLuhan. Tim Leary was a constant presence in the culture—part of what was happening. He hung with the Beat Poets and the Grateful Dead in San Francisco and with Jack Kerouac, Ken Kesey,[4] and Tom Wolfe, author of *The Electric Kool-Aid Acid Test*; he was with the Beatles in India and later with John Lennon and Yoko Ono for the infamous antiwar bed-in in Montreal. When Timothy Leary outlandishly ran for California governor against Ronald Reagan, Leary's campaign theme "Come Together" inspired the legendary John Lennon song. Leary remained close to John and Ringo Starr until his death.

His antiwar activities with the Weathermen and Black Panther movements led to Leary testifying before Congress, being investigated by the CIA and FBI, and serving hard time at Folsom Prison.

In the 1980s, before personal computers became commonplace, Leary developed a fascination with computers, and in 1985, Electronic Arts (EA) released Mind Mirror, a software program that is a blend of Leary's psychological, spiritual, and futurist ideas. Leary said, "The PC is the LSD of the 1990s" and encouraged people to "turn on, boot up, jack in." (Small world: I just missed meeting Leary. I'd interviewed at EA in 1984 to pitch a project called, Self & Other: Assessment Software. EA passed and worked with Leary and I co-founded Acumen).

I find it ironic that Leary, a leader of the antiestablishment movement, today would see so many derivatives of his Interpersonal Circumplex in *establishment* training programs across the world. Just a very few of the very many Circumplex-based personality assessments are shown in Table A.1.

TABLE A.1 | THE LEARY LEGACY: LMAP 360 AND CIRCUMPLEX ASSESSMENTS

Leary (1957)	Schaefer (1959, 1961, 1964)	Lafferty (1971)	Wiggins (1995)	Kaplan & Kaiser (2006)	LMAP 360, Warren (2002, 2006, 2016)
Helpful	Democratic	Humanistic	Helpful	Supports	1. Helpfulness
Affiliation	Cooperative	Affiliative	Sociable	Listens	2. Sociability
Self-Effacing	Accepting	Approval	Absolving	—	3. Approval Seeking
Dependent	Protective	Dependence	Dependent	Empowers—Excessive	4. Dependence
Fearful	—	Avoidant	Abasive	—	5. Tension
Distrustful	Possessive	Oppositional	Rigid	Versatility—Low	6. Rigidity
Hostile	Authoritarian	Power	Dictatorial	Forceful—Excessive	7. Hostility
Aggressive	Authoritarian	Power	Controlling	Takes Charge	8. Need to Control
Competitive	—	Competitive	Competitive	—	9. Competitiveness
Ordering	Persistence	Perfectionism	—	Order	10. Conscientiousness
Responsible	—	Achievement	Ambitious	Executes	11. Achievement Drive
Independent	Imagination	Self-Actualization	Confident	Innovation	12. Innovation
—	—	—	—	—	13. Open to Feedback

Key: — not specifically measured

After Leary's death at 75 years old in 1996, 7 grams of his ashes was launched into outer space on a Pegasus rocket along with the remains of 24 others, including Gene Roddenberry (creator of *Star Trek*). We want to assure readers that Leary's work on the Interpersonal Circumplex took place years *before* his introduction to LSD. More than a half century later, his work remains relevant, reflecting the quality of that work and the ongoing impact of personality at work. While both the business world and the world at large have transformed into a 24/7, globally interconnected world, one thing that has not changed much is people. The same traits and behaviors that operated as assets or liabilities in the industrial age operate similarly in the information age, and we remain essentially *stone age* men and women in the information age (Figure A.1).

FIGURE A.1 | THE INTERPERSONAL CIRCUMPLEX (LEARY, 1955) AND LMAP PROFILE (WARREN, 2001, 2006, 2016)

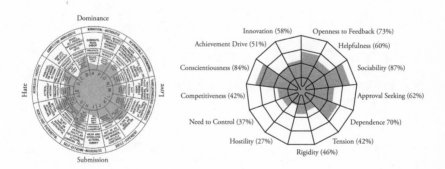

LMAP 360 Effectiveness Ratings

Raters provided ratings on your effectiveness in the domains below, using a 7-point scale.

Performance compared to others in a similar position

	Bottom 2%	Bottom 10%	Bottom 25%	Top 50%	Top 25%	Top 10%	Top 2%		Your Score	Sample Average
	0	1	2	3	4	5	6	7		
Aggregated Feedback						▲			6.11	5.56 ▲
Manager									6.00	
Direct Report									6.25	

Ability to get along with others

	Bottom 2%	Bottom 10%	Bottom 25%	Top 50%	Top 25%	Top 10%	Top 2%		Your Score	Sample Average
	0	1	2	3	4	5	6	7		
Aggregated Feedback					▲				4.66	5.61 ▲
Manager									4.00	
Direct Report									4.50	

Ability to produce results

	Bottom 2%	Bottom 10%	Bottom 25%	Top 50%	Top 25%	Top 10%	Top 2%		Your Score	Sample Average
	0	1	2	3	4	5	6	7		
Aggregated Feedback						▲			5.88	5.69 ▲
Manager									6.00	
Direct Report									5.75	

Leadership ability

	Bottom 2%	Bottom 10%	Bottom 25%	Top 50%	Top 25%	Top 10%	Top 2%		Your Score	Sample Average
	0	1	2	3	4	5	6	7		
Aggregated Feedback					▲				4.66	5.41 ▲
Manager									4.00	
Direct Report									4.50	

Overall effectiveness in his or her current job

	Bottom 2%	Bottom 10%	Bottom 25%	Top 50%	Top 25%	Top 10%	Top 2%		Your Score	Sample Average
	0	1	2	3	4	5	6	7		
Aggregated Feedback						▲			5.88	5.62 ▲
Manager									6.00	
Direct Report									5.75	

Self-Reflection Exercises

For those who do not have the opportunity and access to a quality 360, I put together this self-reflection exercise. I specifically chose the word *exercise* for these profiles because they are *not* assessment profiles, as they lack the reliability, validity, and rigor expected of an assessment.

SELF-REFLECTION EXERCISE 1: SEAT-OF-THE-PANTS SELF-PROFILE

Complete the profile in Figure C.1 by using a light pencil to fill in how much of each trait accurately represents *how you think you behave*. Bear in mind that the center point of the profile equals zero, and the four concentric rings mark the 25th, 50th, 75th, and 100th percentiles. Definitions of each of the 13 traits are found in the latter part of Chapter 3.

REFLECTIONS ON YOUR SEAT-OF-THE-PANTS SELF-PROFILE

When you've completed your prototype Seat-of-the-Pants Self-Profile, put it away for a day and return to it tomorrow to critically evaluate your self-reflections. In the meantime, you may want to return to Chapters 3, 5, and 7 to skim-read about the scale and profile landmarks.

FIGURE C.1 | BLANK SEAT-OF-THE-PANTS SELF-PROFILE

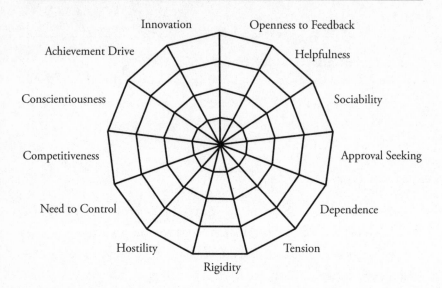

When you come back to your now-completed prototype Seat-of-the-Pants Self-Profile, review it and consider if you were too critical or too generous in your ratings. Make revisions as you see fit. Also, any behaviors that you are unsure how to rate, mark with a question mark. Over the next week, pay attention to these behaviors.

Take one full week to observe your behavior at work. Listen carefully to develop new insights into your motivations, ambitions, relationships, successes, and struggles at work. Remember: if you want to learn from this exercise, take one full week for observations.

Here are some general guidelines for making the most of this exercise:

▶ Pay close attention to what coworkers say or suggest about your personality, your behaviors. Listen and watch for clues on how colleagues and coworkers perceive you:

- Do they mention your enthusiasm for work—or lack of?

- Your decision-making and problem solving styles? Do they see you as a perfectionist or easily satisfied? Urgent or laid back? What are their perceptions of how you delegate? Do you facilitate or impair teamwork? What's their experience of your conflict style?

- What is the style and tone of your communications ... the impact of personality at work is broad. Learn how others perceive your aggressiveness, drive and initiative (or lack thereof). Are you seen as easily influenced or someone who persuades others?

- What's your reputation around social skills? Are you a good listener or more self-focused? Do they see you as more open-minded or stubborn? Friendly or private? More an introvert or extravert? As someone who'll burn out or rust out? Where have they noticed that you flourish and where you derail?

- Formulate and practice your own words in order to be able to say something like: *Please say more about that ... I really am curious... I'm interested in yours and others' perceptions of my work styles and behavior ... to be a better leader (colleague, parent, human being).* If others are skeptical, you might want to ask: *Do you also have curiosity about how others experience your personality and behavior?*

- Also formulate and practice your own words and be prepared to ask: *If I were to change just one thing in my behavior to be more effective, what would you suggest I change?*

GROUND RULES:

1. When the opportunity arises, only ask a follow-up question if you are genuinely curious in hearing more. Don't force

it or be inauthentic. Wait and listen. If you listen, other opportunities will arise.

2. You may inquire *only if* you can do so without getting defensive.

3. It is your sole responsibility to not get defensive, not disagree with anything a work associate says, and to graciously thank them for their candid feedback—even if it was not what you wanted to hear.

4. Stretch your abilities to maintain a positive, curious manner. If your threshold for getting defensive is low, take this opportunity to *prototype a constructive conversation*. Stretch your skills to *get curious and not furious*. Avoid becoming defensive and reframe it as learning from others' insights on how to raise your game. While it's not a 360 assessment, in this learning there is tremendous upside.

5. If you cannot 100 percent commit to maintain a positive, calm, open attitude in listening to their feedback, *don't ask follow-up questions as part of the exercise*. There is great upside in listening as William Mizner observed: *A good listener is not only popular everywhere, but after a while he knows something*.

Take notes or keep a journal to make observations during the week. These notes and seven nights of sleep to unconsciously process the observations (and perhaps feedback) will clarify your thoughts.

▶   Do not peek ahead (or you may bias your responses to the next exercise in an exercise already full of biases!).

▶   After at least one week, compile and reflect on your past week's notes, observations, and insights about your personality at work. What notes and observations suggest high or low scores on the profile? What did you learn about your behaviors and others' perceptions of your personality at work?

▶ When you are ready to move to the next exercise, turn your attention to Exercise 2.

SELF-REFLECTION EXERCISE 2: WHO-DO-I-THINK-THEY-THINK-I-AM PROFILE

First, forget about your Seat-of-the-Pants Self-Profile. Let it go. You may want to return to that profile after this second exercise, but for the moment, drop it.

Given your week of notes, observations, and insights about your behavior, use the Who-Do-I-Think-They-Think-I-Am Profile (Figure C.2), and mark how you think most coworkers would rate you on each of the 13 behavior traits.

FIGURE C.2 | WHO-DO-I-THINK-THEY-THINK-I-AM PROFILE

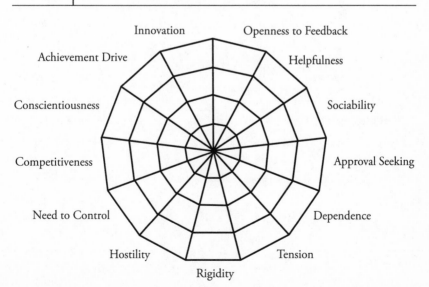

WHAT DID YOU LEARN?

Please do not misunderstand that this self-reflection exercise is anything like 360 feedback. But self-reflection and thinking about how others perceive you will help you develop your empathy and awareness skills, and *Personality at Work* is all about thinking about the character you are and the character you want to be.

INSIGHT INTO ACTION—ONE BEHAVIOR TO START, STOP, OR IMPROVE

You may want to go back to Chapter 16, "Your Best Self—the LMAP Method," and review the section titled "Identify *One* Leadership Development Goal" for an in-depth description of the Leadership Development Goal process we use with the LMAP 360.

There are two guidelines in our Leadership Development Goal process that are transferable here and are recommended that you use:

1. Identify just *one* behavior to start, stop, or improve to raise your effectiveness.

2. Write the goal in positive terms . . . as a goal that any person can *feel proud of* (e.g., start being a great listener, treat everyone with respect and consideration, be more assertive because the team says I have more to contribute, etc.).

Then get to it!

Notes

INTRODUCTION

1. Angela Duckworth, *Grit—the Power of Passion and Perseverance*, Scribner, New York, 2016, p. 172.

CHAPTER 1

1. Steve Wozniak with Gina Smith, *iWoz—Computer Geek to Cult Icon: How I Invented the Personal Computer, Co-Founded Apple, and Had Fun Doing It*, W. W. Norton & Co., New York, 2006, pp. 88–89.
2. Ibid., p. 31.
3. Ibid., p. 14.
4. Ibid., p. 22.
5. Shyness is "the fear of social disapproval or humiliation," and introversion is "a preference for environments that are not overstimulating." Susan Cain, *Quiet: The Power of Introverts in a World That Can't Stop Talking*, Crown, New York, 2012, p. 12.
6. Ibid., p. 44.
7. *iWoz*, p. 57.
8. Ibid., p. 70.
9. Ibid., p. 71.
10. Ibid., pp. 81–83.
11. Ibid., p. 71. In the more extended quote, Woz describes Jobs as extraverted in contrast to his own introversion. In fact, Jobs was more likely also an introvert but, unlike Woz, not shy. Jobs loved to have the stage and the attention and get into promoter mode. Woz, being very shy in those years, would not have been comfortable in that role.
12. Another incident occurred years later when Steve Scott, Apple's then president, assigned Woz employee #1 and Jobs #2. Jobs threw a tantrum, crying and cursing until Scott agreed to make Jobs employee #0. However, because Apple's banking was already set up and required positive integers, Jobs remained #2.
13. Quotes from the documentary *Steve Jobs: The Lost Interview*, an interview with Robert X. Cringley, Magnolia Home Entertainment, 2012.

14. It is ironic that Jobs was *so* impressed by the civility and recognition of the value of employees at HP. Jobs's reputation for his caustic, ungrateful, uncivil behavior illustrates the gap between a leader's self-reported intentions and values and his or her actual behavior.

15. *iWoz*, p. 30.

16. Quotes from *The Lost Interview*.

17. *iWoz*, p. 114.

18. Quotes from *The Lost Interview*.

19. Walter Isaacson, *Steve Jobs*, Simon & Schuster, New York, 2011, p. 43.

20. Isaacson, p. 43.

21. *iWoz*, pp. 147–148.

22. http://applemuseum.bott.org/sections/history.html; Isaacson, pp. 53–54.

23. *iWoz*, p. 143.

24. Ibid., p.193.

25. Ibid., p. 61.

26. To this day, Woz promotes the hacker ethos of technology that contrasts to Jobs's entrepreneurial, proprietary, litigation-enforced, for-profit mentality. In 2011, Woz wrote the foreword to *Ghost in the Wires: My Adventures as the World's Most Wanted Hacker*, by Kevin Mitnick with William L. Simon.

27. Ibid., p. 194.

28. Ron Wayne was brought in partly because he'd started a few companies in California before, a skill that soon was of limited value to the venture.

29. *iWoz*, p. 188.

30. Markkula learned from the Intel Trinity of Robert Noyce, Gordon Moore, and Andy Grove, who were pioneers in start-ups and equity sharing in the Silicon Valley.

31. *iWoz*, p. 197.

32. Ibid., p. 196.

33. Isaacson, p. 77.

34. *iWoz*, p. 199.

35. Isaacson, p. 78.

36. *iWoz*, p. 75.

37. Ibid., p. 206. Years later at Steve Jobs's birthday party, Woz revealed that he was behind this prank, presenting Jobs with a framed copy of the infamous Zaltair handout.

38. *The Lost Interview*. These comments seem to reflect Jobs's idealized notion of wealth. There was a clash between his counterculture-friendly, antiestablishment, cool-California vegan-and-vitamin, I-was-in-a-commune-and-had-long-hair idealized value system and his being clearly seduced by the power, control, beauty and money Jobs had access to by age 23.

39. Isaacson, p. 81.

40. *The Lost Interview*.

41. Nearly 6 million Apple IIs were sold over its 16-year life cycle. *iWoz*, p. 84.

42. Wozniak in an interview with the *Milwaukee Business Journal* at the Flying Car conference in Milwaukee in 2014.

43. Jobs gave his parents $750,000.

44. Dice Insights, an interview with Daniel Kottke, http://insights.dice.com/2013/08/16/early-apple-employees-talk-memories-of-steve-jobs-new-movie-2/.
45. Ibid.
46. *iWoz*, p. 223.
47. Isaacson, pp. 103–104.

CHAPTER 2

1. This is because Grit—initiative, ambition, persistence, and passion—fuels a pathway to leadership (along with intellect, education, specialized knowledge, opportunity, etc.). Whereas Angela Duckworth refers to self-assessed Grit in her research, in this book I refer to Grit as a 360 measure: *being perceived by others* as showing prominent initiative, ambition, persistence, and passion. The differences between self-ratings and 360s are discussed more in Chapters 3 and 7.
2. Geoff Colvin, *Humans Are Underrated: What High Achievers Know That Brilliant Machines Never Will*, Portfolio/Penguin Books, New York, 2015.

CHAPTER 3

1. See Sam Barondes, *Making Sense of People*, which explains the five-factor model and how to apply it to understand other people better.
2. Representative samples are updated every four years. The 2013 U.S. normative sample has 2,214 senior executives assessed by 34,759 feedback raters. In 2015, we developed a global sample: 379 Asians, 338 Europeans, and 330 North Americans assessed by 16,750 raters. The global sample quadrupled in the last two years, and analyses are being run in parallel to publication of *Personality at Work*.
3. Effectiveness ratings are also scored on a normative sample in LMAP 360. See Appendix B.
4. Stanford psychologist Carol Dweck's studies focus on just two important traits or "mindsets." The *Fixed* versus *Growth* mindsets represent two fundamentally different ways of viewing the world and oneself. Those with a fixed mindset believe "your qualities are carved in stone" where those with a growth mindset believe "that your basic qualities are things that you can cultivate through your efforts. See pp. 6–7 Dweck , Carol S., *Mindset*, 2006.
5. Ambiverts are neither introverts nor extraverts, but in between.
6. In the LMAP 360, Conscientiousness is a separate trait from Achievement Drive, whereas in the Big Five, these two traits are intermeshed and split into facets.

CHAPTER 4

1. Larry Bossidy and Ram Charan, *Execution: The Discipline of Getting Things Done*, Crown Business, New York, 2002, p. 141.
2. Rather than just Wall Street banks; Hillary Clinton has stressed this very point.

3. For 79.9 percent of the equity and a controlling interest in AIG.
4. Michael Lewis, "The Man Who Crashed the World," *Vanity Fair*, August 2009.
5. Michael Lewis, *The Big Short: Inside the Doomsday Machine*, W. W. Norton & Co., New York, 2010, p. 86.
6. Lewis, "The Man Who Crashed the World."
7. Ibid.
8. Lewis, *The Big Short*, p. 86.
9. Lewis, "The Man Who Crashed the World."
10. Ibid.
11. Douglas Conant and Mette Norgaard, *TouchPoints: Creating Powerful Leadership Connections in the Smallest of Moments*, Jossey-Bass, San Francisco, 2011, p. xxv.
12. See Conant and Norgaard, chap. 1, p. 17, ftn. 1.
13. Conant and Norgaard, p. 11.
14. Ibid., Preface, p. xxx.
15. Ibid., p. 18.
16. Ibid., p. 19.
17. As Conant stresses, the team was provided with extensive leadership and team development training, coaching, and support.
18. Conant and Norgaard, p. xxvi.
19. Joseph S. Nye, *The Powers to Lead*, Oxford University Press, New York, 2008, p. 90.
20. See Laszlo Bock, *Work Rules! Insights from Inside Google That Will Transform How You Live and Lead* (Hachette, New York, 2015), and Geoff Colvin, *Humans Are Underrated: What High Achievers Know That Brilliant Machines Never Will* (Portfolio/Penguin, New York, 2015), for a discussion of high-value behaviors (empathy, open-mindedness, inquisitiveness, achievement drive, conscientiousness, grit, etc.).
21. Dan Lovallo and Olivier Sibony, "The Case for Behavioral Strategy," *McKinsey Quarterly*, March 2010. Lovallo is a professor at the University of Sydney; Sibony is a director at McKinsey and Co.
22. Chip Heath and Dan Heath, *Decisive: How to Make Better Choices in Life and Work*, Crown Business, New York, 2013, p. 5. Summarizing the work of Lovallo and Sibony.
23. Lovallo and Sibony, p. 7.
24. Ibid., p. 2.
25. "Strong but wrong" was coined by J. Rasmussen of the Risø Laboratory in Denmark, one of the original research theorists to study human error.
26. Lovallo and Sibony, p. 1.
27. Lovallo and Sibony, pp. 3–7.
28. Daniel Kahneman, *Thinking, Fast and Slow* (Farrar, Straus & Giroux, New York, 2011); echoed in Dan Ariely's *Predictably Irrational: The Hidden Forces That Shape Our Decisions* (HarperCollins, New York, 2008) and Richard Thaler and Cass Sunstein's *Nudge: Improving Decisions About Health, Wealth, and Happiness* (Yale University Press, New Haven, CT, 2008).

29. Alex "Sandy" Pentland, "The New Science of Building Teams," *Harvard Business Review*, April 2012.

30. Ibid., p. 3.

31. Ibid.

32. Ibid., p. 4.

33. Ibid.

34. Ibid., p. 6.

35. M. Losada, "The Complex Dynamics of High Performance Teams," *Mathematical and Computer Modeling*, 1999, vol. 30, nos. 9–10, pp. 179–192.

36. The 1999 study is not to be confused with the October 2005 paper published by Barbara Fredrickson and Marcial Losada in *American Psychologist* ("Positive Affect and the Complex Dynamics of Human Flourishing," American Psychologist, vol. 60(7), Oct. 2005, 678-686), which has been retracted from publication. Besides questions about the esoteric statistical methods, the paper was criticized for claiming specific ratios of positivity vs. negativity (2.9:1) that were claimed to be associated with individuals flourishing in their life or not.

    Losada's 1999 studies have been similarly and fairly criticized and *I absolutely concur there are no magic ratios.* However, there is no argument that predominant positivity or negativity has an important impact on our cognition, emotions and behaviors and makes a powerful interpersonal impact.

    John Gottman applied this basic model to marriage/divorce research. He identified four interpersonal behaviors that predict divorce: criticism of partner's personality, contempt, defensiveness, and emotional withdrawal. In contrast, couples that demonstrated more positive, respectful and supportive behaviors had a higher rate of successful marriages. See John Gottman, *The Science of Trust: Emotional Attunement for Couples.* New York: W.W. Norton & Company, 2011.

    And, as noted in Chapter 14, in purely behavioral terms, if one generates a high volume of criticisms and rebukes (punishment) and no encouragement and support (positive reinforcement), then the entire reinforcement schedule is punishment. And that is not an optimal reinforcement schedule for humans.

37. M. Losada & E. Heaphy, "The Role of Positivity and Connectivity in the Performance of Teams: A Nonlinear Dynamics Model, "*American Behavioral Scientist*, 2004, vol. 47, no. 6, pp. 740–765. B. L. Fredrickson and M. Losada, "Positive Affect and the Complex Dynamics of Human Flourishing," *American Psychologist*, 2005, vol. 60, no. 7, pp. 678–686. Along with the work of Fredrickson, Seligman, Csikszentmihalyi, Kahneman, Diener, Salovey, and others, these studies have become anchors in the field of positive psychology.

38. Barbara, L. Fredrickson, *Positivity: Top-Notch Research Reveals the Upward Spiral That Will Change Your Life,* Three Rivers Press, New York, 2009, p. 123.

39. Larry Huston and Nabil Sakkab, "P&G's New Innovation Model," *Harvard Business Review*, March 20, 2006.

40. See Elizabeth Gerber, associate professor of design at Northwestern University.

41. Moreover, research shows that positivity is not the be-all, end-all for leadership interactions: While optimists respond well to positivity when negative events

occur, people with lower self-esteem or a strong followership or relationship orientation tend to respond better to empathy when negative events occur.

42. Having the same flight deck across multiple aircraft platforms simplified one aspect of an increasingly complex flight deck.

43. Robert I. Sutton and Huggy Rao, *Scaling Up Excellence: Getting to More Without Settling for Less*, Crown Business, New York, 2014, p. 81.

44. Ibid., p. 82.

45. Doron Leven, "New GM: Same as It Ever Was?" *Fortune Magazine*, April 28, 2014, pp. 64–68.

46. Bryce G. Hoffman, *American Icon: Alan Mulally and the Fight to Save Ford Motor Company*, Crown Business, New York, 2012, p. 112.

47. Ibid., p. 120.

48. Amy Wilson, as reported in *Automotive News*, March 27, 2007.

49. Hoffman, p. 102.

50. Ibid., p. 112.

51. I met Alan Mulally at an event and was impressed how he showed up in an academics-style, plain brown corduroy sports coat with elbow patches, khaki pants, and functional shoes to an event with other CEOs, bankers, and Ivy academics—all dressed impeccably in slick suits. Mulally was refreshingly plain spoken and immediately credible. I also spoke at length with Mark Fields and one other member of the Executive Management team.

CHAPTER 5

1. The normative sample is over 40,000 ratings.

2. An average of top 15–20 percent makes sense given that the LMAP 360 is mainly used in leadership development with very senior leaders.

3. See John Zenger and Joseph Folkman, *The Extraordinary Leader—Turning Good Managers into Great Leaders*, McGraw-Hill, New York, 2002.

4. Chapter 16, "Your Best Self—the LMAP Method," explains goal setting in greater depth.

5. Malcolm Gladwell references the Fischer and Orasanu studies in "The Ethnic Theory of Plane Crashes" (Chapter Seven in *Outliers, The Story of Success*. Little, Brown & Co. 2008). Gladwell masterfully builds on cultural influences on aviation safety where I focus on the impact of personality. Of course, culture and personality interact and are just two of the multi-dimensional, stochastically complex layers and players that drive human actions and interaction.

CHAPTER 6

1. In 2010, the FAA adopted a no-fault, no-blame go-around procedure. Any crew member can call for a go-around if the flight deviates from a nonstandard approach—with no blame assessed and no fault assigned and without the need for special reports or investigations (as of a decade ago). The standard operating procedure is that flight crews include a go-around plan in the descent briefing to discuss crew roles in normal or emergency conditions. Calling for

a go-around is now positioned as an SOP and good airmanship. Between 0.20 and 0.33 percent of landings are now aborted, and in the United States in 2014, this was about 20 a day.

2. The video re-creation with commercial pilots in a flight simulator can be found in *The Wrong Stuff* on YouTube.

3. National Transportation Safety Board, *Safety Study: A Review of Flightcrew-Involved Major Accidents of U.S. Air Carriers, 1978 Through 1990,* Washington, DC, 1994, NTSB/SS94/01.

4. Ute Fischer and Judith Orasanu, "Cultural Diversity and Crew Communication," 50th Astronautical Congress, Amsterdam, October 1999.

5. Malcolm Gladwell references the Fischer and Orasanu studies in "The Ethnic Theory of Plane Crashes" (Chapter Seven in *Outliers, The Story of Success.* Little, Brown & Co. 2008). Gladwell masterfully builds on cultural influences on aviation safety where I focus on the impact of personality. Of course, culture and personality interact and are just two of the multi-dimensional, stochastically complex layers and players that drive human actions and interaction.

6. Eugen Tarnow, "Towards the Zero Accident Goal: Assisting the First Officer: Monitor and Challenge Captain Errors," *Journal of Aviation/Aerospace Education and Research,* Fall 2000, p. 33.

7. This was prior to FAA changes on missed-approach and go-around procedures in 2010.

CHAPTER 7

1. Calvin S. Hall, Gardner Lindzey, and John B. Campbell, *Theories of Personality,* 4th ed., John Wiley & Sons, Hoboken, NJ, 1997.

2. Raymond Cattell and Paul Kline, *The Scientific Analysis of Personality,* Academic Press, Cambridge, MA, 1977.

3. Richard Arvey, *Fairness in Selecting Employees,* Addison-Wesley, Reading, PA, 1988.

4. Hogan is the retired chair of Industrial Organizational Psychology, University of Oklahoma.

5. Robert Hogan, *Personality and the Fate of Organizations,* LEA Publishers, Princeton, NJ, 2007, pp. 8–9.

6. Ibid., p. 9.

7. David Myers, "The Inflated Self: How Do I Love Me? Let Me Count the Ways," *Psychology Today,* May 1980, p. 16.

8. Justin Kruger and David Dunning, "Unskilled and Unaware of It: How Difficulties in Recognizing One's Own Incompetence Lead to Inflated Self-Assessments, *Journal of Personality and Social Psychology,* 1999, vol. 77, no. 6, pp. 1121–1134.

9. Constantine Sedikides, "Behind Bars but Above the Bar," *British Journal of Social Psychology,* June 2014, vol. 53, no. 2, pp. 396–403.

10. Brian S. Connelly and Ute R. Hülsheger, "A Narrower Scope or a Clearer Lens for Personality? Examining Sources of Observers' Advantages over Self-

Reports for Predicting Performance," *Journal of Personality*, 2012, vol. 80, no. 3, p. 603. DOI:10.1111/j.1467-6494.2011.00744.x. In addition to being an associate professor at the University of Toronto, Connelly is a research and statistical consultant to LMAP.

11. Hogan, pp. 8–10.

12. LMAP 360 Reports are 85+ pages; LMAP Profiles are a few pages, with detailed narrative analyses of Self and Feedback Profiles, effectiveness ratings, and rater comments.

13. See Chapter 17, "Red Teams and WRAP," for a discussion of how deferring personalities may inappropriately defer to dominating personalities, whose own confirmation biases drive their persuasiveness and create problems in decision making.

14. Benjamin Wolman, *Dictionary of Behavioral Science*, Van Nostrand-Rheinhold, 1973.

15. Diagnostic and Statistical Manual of Mental Disorders, DSM-5, May 18, 2013.

16. Ibid.

17. This CEO did not understand that his aggressive, hostile behaviors with the senior managers were having a negative impact on morale and team spirit. Or that the senior managers, like the CEO himself, also had strong internal quality and performance standards that might be better appealed to rather than prodding them with the verbal dressing-downs the CEO sometimes used "as a motivational tool." This was where the coaching would focus.

18. Based on LMAP 360 Leadership Development Goals set in 2014–2015.

19. The author recognizes that operating on "autopilot" is necessary some of the time for some behaviors in order to function in a world of unending stimulus and internal self-talk.

CHAPTER 8

1. Russell Lewis, Estrella Forster, James Whinnery, and Nicholas Webster, "Aircraft-Assisted Pilot Suicides in the United States, 2003–2012" (PDF), Civil Aerospace Medical Institute, Federal Aviation Administration, February 2014; retrieved March 29, 2015.

2. I take the liberty to refer to the last 20 years of DSM diagnostic categories knowing of the unsettled debate in DSM-5 and ICD 10 on whether personality disorders are valid, can be reliably diagnosed, etc. See, for instance, Charles B. Pull's article "Reactions to Removing Versus Retaining Specific Personality Disorders in DSM-5," online at MedScape, September 16, 2016.

3. P.E. Greenberg, T. Sisitsky, R.C. Kessler, et al, "The Economic Burden of Anxiety Disorders in the 1990s." *Journal of Clinical Psychiatry*, 1999, vol. 60, no. 7, pp. 427–435. See also, M.D. Marciniak, M.J. Lage, E. Dunayevich, et al., "The Cost of Treating Anxiety: the Medical and Demographic Correlates that Impact Total Medical Costs," 2005. In *PubMed*, US National Library of Medicine, National Institutes of Health.

4. People who are severely mentally ill (SMI) have chronic, often psychotic, symptoms that are not effectively treated, are often homeless or in jail, have

dual diagnoses, and are nicotine dependent. In regard to the SMI population size: "Depending on how one defines 'seriously mentally ill,' estimates of their number at any given time have ranged from 3 percent to 10 percent of the population." E. Torrey, K. Entsminger, J. Geller, J. Stanley, and D. J. Jaffe, "The Shortage of Public Hospital Beds for Mentally Ill Persons," *A Report of the Treatment Advocacy Center*, 2015, p. 6.

5. Walter Isaacson, *Steve Jobs*, Simon & Schuster, New York, 2011, p. 266.
6. Ibid., p. 119.
7. Bridget F. Grant, S. Patricia Chou, et al., "Prevalence, Correlates, Disability, and Comorbidity of DSM-IV Borderline Personality Disorder: Results from the Wave 2 National Epidemiologic Survey on Alcohol and Related Conditions," *Journal of Clinical Psychiatry*, 2008 Apr, vol. 69, no. 4, pp. 533–545.
8. Belinda Jane Board and Katarina Fritzon, "Disordered Personalities at Work," *Psychology, Crime & Law*, vol. 11, no. 1, March 2005, pp. 17–32.
9. David Dotlich and Peter Cairo, *Why CEOs Fail—The 11 Behaviors That Can Derail Your Climb to the Top—and How to Manage Them.* Jossey-Bass, 2003. Introduction, p.xxiv.
10. A disadvantage of a bad relationship at work versus at home is that at home some of that time is spent asleep!

CHAPTER 9

1. To learn more about leadership in high-risk and crisis situations, see Tom Kolditz, *In Extremis Leadership*, Jossey Bass, San Francisco, 2007.
2. See Joe Palca and Flora Lichtman, *Annoying: The Science of What Bugs Us*, John Wiley & Sons, Hoboken, NJ, 2011.
3. Some organizations have reevaluated the "up-or-out" model, instead creating partnership and professional tracks to allow professionals without high leadership aspirations to continue contributing to the firm.
4. Douglas Conant and Mette Norgaard, *TouchPoints: Creating Powerful Leadership Connections in the Smallest of Moments*, Jossey-Bass, San Francisco, 2011, pp. 78-81.
5. Ashley Whillans, Aaron Weidman, and Elizabeth Dunn, "Valuing Time Over Money Is Associated with Greater Happiness," *Social Psychological & Personality Science*, March 2016, vol. 7, no. 3.
6. Laszlo Bock, *Work Rules! Insights from Inside Google That Will Transform How You Live and Lead*, Hachette Book Group, New York, 2015.
7. Steve Wozniak with Gina Smith, *iWoz—Computer Geek to Cult Icon: How I Invented the Personal Computer, Co-Founded Apple, and Had Fun Doing It*, W. W. Norton & Co., New York, 2006, p. 123.
8. Ibid., p. 148.

CHAPTER 10

1. Robert Hogan, *Personality and the Fate of Organizations*, LEA Publishers, Princeton, NJ, 2007, p. 132.

2. A governor in an engine prevents it from going fast and is a metaphor for those who have an overactive governor on their behavior.

3. In contrast, leaders with prominent Task Mastery traits are more comfortable with persuasion and assertiveness in the service of the work.

4. Susan Scott, *Fierce Conversations: Achieving Success at Work & in Life, One Conversation at a Time*, Berkley Books, New York, 2002, p. 13.

5. Sheryl Sandberg with Nell Scovell, *Lean In: Women, Work, and the Will to Lead*, Knopf, New York, 2013.

6. Patrick Lencioni, *The Advantage: Why Organizational Health Trumps Everything Else*, Jossey-Bass, 2012, p. 48.

7. Ibid., p. 57.

8. Heike Bruch and Sumantra Ghosal, "Beware the Busy Manager," *Harvard Business Review*, February 2002.

9. Their findings identify half as many effective, purposeful leaders as the LMAP research. Distracted managers with high energy and little focus behaved impulsively even when it was best to wait and analyze situations—like LMAP Domineering Profiles. Disengaged managers lacked purpose and used denial to ignore work that needed to get done—like LMAP Bottom-Heavy Profiles. Purposeful managers had focus, energy, and initiative to accomplish important tasks and work well with others—like LMAP Top-Heavy Profiles.

10. See Jeffrey Pfeffer and Robert Sutton, *The Knowing-Doing Gap: How Smart Companies Turn Knowledge into Action*, Harvard Business School Publishing, Boston, 200; Jeffrey Pfeffer and Robert Sutton, *Hard Facts, Dangerous Half-Truths, & Total Nonsense: Profiting from Evidence-Based Management*, Harvard Business School Publishing, Boston, 2006; and Robert Sutton, *Good Boss, Bad Boss: How to Be the Best . . . and Learn from the Worst*, Business Plus, New York, 2010.

11. Jim Collins, *Good to Great: Why Some Companies Make the Leap . . . and Others Don't*, HarperCollins, New York, 2001.

12. Here let's distinguish between deferent leaders who are eager to do work below their pay grade *instead of* addressing key leadership challenges and those who do the hard leadership work *and* also contribute below pay grade work (i.e., Mulally stepping into the shoes of a Ford salesperson and handling sales when he visits adealership).

CHAPTER 11

1. Bill Gates on Steve Jobs, *Business Insider*, January 16, 2015, www.business insider.com/bill-gates-on-steve-jobs-2015-1.

2. Recall, Jobs's adoptive parents had set a pretty good example.

3. Brent Schlender and Rick Tetzeli, *Becoming Steve Jobs: The Evolution of a Reckless Upstart into a Visionary Leader*, Crown Business, New York, 2015, p. 144.

4. Ibid., p. 135.

5. Ibid., p. 137.

6. Ibid., p. 172.

7. Ibid., p. 231.

8. Ibid., p. 141.
9. Ibid., p.173.
10. Isaacson, pp. 561–566.
11. Ibid, p. 178.
12. CNET, August 6, 1997.
13. Richard Carter noted that Gates needed an effective competitor for Microsoft to avoid additional antitrust issues. Making the deal and burying the hatchet with Gates were practical necessities for Jobs. Carter thinks that Gates did the deal for pragmatic and strategic reasons more than altruistic ones.
14. Isaacson, p. 232.
15. Brent Schlender and Rick Tetzeli, *Becoming Steve Jobs*, p. 363.
16. Isaacson, p. 311.
17. Ryan Tate, "What Everyone Is Too Polite to Say About Steve Jobs," gawker.com, November 7, 2011.
18. The rock-and-roll star Neil Young heard Jobs was recovering, and knowing Jobs loved vinyl record albums, he offered to send Jobs his newest collection—as a get-well gesture. Jobs responded, "Fuck Neil Young and fuck his records," because years before, Young had criticized the compressed sound files in iTunes.
19. Isaacson, pp. 511–512.
20. After payments of $20 million+ in prior settlements.
21. Isaacson, p. 327.
22. Ibid., p. 103.
23. "The iPhone 4 Leak Saga from Start to Finish," *Fast Company*, April 20, 2010.

CHAPTER 12

1. Baseline rates of incivility: 30 percent in Britain, per Charlotte Rayner studies; 25–50 percent in Canada, per Christine Pearson's studies; see also C. Porath and C. Pearson, "The Price of Incivility," *Harvard Business Review*, January–February 2013.
2. Zogby Survey, "2007 U.S. Workplace Bullying Survey," published online by the Workplace Bullying Institute.
3. Hornstein, Harvey A., *Brutal Bosses and Their Prey*, Riverhead Trade, 1997.
4. David Campbell, "The Colleges Say Exec Charisma Not All That Charming," *Minneapolis-St. Paul Star Tribune*, January 28, 1990.
5. Loraleigh Keashly, Joel Neuman, and Karen Jagatic have together and independently done well-respected research on workplace and school bullying.
6. Survey by the Workplace Bullying and Trauma Institute.
7. See U.S. Department of Veterans Affairs, Workplace Stress and Aggression Project, 2003. See also Joel Harmon, Dennis J. Scotti, Scott J. Behson, and L. Keashly, "The Impacts of High-Involvement Work Systems on Staff Satisfaction and Service Costs in Veterans Health Care," *Academy of Management Annual Proceedings*, August 2003.
8. Amy C. Edmondson, *Teaming: How Organizations Learn, Innovate, and Compete in the Knowledge Economy*, Jossey-Bass, San Francisco, 2012, pp. 13–14.

9. Robert Sutton, *The No Asshole Rule: Building a Civilized Workplace and Surviving One That Isn't*, Business Plus, New York, p. 9.

10. Ibid., p. 10.

11. Andrew G. Miner, Theresa M. Glomb, and Charles Hulin, "Experience Sampling Mood and Its Correlates at Work: Diary Studies in Work Psychology," *Journal of Occupational and Organizational Psychology*, June 2005, vol. 78, no. 1, pp. 173–193; Bennett J. Tepper, "Consequences of Abusive Supervision," *Academy of Management Journal*, June 2000, vol., 43, no. 2, pp. 178–190; and 1970s studies by Frank Smith on discretionary effort at work.

12. Sutton, *The No Asshole Rule*, p. 47.

13. R. B. Williams, "Hostility: Effects on Health and the Potential for Successful Behavioral Approaches to Prevention and Treatment," in A. Baum, T. A. Revenson, and J. E. Singer, eds., *Handbook of Health Psychology*, Erlbaum, Mahwah, NJ, 2001.

CHAPTER 13

1. Robert Kelly and Janet Caplan, "How Bell Labs Creates Star Performers," *Harvard Business Review*, July–August 1993, pp. 128–139.

2. Linda Grant and Richard Hagberg, "Rambos in Pinstripes: Why So Many CEOs Are Lousy Leaders," *Fortune Magazine*, June 24, 1996.

3. Steve Jobs was a master at this. He could be the most engaging, charming, seductive person one could imagine when he wanted something from someone; but after he got what he wanted, the charm offensive was turned off, and others were shocked by his cold, distant, unfriendly demeanor.

4. Personal communication.

5. Robert Hogan, *Personality and the Fate of Organizations*, LEA Publishers, Princeton, NJ, 2007, chap. 6.

6. See LMAP 360 Methods Summary, available at lmapinc.com.

7. Robert Sutton credits Paul Saffo with the distinction on smart versus wise bosses in *Good Boss, Bad Boss: How to Be the Best . . . and Learn from the Worst* (Business Plus, New York, 2010, p. 73).

8. See Mihaly Csikszentmihalyi, *Flow: The Psychology of Optimal Experience*, HarperPerennial Books, New York, 1990. See also Csikszentmihalyi, *Good Business: Leadership, Flow and the Making of Meaning*, Viking Books, New York, 2003.

9. See Simon Baron-Cohen, *The Science of Evil: On Empathy and the Origins of Cruelty*, Basic Books, New York, 2011.

CHAPTER 14

1. Jill Abramson interview with Katie Couric, July 2014.

2. Dylan Byers, "Jill Abramson Ousted from New York Times," *Politico*, May 14, 2014.

3. Dylan Byers, "Turbulence at the Times," *Politico*, May 23, 2013.

4. *Chief Executive*, October 29, 2012.
5. Lou Solomon, "The Top Ten Complaints from Employees About Their Leaders," *Harvard Business Review*, June 15, 2015.
6. Benjamin Snyder, "Half of Us Have Quit Our Job Because of a Bad Boss," *Fortune Magazine*, April 2, 2015.
7. Nigel Nicholson, "Five Reasons Why Leaders Fail," London Business School, April 28, 2016.
8. Before he was at Yale SOM, Kolditz headed leadership training at West Point and in 2015 became director of the Doerr Institute for New Leaders at Rice University.
9. Richard Carter, PhD, who collaborates with Badham at MGSM, uses a similar model in the MBA and executive education programs at the Australian Institute of Management.
10. As quoted in "Why Humble, Empathic Business Leaders Are More Successful," by Douglas LaBier, *Huffington Post*, December 24, 2014.
11. Mark J. Plotkin, *Tales of a Shaman's Apprentice: An Ethnobotanist Searches for New Medicines in the Amazon Rain Forest*, Viking Penguin, New York, 1993, p. 14.
12. Marshall Goldsmith, *What Got You Here Won't Get You There: How Successful People Become Even More Successful!*, Hyperion Books, New York, 2007.
13. Susan Scott, *Fierce Conversations: Achieving Success at Work & in Life, One Conversation at a Time*, Berkley Books, New York, 2002, p. xvi.
14. Amy Cuddy, *Presence: Bringing Your Boldest Self to Your Biggest Challenges*, Little, Brown and Co., New York, 2015.
15. Joseph S. Nye Jr., *The Powers to Lead*, Oxford University Press, New York, 2008, pp. 70–71.
16. Richard de Crespigny, *QF32*, Pan Macmillan Australia, Sydney, 2012, p. 169.
17. Richard Hackman and Ruth Wageman, "When and How Team Leaders Matter," *Research in Organizational Behavior*, 2005, vol. 26, p. 37.
18. R. F. Baumeister, E. Bratslavsky, C. Finkenauer, C., and K. D. Vohs, "Bad Is Stronger Than Good," *Review of General Psychology*, 2001, vol. 5, pp. 323–370.
19. Readers may be familiar with the "fight-or-flight" sympathetic nervous system circuit, but perhaps less are aware of the opposite, parasympathetic nervous system circuit, known as "woo and screw."
20. Barbara Fredrickson, *Positivity: Top-Notch Research Reveals the 3-to-1 Ratio That Will Change Your Life*, Crown Publishers, New York, 2009. With chapters "Broaden Your Mind," "Decrease Negativity," "Increase Positivity," and "A New Toolkit," the book is a broad resource guide for research and applications of positive psychology.
21. Ram Dass wrote about this phenomenon in his book, *Be Here Now*. Recall that Ram Dass (aka Richard Alpert) was Leary's partner at the Harvard Personality Project.
22. Christensen, Clayton, Allworth, James, Dillon, Karen. *How Will You Measure Your LIfe*, Harper Business, 2012, p. 32.

CHAPTER 15

1. Richard de Crespigny, *QF32*, Pan Macmillan Australia, Sydney, 2012, p. 102.
2. As reported in an article by Andy Pasztor in the *Wall Street Journal*, November 17, 2013, which gives an overview of FAA findings on decreasing pilot skills due to automation and other contributing factors.
3. De Crespigny, pp. 135–136.
4. Ibid., p. 137.
5. De Crespigny, p. 141.
6. Ibid., pp. 140–141.
7. Pilots have annual check rides where their line flying performance is observed, evaluated, and certified by a specially trained "check captain." For this flight, Wubben would be doing an annual flight check of de Crespigny, and Evans would be checking Wubben.
8. *QF 32*, Four Corners video, Australian Broadcasting Company, March 28, 2011. Readers can view this at www.abc.net.au/4corners/special_eds/20110328/qantas/.
9. De Crespigny, pp. 4–5.
11. Quotes from transcript of *QF 32*, Four Corners video, Australian Broadcasting Company.
12. Ibid.
13. De Crespigny, p. 170.
14. Ibid., p. 187.
15. Groupthink is where individuals who see a potential problem do not raise it to the group because they think the group is more intelligent and more correct and someone would have thus raised it if it were important.
16. De Crespigny, p. 169.
17. Ibid., p. 190.
18. De Crespigny, pp. 191–192.
19. For more detailed information on the flight and landing, see the two-part video interview of Richard De Crespigny by the Flight Safety Foundation.
20. De Crespigny, p. 238.
21. Quotes from transcript of *QF 32*, Four Corners video, Australian Broadcasting Company.
22. Quotes from transcript of *QF 32*, Four Corners video, Australian Broadcasting Company.
23. Ironically, the next day, QF32 crew members were aboard a Qantas 747-400 flight to Sydney. At 2,000 feet, there was a loud bang from an engine compressor blade failure. Though it was a nonthreatening equipment failure, nonetheless it required that the plane return to Singapore and was a PR disaster for Qantas.
24. Carey Edwards, *Airmanship*, 2nd ed., Blacker Limited Publisher, East Sussex, U.K., 2013, p. 18.

CHAPTER 16

1. Yale School of Management, Harvard Business School, The Wharton School, Macquarie Graduate School of Management.

2. Temasek Holdings (Singapore), Underwriters Laboratories, PPG, Tupperware Brands.
3. Vergil Metts, PhD; Erica Dawson, PhD; Roger Lipson, EdD; Greg Hiebert; Richard Carter, PhD; and Professor Richard Badham, PhD in Australia.
4. This is not unique to LMAP 360. Even assessments that lack a robust empirical foundation—like the MBTI—provide a common language to talk about behavior.
5. The LMAP 360 Report is computer generated and uses an expert system to select from a library with thousands of pages to generate a highly personalized report. Participants ask if we have psychologists in the LMAP back office writing reports all week long! For years I did write the reports, then coded and stored them, building up the library over eight years.
6. Even after many years, as the LMAP's author I still find this quite astounding, and it makes the hard work of writing all those reports worth it.
7. Lewin is the eighteenth most cited psychologist of the twentieth century.
8. We recommend that the LMAP 360 Report be treated as confidential. This is the norm in North America and in Europe, less so in Asia.
9. Initially thinking through the results and then talking through the results with another person actually activates different parts of the brain.
10. In-house we refer to programs where LMAP 360 is limited to one debrief and no formal follow-up as "hit and runs" or" drive-bys."
11. Marshall Goldsmith, "The Impact of Direct Report Feedback and Follow-Up on Leadership," 2006, www.marshallgoldsmith.com/articles.
12. Clayton Homes is a Berkshire Hathaway Company.
13. Clayton Homes has a broad and deep leadership development program, of which LMAP is just one part.

CHAPTER 17

1. Chip Heath and Dan Heath, *Decisive: How to Make Better Choices in Life and Work*, Crown Business, New York, 2013.
2. U.S. Army Command Center website.
3. Andrew Zolli and Ann Marie Healy, *Resilience: Why Things Bounce Back*, Simon & Schuster, New York, 2012, chap. 6, p. 200.
4. Scott Page is a professor of complex systems, political science, and economics at the University of Michigan.
5. Heath and Heath, pp. 6–7.
6. Ibid., p. 8.
7. For more, see Wendy Smith, Marianne Lewis, and Michael Tushman, "'Both/And' Leadership," *Harvard Business Review*, May 2016.
8. The story is from Heath and Heath quoting Andy Grove from his book *Only the Paranoid Survive*, p. 14.

CHAPTER 18

1. Bernard Roth, *The Achievement Habit: Stop Wishing, Start Doing, and Take Command of Your Life*, HarperCollins, New York, 2015.

2. Bill Burnett and David Evans, *Designing Your Life: How to Build a Well-Lived, Joyful Life*, Knopf, New York, 2016.

3. Steven Kurutz, "Want to Find a Fulfillment at Last? Think Like a Designer," *New York Times*, September 17, 2016.

4. Susan Scott, *Fierce Conversations: Achieving Success at Work & in Life, One Conversation at a Time*, Berkley Books, New York, 2002, p. xv.

5. It can help to shift your situational awareness to not focus on your immediate here and now, but instead to see and appreciate your moment in time, in our species' time and place —in evolutionary time—a perspective with a span of millions of years. See Yuval Noah Harari, *Sapiens: A Brief History of Humankind* (HarperCollins, New York, 2015), for more on this perspective.

APPENDIX A

1. Erik Erikson, a student of Freud, considered one of the great psychologists of the twentieth century, taught at Yale, Harvard, and Berkeley though never graduated from college.

2. Timothy Leary, Frank Barron, 1955, at Kaiser Hospital.

3. Torgoff, Martin, *Can't Find My Way Home: America in the Great Stoned Age*, Simon and Schuster, 2004, p. 72.

4. Ken Kesey, *One Flew over the Cuckoo's Nest*, Viking, New York, 1962.

Index

About the Author

RON WARREN's first real job, at age 13, was holiday help at Smoky Joe's Menswear on South State Street, Chicago, followed by grocery clerk, union janitor, cook, jack hammerer (at Esalen Institute), waiter, camp counselor, clinical psych researcher, intern, fellow. After parole with a PhD from The University of Chicago, Committee on Human Development, Ron specialized in clinical psychology, differential diagnosis, and thought disorders. Ron was recruited to a Silicon Valley start-up, Human Edge Software, to do totally unrelated work: design its first software: The Sales Edge, the first personal computer self-assessment for professional development. *Newsweek* wrote a strong review called "Shrink on a Disk." Ron exited the firm after repeatedly making non-Freudian slips by referring to it as Human Dredge Software.

From 1984 and through the next 14 years Ron directed R&D at Acumen. The Center for Creative Leadership recognized both of Acumen's personality and competency 360s as sound, quality psychometric tools (out of 18 selected). Clients included UPS, Apple Computer, Silicon Graphics, FAA, Consumer's Union, Merck, BMW, Hyatt Hotels, JPMorgan Chase, Capgemini, and Bain Capital. Ron also developed assessments for UPS Air and British Airways for commercial pilot training.

After leaving Acumen, Ron completed a Balanced Scorecard study for a Fortune 50 firm and then in 1997 self-funded LMAP 360 development. Two years later, Ron joined the Kenexa assessment team and gained exposure to smart people and technologies and divergent perspectives, and Kenexa generously supported further development of the LMAP 360.

Ron hit a big road bump after 911; the recession hit hard and led to 13 months of unemployment until Ron turned to clinical work in 2003. This work was intense, immediate, and fulfilling, and Ron appreciated having education and skills in demand by folks with a rougher lot in life than himself and his family. Within a year, Ron became director of the PACE Dual Diagnosis Program at Family Services Agency of Marin. PACE was a Medi-Cal program with private pay clients and was profitable for six years . . . while slowly, organically, a client base grew for LMAP 360.

When Yale School of Management (SOM) integrated LMAP 360 in Executive Education programs in 2006, it was a game changer for the firm, and Ornaith Keane—who had worked with Ron for 7 years at Acumen—joined and co-founded LMAP llc. Ornaith manages operations, and Ron does psychology.

Ron is a Guest Lecturer and Executive Coach at Yale SOM, Harvard Business School, and previously, The Wharton School. From November 2014 to January 2017, Ron's full-time job was to write *Personality at Work*. It is his second book.